Instructor's Resource Guide

THE AMERICAN PAGEANT

TWELFTH EDITION

Mel Piehl
Valparaiso University

HOUGHTON MIFFLIN COMPANY   BOSTON   NEW YORK

Sponsoring Editor: Colleen Shanley Kyle
Editorial Associate: Michael Kerns
Production Design Coordinator: Christine Gervais
Senior Manufacturing Coordinator: Marie Barnes
Senior Marketing Manager: Sandra McGuire

Copyright © 2002 by Houghton Mifflin Company. All rights reserved.

Houghton Mifflin Company hereby grants you permission to reproduce the Houghton Mifflin material contained in this work in classroom quantities, solely for use with the accompanying Houghton Mifflin textbook. All reproductions must include the Houghton Mifflin copyright notice, and no fee may be collected except to cover the cost of duplication. If you wish to make any other use of this material, including reproducing or transmitting the material or portions thereof in any form or by any electronic or mechanical means including any information storage or retrieval system, you must obtain prior written permission from Houghton Mifflin Company, unless such use is expressly permitted by federal copyright law. If you wish to reproduce material acknowledging a rights holder other than Houghton Mifflin Company, you must obtain permission from the rights holder. Address inquiries to College Permissions, Houghton Mifflin Company, 222 Berkeley Street, Boston, MA 02116-3764.

Printed in the U.S.A.

ISBN: 0-618-10358-9

456789-VGI-07 06 05 04 03

Contents

Foreword v

Chapter 1	New World Beginnings, 33,000 B.C.–A.D. 1769	*1*
Chapter 2	The Planting of English America, 1500–1733	*6*
Chapter 3	Settling the Northern Colonies, 1619–1700	*10*
Chapter 4	American Life in the Seventeenth Century, 1607–1692	*16*
Chapter 5	Colonial Society on the Eve of Revolution, 1700–1775	*21*
Chapter 6	The Duel for North America, 1608–1763	*27*
Chapter 7	The Road to Revolution, 1763–1775	*31*
Chapter 8	America Secedes from the Empire, 1775–1783	*37*
Chapter 9	The Confederation and the Constitution, 1776–1790	*41*
Chapter 10	Launching the New Ship of State, 1789–1800	*48*
Chapter 11	The Triumphs and Travails of Jeffersonian Democracy, 1800–1812	*55*
Chapter 12	The Second War for Independence and the Upsurge of Nationalism, 1812–1824	*60*
Chapter 13	The Rise of a Mass Democracy, 1824–1840	*65*
Chapter 14	Forging the National Economy, 1790–1860	*73*
Chapter 15	The Ferment of Reform and Culture, 1790–1860	*78*
Chapter 16	The South and the Slavery Controversy, 1793–1860	*85*
Chapter 17	Manifest Destiny and Its Legacy, 1841–1848	*91*
Chapter 18	Renewing the Sectional Struggle, 1848–1854	*95*
Chapter 19	Drifting Toward Disunion, 1854–1861	*99*
Chapter 20	Girding for War: The North and the South, 1861–1865	*103*
Chapter 21	The Furnace of Civil War, 1861–1865	*107*
Chapter 22	The Ordeal of Reconstruction, 1865–1877	*113*
Chapter 23	Political Paralysis in the Gilded Age, 1869–1896	*118*

Chapter 24	Industry Comes of Age, 1865–1900	*123*
Chapter 25	America Moves to the City, 1865–1900	*128*
Chapter 26	The Great West and the Agricultural Revolution, 1865–1896	*133*
Chapter 27	The Path of Empire, 1890–1899	*142*
Chapter 28	America on the World Stage, 1899–1909	*148*
Chapter 29	Progressivism and the Republican Roosevelt, 1901–1912	*153*
Chapter 30	Wilsonian Progressivism at Home and Abroad, 1912–1916	*157*
Chapter 31	The War to End War, 1917–1918	*162*
Chapter 32	American Life in the "Roaring Twenties," 1919–1929	*168*
Chapter 33	The Politics of Boom and Bust, 1920–1932	*173*
Chapter 34	The Great Depression and the New Deal, 1933–1938	*177*
Chapter 35	Franklin D. Roosevelt and the Shadow of War, 1933–1941	*182*
Chapter 36	America in World War II, 1941–1945	*188*
Chapter 37	The Cold War Begins, 1945–1952	*193*
Chapter 38	The Eisenhower Era, 1952–1960	*199*
Chapter 39	The Stormy Sixties, 1960–1968	*204*
Chapter 40	The Stalemated Seventies, 1968–1980	*211*
Chapter 41	The Resurgence of Conservatism, 1980–2000	*216*
Chapter 42	The American People Face a New Century	*223*

Foreword

This *Instructor's Resource Guide* is a unique supplement for instructors using *The American Pageant*. The *Guide* offers a variety of material designed to focus and highlight the text for teaching purposes. It also suggests approaches and tips for teaching the history presented in the text and provides handy resources for expanding and enlivening classroom work. Most centrally, the *Guide* equips instructors with ideas for building on the clarity, liveliness, and "personality" that constitute the special virtues of *The American Pageant,* while recognizing that each instructor has his or her own way of using the text.

The forty-two chapters of the *Instructor's Resource Guide* correspond with the chapters of *The American Pageant*. Each *Guide* chapter follows the same format. Eight chapters contain a special additional feature, "Great Debates in American History."

The first three features of each chapter, "Chapter Themes," "Chapter Summary," and "Developing the Chapter," underscore the essential core material presented in that chapter of the text. "Chapter Themes" states the central idea or ideas of the corresponding text chapter. "Chapter Summary" provides a capsule of the narrative. "Developing the Chapter" suggests ways in which to emphasize and amplify the major chapter themes in class, whether by lecture or by discussion methods. Each suggested topic also contains a reference to pertinent historical material.

"For Further Interest" and "Questions for Class Discussion" offer ideas for sparking students' interest by taking innovative or provocative approaches to the history presented in *The American Pageant*. In some cases, the ideas provided are also directly related to the "Chapter Themes," but more often they suggest approaches to the chapter's material that students might find intrinsically interesting (for example, the "image" of various historical events or the experiences of ordinary Americans). Some of these topics or questions might serve as the basis for informational lectures or presentations; others might stimulate "open-ended" discussions or writing assignments. In any case, they seek to whet students' curiosity and to show them that history is not, as folklore has it, a dull subject.

The *Instructor's Resource Guide* also contains questions and suggestions for incorporating the text's "Makers of America" essays into classroom activities and student projects. Many of the questions focus on the comparative dimensions of immigration and ethnicity suggested by these illustrated essays.

"Character Sketches," along with "Great Debates in American History" and "Expanding the Varying Viewpoints," offer readily accessible resources for busy instructors who may want to add spice to the classroom and build on the special lively qualities of *The American Pageant*. "Character Sketches" further develops the text's sprightly characterization of historical personalities. By including nearly 150 profiles of historical figures—each accompanied by a biographical reference and quotation—the *Instructor's Resource Guide* offers engrossing biographical material with which to enhance and enliven historical understanding. "Character Sketches" might serve as a rich resource for those wishing to (1) incorporate interesting details, anecdotes, and quotations into class presentations, lectures, or discussions; (2) make abstract issues especially vivid by treating them in personal terms; (3) stimulate students to investigate significant historical personages and events in depth by reading biographies or carrying out other historical inquiry; and (4) use quotations or anecdotes as the basis for examination questions, essay assignments, and so on. Above all, the sketches should aid instructors in communicating to students the crucial realization that history always concerns real—and interesting—human beings.

The special resource feature, "Great Debates in American History," spotlights those periods when fundamental issues facing the country became the subject of great national controversies. By schematically presenting the two sides' positions, "Great Debates" allows instructors to build on the description of these conflicts in *The American Pageant* and thus to make the issues of the past meaningful for students. These debates might also inspire classroom simulations or similar teaching techniques.

"Expanding the Varying Viewpoints" and "Questions About the Varying Viewpoints" build on the feature of *The American Pageant* that raises issues of historical interpretation and disagreement. These complementary elements of the *Guide* demonstrate the differences in historical interpretation by supplying quotations from two of the "varying" historians described in the text and pose questions that highlight the significance of the disagreement. Instructors might use this material to illustrate historical interpretation, provoke discussion (especially for advanced or honor students), or refresh their own appreciation of the most fundamental issues of current historical interpretation.

Each instructor is different, and so is each class; thus, no two instructors will use this *Guide* in precisely the same way. Here, we hope to offer a resource filled with diverse enough materials that everyone can make his or her teaching of history more rewarding and successful.

M.P.

1

New World Beginnings, 33,000 B.C.–A.D. 1769

CHAPTER THEMES

Theme: The first discoverers of America, the ancestors of the American Indians, were small bands of hunters who crossed a temporary land bridge from Siberia and spread across both North and South America. They evolved a great variety of cultures, which ranged from the sophisticated urban civilizations in Mexico and Central and South America to the largely seminomadic societies of North America.

Theme: Motivated by economic and technological developments in European society, Portuguese and Spanish explorers encountered and then conquered much of the Americas and their Indian inhabitants. This "collision of worlds" deeply affected all the Atlantic societies—Europe, the Americas, and Africa—as the effects of disease, conquest, slavery, and intermarriage began to create a truly "new world" in Latin America, including the borderlands of Florida, New Mexico, and California, all of which later became part of the United States.

CHAPTER SUMMARY

Millions of years ago, the two American continents became geologically separated from the Eastern Hemisphere land masses where humanity originated. The first people to enter these continents came across a temporary land bridge from Siberia about 35,000 years ago. Spreading across the two continents, they developed a great variety of societies based largely on corn agriculture and hunting. In North America, some ancient Indian peoples like the Pueblos, the Anasazi, and the Mississippian culture developed elaborate settlements. But on the whole, North American Indian societies were less numerous and urbanized than those in Central and South America, though equally diverse in culture and social organization.

The impetus for European exploration came from the desire for new trade routes to the East, the spirit and technological discoveries of the Renaissance, and the power of the new European national monarchies. The European encounters with America and Africa, beginning with the Portuguese and Spanish explorers, convulsed the entire world. Biological change, disease, population loss, conquest, African slavery, cultural change, and economic expansion were just some of the consequences of the commingling of two ecosystems.

After they conquered and then intermarried with Indians of the great civilizations of South America and Mexico, the Spanish *conquistadores* expanded northward into the northern border territories of Florida, New Mexico, and California. There they established small but permanent settlements in competition with the French and English explorers who also were venturing into North America.

DEVELOPING THE CHAPTER: SUGGESTED LECTURE OR DISCUSSION TOPICS

- Using globes and maps, examine the impact of geology and geography on the prehistory and history of the Americas. Point out the areas of relatively dense Indian population and civilization before 1492, and emphasize the ways in which geography shaped the subsequent pattern of European exploration and conquest—in both South and North America.

    REFERENCE: D. W. Meinig, *The Shaping of America: A Geographical Perspective on 500 Years of Atlantic America* (1986).

- Explore what has been learned from history, anthropology, and archaeology regarding the life of American Indians before 1492. Emphasize that these societies were varied and dynamic, and had undergone significant conflicts and changes over many centuries. Perhaps select one North American Indian culture that had disappeared by the time of the Columbian encounter (e.g., the Anasazi culture that built Mesa Verde and Chaco Canyon in the Southwest), and compare their ways of life with those of the Indians that the Europeans first met when they arrived.

    REFERENCE: Brian M. Fagan, *Kingdoms of Gold, Kingdoms of Jade: The Americas Before Columbus* (1991).

- Analyze in more depth the condition of European societies at the beginning of the age of exploration. Consider, for example, the ways in which Europe was still "medieval" in its outlook around 1500 or so, and the ways in which it was being affected by more "modern" developments. Point out the changes in Europe that were occurring almost simultaneously with the age of discovery—particularly the Protestant Reformation and Catholic Counter-Reformation, the Italian Renaissance, the unification of Spain, the reign of Henry VIII—and consider their impact on the Americas.

    REFERENCE: Immanuel Wallerstein, *The Modern World-System* (1974).

- Discuss the "exchanges" involved in the encounter of Europeans, Native Americans, and Africans in the New World. Focus particularly on the ways in which all parties in the process—the "conquerors" as well as the "conquered"—were changed. The emphasis could be on issues of population, intermarriage, agriculture, and the like, or on the new forms of society that developed in both Hispanic America and North America as a result of the events of 1492 and after.

    REFERENCES: Karen Ordahl Kupperman, *Settling with the Indians: The Meeting of English and Indian Cultures in America, 1580–1640* (1980); Ramon A. Gutierrez, *When Jesus Came, The Corn Mothers Went Away* (1991).

FOR FURTHER INTEREST: ADDITIONAL CLASS TOPICS

- Consider the whole story of the settlement and discovery of America from the Indians' point of view. Examine the controversies over Columbus's role in the discovery and the actions of subsequent Spanish *conquistadores*.

- Compare the development and subsequent history of the Spanish in Mexico with that of the English in North America. Consider particularly the impact of the "mestizo factor" in Mexican history (a result of the intermarriage of Spanish and Indians) compared to the quite different pattern of English relations with the Indians in North America.

- Discuss the different historical perspective obtained by considering the role of the Spanish borderlands of Florida, New Mexico, and California as part of the history of colonial America (as distinct from examining only the later English settlements along the Atlantic coast). How does our understanding of American history alter if we consider developments in these areas to be of equal importance?

CHARACTER SKETCHES

Christopher Columbus (1451–1506)

Although his encounter with continents and peoples previously unknown to Europeans transformed world history, Columbus, the Genoese sailor who discovered America for the Spanish monarchy, never really understood the nature or significance of his accomplishment.

Having sailed under the flags of many nations, including Portugal, Columbus was already a well-known, successful voyager when he became obsessed with the idea of reaching Cathay (China) and the Indies by sailing west. His frustrating inability to gain backing for the venture ended when Ferdinand and Isabella agreed to supply him three ships.

The great achievement of Columbus's first voyage was not only to navigate unknown waters under unprecedented conditions but to keep his crews from mutiny—especially when the ships were becalmed after nearly sixty days. Although well aware during all his voyages that he was not in China or India, Columbus became firmly convinced that he had found islands just off the Asian coast and that the rich cities of Japan and China were not far away. This notion was reinforced by his desperate need to obtain continuing funding from the Spanish rulers, who pressed ever harder for concrete economic gains from the voyages.

Quote: "The inhabitants of this and of all the other islands I have found or gained intelligence of, both men and women, go as naked as they were born, with the exception that some of the women cover one part only with a single leaf or grass with a piece of cotton, made for that purpose.... I gave away a thousand good and pretty articles which I had brought with me in order to win their affection, and that they might be led to become Christians, and be well inclined to love and serve their highnesses and the whole Spanish nation...." (Letter on the first voyage, 1493)

REFERENCE: John Stewart Wilford, *The Mysterious History of Columbus* (1991).

Moctezuma II (1466–1520)

Moctezuma II (also called Montezuma II) was the Aztec ruler who succumbed to Cortés's invasion of Mexico.

He was the tenth in the line of Aztec emperors who controlled the vast regions and diverse peoples of Mexico from their rich capital at Tenochtitlán. Like other members of the royal aristocracy, he lived in luxury and served as a high priest of the elaborate but cruel Aztec religion. He succeeded to the throne in 1502 on the death of his uncle Ahuitzotl.

Before Cortés arrived, Moctezuma had expanded the Aztec realm, yet controlling the increasingly restless subordinate peoples of the empire demanded more and more of his energy. He was particularly devoted to the god Huitzilpochtli, but also came under the influence of astrologers and readers of portents. Their pessimistic predictions about his fate evidently weakened his will to resist the Spanish invaders.

After Cortés and his men seized Moctezuma and held him under house arrest, the people of Tenochtitlán became increasingly hostile to their leader. When Moctezuma appeared in public for the first time in nearly a year in early 1520, the angry populace showered him with stones before he could retreat indoors. The Spanish claimed that the wounded ruler died shortly thereafter from the stoning, but many Aztecs believed that the Spanish killed him. The truth remains unknown.

Quote: "I have in truth seen you and have now set eyes upon your force. You have come between mists and clouds, and now it has come to pass. Now you have arrived, with much fatigue and toil. Come to our land, come and repose." (Message to Cortés as he approached Tenochtitlán, 1519)

REFERENCE: Hugh Thomas, *Conquest: Montezuma, Cortes, and the Fall of Old Mexico* (1994).

Hernán Cortés (1485–1547)

Like many *conquistadores*, Cortés was born into a noble family but as a younger son failed to inherit extensive lands and wealth. As a youth, he was restless, ambitious, and nearly uncontrollable. In 1504, at age nineteen, he sailed for the island of Hispaniola (today's Dominican Republic and Haiti), at that time the headquarters of Spanish activity in the New World.

Cortés farmed and worked as a minor town official for six years, but he longed for greater adventures. In 1511, he joined a successful expedition to Cuba and then used a commission from the governor of Cuba, Velazquez, to assemble an expedition of eleven ships, five hundred soldiers, and sixteen horses. Although Velazquez soon changed his mind, Cortés had already sailed for Mexico. Cortés's brilliant, if treacherous, combination of military, political, and psychological tactics overcame Aztec resistance and gained him an empire larger than Spain. His reports of his conquests, contained in five lengthy letters to King Charles V of Spain, are full of fascinating detail, as well as much boasting and exaggeration.

Cortés was a talented administrator, but peaceful pursuits did not suit him, and in 1524 he headed for Honduras in search of further glory. There, he succeeded only in ruining his health and undermining his position in Mexico City. He retired to his estate in Cuernavaca, Mexico in 1528, and in 1540 returned to Spain to die, a broken man.

Quote: "Touching Montezuma's palace and all that was remarkable in his magnificence and power, there is so much to describe that I do not know how to begin….There could be nothing more magnificent than that this barbarian lord should have all the things of heaven to be found under his domain, fashioned in gold and silver and jewels and feathers." (Second letter to King Charles V, 1521)

REFERENCE: Jon White, *Cortés and the Downfall of the Aztec Empire: A Study in the Conflict of Cultures*, rev. ed. (1989).

QUESTIONS FOR CLASS DISCUSSION

1. How did Indian societies of South and North America differ from European societies at the time the two came into contact? In what ways did Indians retain a "world view" different from that of the Europeans?

2. What role did disease and forced labor (including slavery) play in the early settlement of America? Is the view of the Spanish and Portuguese as especially harsh conquerors and exploiters valid—or is this image just another version of the English "black legend" concerning the Spanish role in the Americas?

3. Are the differences between Latin America and North America due primarily to the differences between the respective Indian societies that existed in the two places, or to the disparity between Spanish and English culture? What would have happened if the English had conquered densely settled Mexico and Peru, and the Spanish had settled more thinly populated North America?

4. In what ways are the early (pre-1600) histories of Mexican and the present-day American Southwest understood differently now that the United States is being so substantially affected by Mexican and Latin American immigration and culture? To what extent should this now be regarded as part of our American history?

MAKERS OF AMERICA: THE *CONQUISTADORES*

Questions for Class Discussion

1. Should the Spanish *conquistadores* be especially blamed for the cruelties and deaths (including those by disease) inflicted on the original Indian populations of the Americas? Is it possible to make such criticisms without falling into the traditional English fallacies of the "black legend"? (See text, p. 23)

2. What is the long-term significance for Latin America of the "immortality" achieved by the *conquistadores* through intermarriage with Indian women?

Suggested Student Exercises

- Examine the careers of Hernán Cortés and Francisco Pizarro in both Spain and the New World, and assess the reasons for their "success."

- Examine some visual portrayals of the conquests of Mexico and Peru from the past and present, and compare how, over time, artists of various political outlooks have depicted the *conquistadores* and their victims.

Copyright © Houghton Mifflin Company. All rights reserved.

2

The Planting of English America, 1500–1733

CHAPTER THEMES

Theme: After a late start, a proud, nationalistic England joined the colonial race and successfully established five colonies along the southeastern seacoast of North America. Although varying somewhat in origins and character, all these colonies exhibited plantation agriculture, indentured and slave labor, a tendency toward strong economic and social hierarchies, and a pattern of widely scattered, institutionally weak settlement.

Theme: The early southern colonies' encounters with Indians and African slaves established the patterns of race relations that would shape the North American experience—in particular, warfare and reservations for the Indians and lifelong slave codes for African-Americans.

CHAPTER SUMMARY

The defeat of the Spanish Armada and the exuberant spirit of Elizabethan nationalism finally drew England into the colonial race. After some early failures, the first permanent English colony was established at Jamestown, Virginia. Initially it faced harsh conditions and Indian hostility, but tobacco cultivation finally brought prosperity and population growth.

The early encounters of English settlers with the Powhatans in Virginia established many of the patterns that characterized later Indian-white relations in North America. Indian societies underwent their own substantial changes as a result of warfare, disease, trade, and the mingling and migration of Indians from the Atlantic coast to inland areas.

Other colonies were established in Maryland and the Carolinas. South Carolina flourished by establishing close ties with the British sugar colonies in the West Indies. It also borrowed the West Indian pattern of harsh slave codes and large plantation agriculture. North Carolina developed somewhat differently, with fewer slaves and more white colonists who owned small farms. Latecomer Georgia served initially as a buffer against the Spanish and a haven for debtors.

Despite some differences, all the southern colonies depended on staple plantation agriculture for their survival and on the institutions of indentured servitude and African slavery for their labor. With widely scattered rural settlements, they had relatively weak religious and social institutions and tended to develop hierarchical economic and social orders.

DEVELOPING THE CHAPTER: SUGGESTED LECTURE OR DISCUSSION TOPICS

- Examine the condition of England at the time of the nation's early colonization efforts. Focus especially on the rise of the Elizabethan monarchy and the spirit of the English renaissance (for example, Shakespeare, Sir Walter Raleigh) in London and other commercial centers, as well as the social upheaval in the countryside ("enclosure"). Show how these factors—as well as religious rivalry with Spain—lay behind the colonization effort.

REFERENCE: Carl Bridenbaugh, *Vexed and Troubled Englishmen, 1590–1642* (1968).

- Consider the traditional Indian cultures of the south Atlantic coastal regions, and examine the transformations they underwent in response to English colonization. Explain the particular changes that affected the Powhatans of Virginia in relation to the larger patterns of English-Indian encounters that shaped subsequent American history.

    REFERENCE: Helen Rountree, *The Powhatans of Virginia: Their Traditional Culture* (1989).

- Examine the issue of race relations in the early southern colonies, showing how the early patterns established there set a course for subsequent American history. Focus particularly on the policies of driving out the Indians and of importing African slaves as a solution to the labor shortages in the New World.

    REFERENCE: Timothy Silver, *A New Face on the Countryside: Indians, Colonists, and Slaves in South Atlantic Forests 1500–1800* (1990).

FOR FURTHER INTEREST: ADDITIONAL CLASS TOPICS

- Contrast the pattern of English colonization with that of Spain described in Chapter 1 (or, perhaps, with that of France described in Chapter 6). Examine similarities and differences in motivation, population patterns, race relations, economic development, and the like.

- Compare the legends of early English colonization with the often harsh realities: for example, the tale of John Smith and Pocahontas with the actual patterns of relations between whites and Indians in Virginia. Consider why many early settlers tried to paint a rosier portrait of the colonies than their actual conditions warranted (to satisfy investors and lure new colonists).

- Contrast other English New World settlements, particularly in the West Indies, with those on the North American mainland. Note especially how in the West Indies many white plantation owners became absentees who spent much of their time in England, whereas the North American colonies developed as more complete, autonomous societies. (South Carolina can be used as an example of a partially West Indian pattern in North America.)

CHARACTER SKETCHES

John Smith (1580–1631)

The adventures that are popularly identified with Capt. John Smith—Pocahontas's saving of his life and Smith's own rescue of the infant Jamestown colony from ruin—were first recorded by Smith himself. Whether these events were invention or fact, one thing is certain: Smith lived an extraordinarily dramatic life.

According to Smith's autobiography, he left England at an early age to become a soldier of fortune. His many escapades included being enslaved, murdering his master, and being seduced by the wife of the pasha of Turkey. The trouble with these and other of Smith's tales is that their only source is Smith himself; in fact historians have shown that some of his stories were made up. He was, however, a talented soldier and administrator, whose effort in organizing the Jamestown colonists and in obtaining corn from the Indians clearly helped save the colony from starvation in the winter of 1608–1609.

Smith's writings, including *The Generall Historie of Virginia, New-England, and the Summer Isles* (1624), are fascinating, even if they are more fiction than history. Actually, most historians today believe that the *core* of his narrative is true, but that Smith simply embellished and altered particular events to increase their dramatic effect.

Quote: "Pocahontas, the King's most dear and well-beloved daughter, being but a childe of twelve or thirteen years of age, whose compassionate, pitiful heart, of my desperate estate, gave me much cause to respect her.... After some six weeks fatting amongst those savage courtiers, at the minute of my execution, she hazarded the beating out of her own brains to save mine; and not only that, but so prevailed with her father that I was safely conducted to Jamestown, where I found about eight and thirty miserable, poor and sick creatures.... Such was the weakness of this poor Commonwealth, as had the savages not fed us, we directly had starved." (1624)

REFERENCE: Philip Barbour, *The Three Worlds of Captain John Smith* (1964).

Pocahontas (1595–1617)

Although the story of Pocahontas's rescue of John Smith from death at the hands of her father, the great chief Powhatan, may or may not be true (most likely not), it is certain that she played an important role in the Virginia colony's early years as a kind of ambassador between the English and the Powhatan Indians—a role that Powhatan himself likely arranged. The children of powerful chiefs frequently played such intermediary roles in eastern Indian cultures. It is also known that she visited Jamestown often, sometimes to negotiate prisoner releases.

Her formal tribal name was Matoaka, meaning "playful." (Pocahontas ["frolicsome"] was a pet name.) In 1613 she was "kidnapped" by Capt. Samuel Argall and taken to live with a clergyman, though it may be that she collaborated in this arrangement as well. Shortly after, she was instructed in Christianity and baptized. She married John Rolfe, the promoter of tobacco, in 1614.

Rolfe took her to England in 1616, where she was badly affected by the climate and urban environment of London. She was presented to King James I at court, but as she boarded ship to return to Virginia, she became ill and died. Many later writers and poets—including Stephen Vincent Benét—have celebrated her brief but romantic life.

REFERENCE: Peter Lampe, *Pocahontas* (1995).

John Rolfe (1585–1622)

Rolfe was born in the county of Norfolk, England. Unhappy with his economic prospects, he sailed for Virginia in 1609 with his first wife but was shipwrecked in Bermuda, where his wife died. Rolfe pushed on to Virginia and arrived the following year. In 1612, he began experimenting with a "sweeter" variety of tobacco from the West Indies. (The native leaf smoked by the Powhatans of Virginia was too bitter for English tastes.) Despite the strong hostility to smoking felt by many English authorities, including King James I, the new tobacco caught on quickly and saved the colony's economy.

In 1614, Rolfe's status as the promoter of tobacco persuaded Pocahontas's father and Virginia governor Thomas Dale to grant Rolfe permission to marry the Indian princess. Before her death in England, Pocahontas gave birth to a son, Thomas, whom an uncle in England raised.

Rolfe returned to Virginia, married again, and served on the colony's Council of State. He was killed by Indians in the Second Anglo-Powhatan War (1622). In 1640, his son, Thomas, returned to Virginia, where his many descendants continued to live.

Quote: "Likewise, add hereunto her great appearance of love to me, her desire to be taught and instructed in the knowledge of God, her capableness of understanding, and her aptness and willingness to receive any good impression, besides her own incitements stirring me up." (Letter to Governor Thomas Dale, 1614, explaining reasons for wanting to marry Pocahontas).

REFERENCE: Philip Barbour, *Pocahontas and Her World* (1970)

QUESTIONS FOR CLASS DISCUSSION

1. What did England and the English settlers really want from colonization? National glory? Wealth? Adventure? A solution to social tensions? New sources of goods and trade? Did they get what they wanted?

2. Were the English colonizers crueler or more tolerant than the Spanish *conquistadores*? Why did the Spanish tend to settle and intermarry with the Indian population, whereas the English either killed the Indians, drove them out, or confined them to separate territories? How did this pattern of interaction affect both white and Indian societies?

3. Was the development of African slavery in the North American colonies inevitable? (Consider that it never developed in some other colonial areas, for example, Mexico and New France.) How would the North American colonies have been different without slavery?

4. How did the reliance on plantation agriculture affect the southern colonies? Were their societies relatively "loose" because they were primarily rural, or because they tended to rely on forced labor systems?

MAKERS OF AMERICA: THE IROQUOIS

Questions for Class Discussion

1. It is sometimes suggested that the Iroquois Confederacy may have provided a model for the union of states into the United States of America. What similarities and differences are there between the two confederations?

2. What role did the Iroquois play in the politics and warfare of British North America? Was the decision of most Iroquois to side with the British in the Revolutionary War the most decisive moment in their history? Why or why not?

Suggested Student Exercises

- Use a map of upstate New York to locate the traditional Iroquois lands as well as present-day areas of settlement. Examine materials on the efforts of today's Iroquois to recover lands and obtain governmental recognition in both New York state and Canada.

- Look at the conflict between Britain and the American colonies from an Iroquois perspective. Ask students to consider how subsequent history might have been different had the British defeated the Americans in the Revolution.

3

Settling the Northern Colonies, 1619–1700

CHAPTER THEMES

Theme: The Protestant Reformation, in its English Calvinist (Reformed) version, provided the major impetus and leadership for the settlement of New England. The New England colonies developed a fairly homogeneous social order based on religion and semicommunal family and town settlements.

Theme: The middle colonies of New Netherland (New York), Pennsylvania, New Jersey, and Delaware developed with far greater political, ethnic, religious, and social diversity, and they represented a more cosmopolitan middle ground between the tightly knit New England towns and the scattered, hierarchical plantation South.

CHAPTER SUMMARY

The New England colonies were founded by English Puritans. While most Puritans sought to "purify" the Church of England from within, and not to break away from it, a small group of Separatists—the Pilgrims—founded the first small, pious Plymouth Colony in New England. More important was the larger group of nonseparating Puritans, led by John Winthrop, who founded the Massachusetts Bay Colony as part of the "great migration" of Puritans fleeing persecution in England in the 1630s.

A strong sense of common purpose among the first settlers shaped the Massachusetts Bay Colony. Because of the close alignment of religion and politics in the colony, those who challenged religious orthodoxy, among them Anne Hutchinson and Roger Williams, were considered guilty of sedition and driven out of Massachusetts. The banished Williams founded Rhode Island, by far the most religiously and politically tolerant of the colonies. Other New England settlements, all originating in Massachusetts Bay, were established in Connecticut, Maine, and New Hampshire. Although they shared a common way of life, the New England colonies developed with a substantial degree of independence.

The middle colonies took shape quite differently. New York, founded as New Netherland by the Dutch and later conquered by England, was economically and ethnically diverse, socially hierarchical, and politically quarrelsome. Pennsylvania, founded as a Quaker haven by William Penn, also attracted an economically ambitious and politically troublesome population of diverse ethnic groups.

With their economic variety, ethnic diversity, and political factionalism, the middle colonies were the most typically "American" of England's thirteen Atlantic seaboard colonies.

DEVELOPING THE CHAPTER: SUGGESTED LECTURE OR DISCUSSION TOPICS

- Explain Puritanism in terms of the "Puritan dilemma" of trying to pursue high religious ideals while somehow remaining practically effective and involved in the world. Emphasize how the Puritans believed that their "errand into the wilderness" in New England would enable them to build an idealistic "City upon a Hill" that would inspire a corrupt world.

    REFERENCE: Andrew Delbanco, *The Puritan Ordeal* (1989).

- Examine the relationship between Puritan theology, the ideas of government its educated leaders promoted, and the religious beliefs and experience of the more ordinary settlers of the Massachusetts Bay Colony. Consider the ways in which Puritanism created both strong communal ideals, while almost guaranteeing tensions and conflicts at the boundaries of church and society.

    REFERENCE: David Hall, *Worlds of Wonder, Days of Judgment: Popular Religious Beliefs in Early New England* (1989).

- Explore the development of religious, political, and social freedom in New England and the middle colonies. Examine the role that the fight against religious intolerance in New England played in the developing ideas of American religious liberty, and the particular role that dissenters like Quakers and Baptists played in that development in New England, Pennsylvania, and Virginia.

    REFERENCES: Carla Gardina Pestana, *Quakers and Baptists in Colonial Massachusetts* (1991).

- Consider the relations of the New England settlers and their Puritan leadership to the Indians. Examine how they adjusted, or failed to adjust, their understanding of covenant and the communal role of town government to those on the frontier of settlement. Analyze episodes like King Philip's War and the Pequod War to discover what they revealed about the roles of "insiders" and "outsiders" in defining American identity and culture.

    REFERENCE: Jill Lepore, *The Name of War: King Philip's War and the Origin of American Identity* (1998).

- Examine the origins of ethnic and social diversity in America by focusing on the early middle colonies, especially New York and Pennsylvania. Contrast the ethnic and religious diversity of those two colonies with the Anglo-Saxon, Puritan character of New England and relate this to the more turbulent politics of the middle colonies. Consider how the middle colonies' ethnic variety laid the basis for later American immigration and ethnicity.

    REFERENCE: Michael Zuckerman, ed., *Friends and Neighbors: Group Life in America's First Plural Society* (1982).

FOR FURTHER INTEREST: ADDITIONAL CLASS TOPICS

- Focus on the "Thanksgiving image" of the Pilgrims and Puritans and compare it with the historical reality. Consider the enduring influence of the Puritans on America and the American self-image.

- Focus on Anne Hutchinson as a complex instance of religious, political, and perhaps gender-based dissent. Consider to what extent the hostility to her religious opinions might have been strengthened because she was a woman challenging the male religious and political establishment.

- Compare the colonizing effort of the Dutch in New Netherland with that of their English neighbors. Note particularly how Peter Stuyvesant's absolutist religious and political controls differed from the much "looser" quality of English colonialism.

- Consider William Penn and the Quakers as a case study in religious influence on colonial origins, and compare the Quakers with the New England Puritans. Examine the influence on Pennsylvania of particular Quaker belief—such as each individual's "inner light," social equality, and nonviolence—as well as how circumstances altered the implementation of such beliefs.

CHARACTER SKETCHES

John Winthrop (1588–1649)

John Winthrop was the leader of the great Puritan migration to Massachusetts Bay in 1630 and the dominant influence in the early colony. His personality and political policies reflected the complex nature of New England Puritanism: intense, high-minded, sober, driven, intellectual, intolerant.

A very well-off country gentleman and attorney, Winthrop began to experience career difficulties in England because of his strong Puritan leanings. He grew deeply pessimistic about the future, especially after the dismissal of Parliament in 1629, and joined as one of the twelve influential Puritans who organized the migration to the New World.

Winthrop was elected governor before sailing on the *Arbella* (1630) and reelected nearly every year until his death. Pious, humorless, and extremely stern toward dissenters, he skillfully managed the colony's affairs, successfully negotiating with Puritans and others in England—while putting Massachusetts Bay on a sound economic and political footing.

Quote: "The Lord will be our God and delight to dwell among us as his own people and will command a blessing upon us all in our ways.... And he shall make us a praise and glory, that men shall say of succeeding plantations: the Lord make it like that of New England. For we must consider that we shall be as a City upon a Hill; the eyes of all people are upon us." (Sermon aboard the *Arbella*, 1630)

REFERENCE: Lee Schweninger, *John Winthrop* (1990).

Anne Hutchinson (1591–1643)

Anne Hutchinson was the strong-minded religious dissenter whose challenge to Massachusetts Bay authorities from 1636 to 1638 shook the infant colony to its foundation and led to her banishment.

The second of thirteen children of a Puritan minister, from whom she received a strong education in theology and Scripture, she married William Hutchinson, a well-to-do merchant, and bore fourteen children between 1613 and 1636, of whom eleven survived infancy.

Hutchinson's twice-weekly meetings in her home to discuss sermons and Scripture won her an enthusiastic following throughout Massachusetts Bay, and for a time it appeared that she and her clerical allies might take over the colony. But her enemies gained control of the General Court in 1637, and she was excommunicated from the church and banished from the colony, despite her clever defense. She first went to Rhode Island, but after her husband died in 1642, she moved with her children to Pelham, New Netherland (now in the Bronx), where she and all but one of her children were killed by Indians in 1643.

Quote:

Court: "See how your argument stands. Priscilla, with her husband, took Apollo home to instruct him privately. Therefore Mistress Hutchinson, without her husband, may teach sixty or eighty."

Hutchinson: "I call them not, but if they come to me, I may instruct them."

Court: "Yet you show us not a rule."

Hutchinson: "I have given you two places of Scripture."

Court: "But neither of them will suit your practice."

Hutchinson: "Must I show you my name written therein?"

(Excerpt from Hutchinsons's trial, 1637)

REFERENCE: Amy Schrager Lang, *Prophetic Woman: Anne Hutchinson and the Problem of Dissent in the Literature of New England* (1987).

William Penn (1644–1718)

Although this English Quaker who founded Pennsylvania engaged in frequent quarrels with the colony's settlers, his basic policies of liberality, tolerance, and free immigration had a lasting effect on Pennsylvania and eventually on other American colonies, as well.

In his youth, Penn developed nonconformist religious leanings that angered his father, the great Admiral Sir William Penn, and eventually landed the younger Penn in the Tower of London. Reconciled to his father on Sir William's deathbed, he obtained the charter for Pennsylvania because of debts owed to his father by King Charles II.

Although Pennsylvania was a great economic success, Penn benefited little from it. His friendship with King James II caused him to lose political influence after the Glorious Revolution, and his dissolute son wasted much of his fortune, so that he ended up in debtor's prison.

Penn was considered handsome, courtly, and well read—a remarkable combination of religious visionary, charming courtier, and practical statesman. In the words of a contemporary: "a man of great abilities, of an excellent disposition, quick of thought and ready of utterance, full of true discipleship, even Love, without dissimulation."

Quote: "I am sorry at heart for your animosities. For the love of God, me, and the poor country, be not so governmentish, so noisy, and so open in your dissatisfactions." (Letter to settlers, 1701)

REFERENCE: Richard and Mary Dunn, eds., *The World of William Penn* (1986).

QUESTIONS FOR CLASS DISCUSSION

1. Did the Puritans really come to America seeking religious freedom? How did they reconcile their own religious dissent from the Church of England with their persecution of dissenters like Hutchinson and Williams? Does their outlook make them hypocrites?

2. How were government and religion—or church and state—related in New England and the middle colonies? How does the colonial view of these matters compare with more recent understandings?

3. How does the founding of the New England colonies compare with the origin of the middle colonies? In what ways were New England and the middle colonies each like the South, and in what ways were they different?

4. In what ways were the middle colonies of New York more "open" and diverse than New England? In what ways were they less democratic?

MAKERS OF AMERICA: THE ENGLISH

Questions for Class Discussion

1. In what areas of their lives did the Puritans seem to draw on their old local English traditions, and in what areas did they draw on their religion? In what ways did the two conflict, and in what ways did they support one another?

2. How does this material fit with the idea of America as a "new world" different from England? Was there a fundamental difference between those Englishmen who essentially tried to re-create their old way of life and those who saw life in America as a radical departure? What tensions might result between these two groups?

Suggested Student Exercises

- Use maps of "old" England and New England to identify where exactly in England various New England names (often beginning with "New") originated (for example, Dedham, Cambridge, Waterbury). See if you can identify any patterns or concentrations of early English settlements in certain areas.

- Draw map sketches of a local farming village like Rowley, Massachusetts, *with* common lands, and of a town like Watertown, Massachusetts, *without* such common lands.

EXPANDING THE "VARYING VIEWPOINTS"

- Thomas J. Wertenbaker, *The Founding of American Civilization* (1938).

    A view of America as the product of European culture:

    "The most stupendous phenomenon of all history is the transit of European civilization to the two American continents. For four and a half centuries Europeans have been crossing the Atlantic to establish in a new world their blood, languages, religions, literatures, art, customs. This movement, involving many nations and millions of men and women, has been termed the expansion of a new Europe in America. The Indian civilizations have been overwhelmed or subordinated, and in their place have arisen great nations speaking English, Spanish, Portuguese, or French, whose peoples profess the Christian religion, are partly or entirely European in blood, accept Shakespeare or Cervantes or Molière or even Tolstoy as their own. . . . Historians have been too prone to neglect the factor of inheritance in interpreting the United States, especially the multiple inheritance which makes it the child, not of England, but of Europe."

- Gary Nash, *Red, White, and Black: The People of Early America* (1974).

    A view of America as the product of the meeting of Indian, European, and African cultures:

    "The pathways of power did not strictly dictate the history of cultural interchange—a point that is obscured if we mistakenly assume that under conditions of oppression and exploitation, acculturation occurs in only one direction. The cultures of Africans and Indians—their agricultural techniques, modes of behavior, styles of speech, dress, food preference, music, dance, and other aspects of existence—became commingled with European culture.... A New World it is...for those who became its peoples remade it, and in the process they remade themselves, whether red, white, or black."

QUESTIONS ABOUT THE "VARYING VIEWPOINTS"

1. How does Wertenbaker represent the older and now generally unaccepted view that American society is essentially an extension of European civilization?

2. How does Nash combine a recognition of European "exploitation" with a belief that *all* the peoples of America created a genuinely new culture?

3. How is our view of subsequent American history altered if one adopts the "diversity" rather than the "Europeanist" perspective?

4

American Life in the Seventeenth Century, 1607–1692

CHAPTER THEMES

Theme: In the Chesapeake region, seventeenth-century colonial society was characterized by disease-shortened lives, weak family life, and a social hierarchy that included hardworking planters at the top and restless poor whites and black slaves at the bottom. Despite the substantial disruption of their traditional culture and the mingling of African peoples, slaves in the Chesapeake developed a culture that mixed African and new-world elements, and developed one of the few slave societies that grew through natural reproduction.

Theme: By contrast, early New England life was characterized by healthy, extended life spans, strong family life, closely knit towns and churches, and a demanding economic and moral environment.

CHAPTER SUMMARY

Life was hard in the seventeenth-century southern colonies. Disease drastically shortened life spans in the Chesapeake region, even for the young single men who made up the majority of settlers. Families were few and fragile, with men greatly outnumbering women, who were much in demand and seldom remained single for long.

The tobacco economy first thrived on the labor of white indentured servants, who hoped to work their way up to become landowners and perhaps even become wealthy. But by the late seventeenth century, this hope was increasingly frustrated, and the discontents of the poor whites exploded in Bacon's Rebellion.

With white labor increasingly troublesome, slaves (earlier a small fraction of the workforce) began to be imported from West Africa by the tens of thousands in the 1680s, and soon became essential to the colonial economy. Slaves in the Deep South died rapidly of disease and overwork, but those in the Chesapeake tobacco region survived longer. Their numbers eventually increased by natural reproduction and they developed a distinctive African-American way of life that combined African elements with features developed in the New World.

By contrast with the South, New England's clean water and cool air contributed to a healthy way of life, which *added* ten years to the average English life span. The New England way of life centered on strong families and tightly knit towns and churches, which were relatively democratic and equal by seventeenth-century standards. By the late seventeenth century, however, social and religious tensions developed in these narrow communities, as the Salem witch hysteria dramatically illustrates.

Rocky soil forced many New Englanders to turn to fishing and merchant shipping for their livelihoods. Their difficult lives and stern religion made New Englanders tough, idealistic, purposeful, and resourceful. In later years they spread these same values across much of American society.

Seventeenth-century American society was still almost entirely simple and agrarian. Would-be aristocrats who tried to recreate the social hierarchies of Europe were generally frustrated.

DEVELOPING THE CHAPTER: SUGGESTED LECTURE OR DISCUSSION TOPICS

- Explain the search for a suitable labor supply in the plantation colonies, contrasting the relative advantages and disadvantages of white indentured servants and slaves (from the planters' point of view). Perhaps use Bacon's Rebellion as the clearest illustration of why planters feared uncontrolled laborers and turned increasingly to slavery.

    REFERENCE: Edmund Morgan, *American Slavery, American Freedom* (1975).

- Explore the origins of American race relations by examining the closely linked development of slavery and racial prejudice in the seventeenth century. The emphasis might be on how slavery, once established, tended to reinforce prejudice, while prejudice justified slavery.

    REFERENCE: Winthrop Jordan, *White over Black* (1968).

- Provide a portrait of a "typical" New England town, focusing on the close connection between town and church and on family life, particularly the role of women and the relation of farming and trade in the region. Several towns have been studied in detail and the various social roles of men and women can be traced over time.

    REFERENCE: Stephen Innes, *Creating the Commonwealth: The Economic Culture of Puritan New England* (1995).

- Explore the Salem witch trials in more depth. The rich literature on the trials can be used to illuminate seventeenth-century New England history from numerous perspectives: town life, religion, the beliefs and actions of common people, generational conflict, and so on. Perhaps the most interesting is the light it sheds on the condition of women—both ordinary women and the extraordinary "witches"—and on gender relations and ideas in seventeenth-century America.

    REFERENCE: Carol F. Karlsen, *The Devil in the Shape of a Woman: Witchcraft in Colonial New England* (1987).

FOR FURTHER INTEREST: ADDITIONAL CLASS TOPICS

- Focus on the nature of colonial family life, particularly as it was affected by different demographic patterns (for example, frequent childbearing, frequent remarriage, and strong competition for women). A particular focus might be on attitudes toward children in an age of large families and infant deaths.

- Focus on the slave trade from Africa, considering how it affected those Africans who were caught in it as well as their descendants. A particular question might be that of the survival of African cultural elements among the slaves.

- Discuss women's lives in the seventeenth century, including economic functions, religion, marriage, and child raising. The focus might be on the economic and social importance of women in agrarian colonial communities, as well as on the legal and political restrictions that kept them tied to men.

- Explore the values of the traditional New Englander as both morally rigid "Puritan" and hard-bargaining "Yankee." Examine the "expansion of New England" in the spread of settlements west. (Places like northern Ohio, Kansas, Oregon, and later Hawaii had a high proportion of New Englanders in their populations.)

CHARACTER SKETCHES

Nathaniel Bacon (1647–1676)

Although his followers were mostly poor, landless white farmers who hated the planter aristocrats, rebel leader Nathaniel Bacon was himself a well-off planter.

Bacon, descended from a famous English family, immigrated to Virginia in 1674 after obtaining a gentlemanly education at Cambridge University and the Inns of Court in London. After the initial phase of his "rebellion," which consisted of leading unauthorized attacks on Indians, he was arrested by Governor Berkeley but then pardoned and even appointed to the colonial council in an attempt to appease him. But he and his supporters refused to be conciliated, and when Berkeley tried to suppress them, they went on a rampage that ended in the burning of Jamestown. Bacon seemed on the verge of seizing complete control of the colony when he suddenly died of illness—a development that enabled Berkeley to crush the leaderless rebels.

Quote: "For having upon specious pretences of publick works raised greate unjust taxes upon the commonality for the advancement of private favorites and other sinister ends…for having wronged his Majesty's prerogative and interesting by assuming monopoly of the beaver trade…and for having protected, favored, and imboldened the Indian's against his Majesty's loyall subjects…we do demand that the said Sir William Berkeley…be forthwith delivered up or surrender [himself] within four days of this notice forthwith." (Declaration of the People, 1676)

REFERENCE: Wilcomb E. Washburn, *The Governor and the Rebel* (1957).

Cotton Mather (1662–1728)

Cotton Mather's notorious involvement in the Salem witch trials was only one episode in his long, remarkable career, but it showed many of the contradictions of his complex personality.

The influential Puritan minister's role in the Salem witch trials arose partly because of his strong "scientific" interest in spirits and the invisible world. Even before the trials, he took into his home a girl believed to be a victim of witchcraft so that he could study her case in detail. By seventeenth-century standards Mather was actually quite cautious about witchcraft. He believed that where witchcraft existed, it should be treated by prayer and fasting, not by prosecutions and executions. But once the Salem trials got under way, he defended them in public, despite his apparent private belief that the evidence was questionable and the executions unjust.

Mather was hot-tempered, arrogant, and power-hungry but also extremely introspective and given to anxiety and self-doubt. Although he sometimes experienced hallucinations and severe depressions, and engaged in harsh attacks on his enemies, some of his writings are brilliant.

Quote: "Albeit the business of this witchcraft may be very much transacted upon the stage of imagination, yet we know that, as in treason, there is an imagining which is a capital crime, and here also the business, though managed in imagination, yet may not be called imaginary. The effects are dreadfully real.… Our neighbors at Salem Village are blown up, after a sort, with an infernal gunpowder; the train is laid in the laws of the kingdom of darkness.... Now the question is, who gives fire to this train? And by what acts is the match applied?" (1692)

REFERENCE: Kenneth Silverman, *The Life and Times of Cotton Mather* (1984).

Rachel Clinton (1629–1694)

Clinton is one of the few Salem "witches" whose biography historians have been able to reconstruct. Her childhood was extremely unhappy, as, evidently, was the rest of her life. After both her parents died when she was very young, she was placed under the control of her mentally unstable stepmother. Her father had left a substantial estate; but Clinton was never able to get a fair share of it because she was constantly exploited by others, including Thomas Clinton, her brother-in-law, whom she married at age thirty-six (he was twenty-two at the time). After her divorce from Thomas Clinton, she was reduced to poverty and dependency, which likely made her extremely bitter and hostile. It is known that she threw stones at people and called them names like "hellhound" and "whoremasterly rogue." Among the "witchcraft" activities she was accused of, even before the Salem trials, were taking away a girl's power of speech for three hours, sending animals to cross people's paths, and making beer disappear from kegs.

Although convicted in the Salem trials and imprisoned for several months, Clinton was not executed. Released from prison in 1693, she died the following year.

REFERENCE: John Demos, *Entertaining Satan* (1982).

QUESTIONS FOR CLASS DISCUSSION

1. Why was family life in New England so different from family life in the South?

2. Why did slavery grow to be such an important institution in colonial America? What were the effects of slavery on the Africans who were brought to the New World?

3. What was attractive and unattractive about the closely knit New England way of life?

4. Were the Salem witch trials a peculiar, aberrant moment in an age of superstition, or did they reflect common human psychological and social anxieties that could appear in any age? How harshly should those who prosecuted the "witches" be condemned?

MAKERS OF AMERICA: FROM AFRICAN TO AFRICAN-AMERICAN

Questions for Class Discussion

1. How did African-Americans work to adapt their native traditions under the conditions of New World slavery? What kinds of traditions were most successfully preserved?

2. What enabled African-Americans in the Chesapeake region to develop societies where—unusually for the history of slavery—the population reproduced and grew through natural increase? What does this suggest about the nature of families under slavery? How might these circumstances have affected the relationship between slaves and slaveholders?

Copyright © Houghton Mifflin Company. All rights reserved.

Chapter 4

Suggested Student Exercises

- Use photographs of art objects or other materials from one of the particular cultures or regions of Africa from which a substantial number of slaves came to America (e.g., the Guinea Coast, Benin, Ivory Coast, or Angola), and have students consider characteristics that may have passed into African-American culture.

- Examine some of the areas along the Atlantic coast where economic and social conditions, including the density of slave populations, made for a more extensive survival of African elements within African-American cultures. (The most famous and well-studied is the Gullah culture on the Georgia and South Carolina sea islands.)

5

Colonial Society on the Eve of Revolution, 1700–1775

CHAPTER THEMES

Theme: Compared with its seventeenth-century counterpart, eighteenth-century colonial society became more complex and hierarchical, more ethnically and religiously diverse, and more economically and politically developed.

Theme: Colonial culture, while still limited, took on distinct American qualities in such areas as evangelical religion, education, press freedom, and self-government.

CHAPTER SUMMARY

By 1775 the thirteen American colonies east of the Appalachians were inhabited by a burgeoning population of two million whites and half a million blacks. The white population was increasingly a melting pot of diverse ethnic groups.

Compared with Europe, America was a land of equality and opportunity (for whites); but relative to the seventeenth-century colonies, there was a rising economic hierarchy and increasing social complexity. Ninety percent of Americans remained agriculturalists. But a growing class of wealthy planters and merchants appeared at the top of the social pyramid, in contrast with slaves and "jayle birds" from England, who formed a visible lower class.

By the early eighteenth century, the established New England Congregational church was losing religious fervor. The Great Awakening, sparked by fiery preachers like Jonathan Edwards and George Whitefield, spread a new style of emotional worship that revived religious zeal. Colonial education and culture were generally undistinguished, although science and journalism displayed some vigor. Politics was everywhere an important activity, as representative colonial assemblies battled on equal terms with politically appointed governors from England.

DEVELOPING THE CHAPTER: SUGGESTED LECTURE OR DISCUSSION TOPICS

- Expand on the economic activities and relationships of the different parts of the colonial "social pyramid" discussed in the text on pp. 87, 90. Explain especially the trend toward greater hierarchy, with a wealthy elite on the top and "jayle birds" and others on the bottom. The focus might be on the concern this tendency would have aroused among the "middle class" of colonists.

  REFERENCE: John J. McCusker and Russell R. Menard, *The Economy of British America, 1607–1789* (1991).

- Show how the Great Awakening marked a key transition from the lukewarm style of religion fostered by "established" (tax-supported) colonial churches to the strong commitment required by the "voluntary" (member-supported) churches that later became the American norm. The focus might be on how a religious "revival" like the Great Awakening could arouse marked fervor among some colonists while also causing opposition among those who distrusted emotional religion. Consider the arguments regarding the role that evangelical Protestantism played in promoting the American Revolution. Consider the contentions of some historians like Jon Butler that the Great Awakening did not have the extensive influence usually attributed to it.

REFERENCE: Ronald Hoffman and Peter J. Albert, eds., *Religion in a Revolutionary Age* (1994); Jon Butler, *Awash in a Sea of Faith*: *Christianizing the American People* (1990).

- Examine the ordinary social lives of colonial Americans. Consider the relationship between the way average people lived in the eighteenth century and the kinds of public concerns they had in the areas of politics, religion, economics, and culture.

  REFERENCES: Stephanie G. Wolf, *As Various as Their Land: Everyday Lives of 18th Century Americans* (1994); Bruce Daniels, *Puritans at Play: Leisure and Recreation in Colonial New England* (1995).

- Explain more fully the evolution of colonial politics and why politics was especially important to colonists jealously trying to control their own affairs. The emphasis might be on the development of a distinctively American type of "opposition" politics, which was anxious to preserve local liberties and fearful of centralized or corrupt governmental power—such as the royal governors represented.

  REFERENCE: Bernard Bailyn, *The Origins of American Politics* (1967).

FOR FURTHER INTEREST: ADDITIONAL CLASS TOPICS

- Compare the social structure and social life of the eighteenth century with that of the seventeenth century as described in Chapter 4. Discuss what factors caused the transition toward greater social diversity and complexity and whether the development was an inevitable result of population growth and expansion.

- Focus on the issue of racial, ethnic, and religious diversity in the colonies. The discussion might emphasize the question of how diverse the colonies really were, since the ethnic groups were all northern European—except for blacks—and the religious groups almost all Protestant.

- Select a particular colonial occupation and consider how the activities of those who performed it might differ from those of later, twentieth-century practitioners. Among the occupations that could be discussed in this way: farmer, merchant, lawyer, minister, printer, schoolteacher, doctor. Benjamin Franklin as printer might form a good focus, with further emphasis on how he combined this role with so many others, such as scientist, politician, and diplomat.

- Use the example of Jonathan Edwards as preacher, pastor, theologian, and educator in order to explain the motivations and impact of the Great Awakening. A sermon like "Sinners in the Hands of an Angry God" (which some students know from literature classes) might be compared with some of Edwards's other writings.

CHARACTER SKETCHES

Jonathan Edwards (1703–1758)

Edwards was the great preacher, revivalist, theologian, and philosopher of eighteenth-century New England. Even as a child he showed personal piety and intellectual brilliance: at age seven he began leading other children into the woods for prayer, and by age fourteen he was reading John Locke and Isaac Newton.

Despite his later learned writings on subjects like the nature of the mind and its relation to the natural world, he remained a parish pastor in Northampton, Massachusetts. In 1734, his intense preaching, first considered "old-fashioned," began producing emotional conversions that soon numbered thirty a week. His fame spread throughout the colonies. By 1741 he became concerned about the excesses of the Great Awakening, especially as conducted by uneducated revivalists, but he still defended it strongly.

Tall, slender, with piercing eyes and a soft but perfectly modulated voice, Edwards rose daily at 4:00 A.M. and devoted thirteen hours to study. His later years were absorbed by controversies with parishioners who objected to his strong moral demands on them. In 1750 a majority voted to dismiss him, and he was left jobless and in debt. In 1757 he was appointed president of Princeton University but died of a smallpox inoculation before taking office.

Quote: "All will allow that true virtue or holiness has its seat chiefly in the heart, rather than in the head: it therefore follows….that it consists chiefly in holy affections….Now if such things are enthusiasm, and the fruits of a distempered brain, let my brain be evermore possessed of that happy distemper! If this be distraction, I pray God that the world of mankind may be all seized with this benign, meek, beneficent, beatifical, glorious distraction!" (1742)

REFERENCE: J.E. Smith, *Jonathan Edwards: Puritan, Preacher, Philosopher* (1992).

Benjamin Franklin (1706–1790)

Franklin, the most famous American of the eighteenth century and a great cultural hero in Europe as well as in his own country, was born to a Boston soapmaker. In 1718 he became a printer's apprentice under his brother James. At age seventeen he moved to Philadelphia, which became his permanent home.

Once Franklin had made a substantial fortune from *Poor Richard's Almanack* and other publishing business ventures, he concentrated on science, philosophy, and politics. Although largely self-taught (he learned five languages on his own), he was immensely knowledgeable in many areas. Besides electricity, he studied meteorology, hydrology (water), geology and demographics (population).

While serving as a colonial agent in England in the 1760s, he considered permanently moving to that country, and in America he was suspected of favoring the Stamp Act until he testified against it in Parliament. When he served as minister to France during the Revolution, his portrait was put in shop windows and on medals, rings, watches, snuffboxes, and bracelets. His charm and "simple" democratic manners endeared him to everyone, especially aristocratic French ladies. Practical, skeptical, cool-minded, insatiably curious, sexually passionate, uninhibited, plainspoken, and above all humorous, Franklin was at ease with all kinds and levels of people, from kings to tavern maids.

Quote: "It was wise counsel given to a young man, 'Pitch upon that course of life which is most excellent, and custom will make it the most delightful.' But many pitch on no course of life at all, nor form any scheme of living, by which to attain any valuable end; but wander perpetually from one thing to another." (From *Poor Richard,* 1749)

REFERENCE: H.W. Brands, *The First American: The Life and Times of Benjamin Franklin* (2000).

Charles W. Peale (1741–1827)

Peale was one of the best-known American painters of the eighteenth century and one of the few to make his career in the United States rather than Europe. Originally apprenticed as a saddler, he was forced out of that trade because he joined the Sons of Liberty and most of his customers were Loyalists. He then became interested in art and studied under John Singleton Copley in Boston and Benjamin West in London. Besides art, he was a prominent museum curator, essayist, civic leader, silversmith, and landscape gardener. Because of his diverse talents, he was sometimes called "the American Leonardo da Vinci."

Serving as an army captain during the Revolution, he executed numerous portraits of his fellow officers. He painted Washington from life seven times and made more than fifty other portraits of him as general and president. He usually portrayed Washington more realistically and less heroically than other painters, showing his high cheekbones, sloping shoulders, and long arms and legs. Yet his portraits were very popular with Washington and others.

Quote: "A good painter of either portrait or history must be well acquainted with the Grecian or Roman statues, to be able to draw them at pleasure by memory. . . . these are more than I shall ever have time or opportunity to know." (1772)

REFERENCE: Charles Coleman Sellers, *Charles Willson Peale* (1969).

Phillis Wheatley (c. 1753–1784)

Wheatley, the gifted black poet who published admired verse in late-eighteenth-century America and England, was brought as a slave from Africa to Boston in 1761, when she was about eight years old, and bought by John Wheatley, a tailor. She was made Mrs. Wheatley's personal servant but quickly impressed her master with her remarkable intelligence, which he cultivated.

She began writing poems at age thirteen; the first is called "On Being Brought from Africa to America." Her first published poem (on George Whitefield's death) was composed at age seventeen, and she soon gained renown in Boston and then elsewhere. Her master's daughter took her to England in 1773, where she was introduced to many literary people.

Four years after her return to America in 1774, she contracted a disastrous marriage to John Peters, a black baker. He apparently treated her badly, and she wrote no more poems. She bore three children, two of whom died before her own death in 1784.

Quote: "On Being Brought from Africa to America"
"'Twas mercy brought me from my pagan land
Taught my benighted soul to understand
That there's a God, that there's a savior, too;
Once I redemption neither sought nor knew.
Some view our sable race with scornful eye,
'Their color is a diabolic lie.'
Remember, Christians, Negroes black as Cain
May be refined and join the angelic train."
(1766)

REFERENCE: Julian D. Mason, Jr., *The Poems of Phillis Wheatley* (1966).

QUESTIONS FOR CLASS DISCUSSION

1. How democratic was colonial American society? Why was it apparently becoming less equal?

2. How were the various occupations and activities of colonial America related to the nature of the economy? Why were occupations like lawyer, printer, and artisan taking on greater importance?

3. What were the causes and effects of the Great Awakening? How did such an intense religious revival affect those who experienced "conversion" as well as those who did not? How did the Awakening help to create a sense of shared American identity?

4. In what ways was colonial life attractive, and in what ways would it seem tedious and dull to the average twenty-first-century American? How were the educational, cultural, and leisured sides of colonial life affected by the basic nature of the economy?

MAKERS OF AMERICA: THE SCOTS-IRISH

Questions for Class Discussion

1. What characteristics did the Scots-Irish develop from their history *before* arriving in America? How did their American experience relate to that earlier history?

2. Why were the Scots-Irish likely to be especially fervent patriots in the American Revolution? What issues might separate them from other American revolutionists, like the New Englanders or the Virginia planters?

Suggested Student Exercises

- Locate both the Scottish lowlands and Ulster (Northern Ireland) on a map of the British Isles. Point out how and why the Protestant Scots-Irish in Northern Ireland differ from the Roman Catholic Irish in Ireland.

- Use a relief map of the Appalachian Mountains to trace the migration of the Scots-Irish south and southwest from Pennsylvania, as they moved down through the valleys of the region. Show why the Scots-Irish did not generally migrate west to Ohio and Indiana.

EXPANDING THE "VARYING VIEWPOINTS"

- Richard Bushman, *From Puritan to Yankee* (1967).

    A view of eighteenth-century society as becoming more open and democratic:

    "...[T]he law and authority embodied in governing institutions gave way under the impact first of economic ambitions and later of the religious impulses of the Great Awakening....As, in the expanding eighteenth century, merchants and farmers felt free to pursue wealth with an avidity dangerously close to avarice, the energies released exerted irresistible pressures against traditional bounds. When the Great Awakening added its measure of opposition, the old institutions began to crumble."

- Gary Nash, *The Urban Crucible* (1979).

    A view of eighteenth-century society as becoming more closed and undemocratic:

    "What has led early American historians to avoid questions about class formation and the development of lower-class political consciousness is not only an aversion to Marxist conceptualizations of history but also the myth that class relations did not matter in early America because there were no classes....By the end of the Seven Years' War, poverty on a scale that urban leaders found appalling had appeared in New York and Philadelphia. Many urban Americans, living amidst historical forces that were transforming the social landscape, came to perceive antagonistic divisions based on economic and social position;...they began to struggle around these conflicting interests; and through these struggles they developed a consciousness of class."

QUESTIONS ABOUT THE "VARYING VIEWPOINTS"

1. Where do both viewpoints agree concerning eighteenth-century society, and where do they disagree?

2. What might each of these historians see as the social background of the American Revolution?

3. Are these viewpoints primarily focused on society in the middle and northern colonies? How would these perspectives appear if slavery is included in the equation? Does Edmund Morgan's belief that slavery actually promoted equality and solidarity among whites offer a serious challenge to these views of colonial America?

6

The Duel for North America, 1608–1763

CHAPTER THEMES

Theme: As part of their worldwide rivalry, Great Britain and France engaged in a great struggle for colonial control of North America, culminating in the British victory in the French and Indian War (Seven Years' War) that drove France from the continent. The French defeat created conditions for a growing conflict between Britain and its American colonies.

CHAPTER SUMMARY

Like Britain, France entered late into the American colonial scramble, eventually developing an extensive though thinly settled empire economically based on the fur trade. During much of the seventeenth and eighteenth centuries, Britain and France engaged in a bitter power struggle that frequently erupted into worldwide wars. In North America these wars constituted an extended military duel for imperial control of the continent.

The culminating phase of this struggle was inaugurated by young George Washington's venture into the sharply contested Ohio country. After early reversals in this French and Indian War (the Seven Years' War in Europe), the British under William Pitt revived their fortunes and won a decisive victory at Quebec, finally forcing the French from North America.

The American colonials, who had played a large part in Britain's imperial wars with France, emerged with increased confidence in their own abilities. The removal of the French and Spanish threat to British control of North America kindled increasing tensions between the colonists and Britain. The Ottawa chief Pontiac's unsuccessful uprising in 1763 convinced the British of the need to continue stationing troops in America. But with foreign threats gone, the colonists were unwilling to pay taxes for British protection and increasingly resented Britain's authority over them.

DEVELOPING THE CHAPTER: SUGGESTED LECTURE OR DISCUSSION TOPICS

- Compare the French empire in America with those of Britain and Spain. The emphasis of the comparison might be on showing that France's empire was like Spain's in having close relations with the Indians, like Britain's in developing settler colonization, but different from both in focusing on trade and missions rather than on precious metals or agriculture.

  REFERENCE: W. J. Eccles, *France in America* (1972).

- Explain how and why the British won the French and Indian War. The focus might be on the reasons for the early French successes (particularly the alliance with the Indians) as well as the reasons for the eventual British triumph (superior numbers, resources, leadership, and strategy—especially in the Battle of Quebec).

REFERENCE: Francis Jennings, *Empire of Fortune: Crowns, Colonies, and Tribes in the Seven Years War in America* (1988).

- Examine the French and Indian War, and the other colonial struggles, from the perspective and the historical situation of the Indians. Consider how they viewed the struggles between European powers, and how they tried to make tensions between settlers and colonial governments work to their advantage.

    REFERENCE: Richard White, *The Middle Ground: Indians, Empires, and Republics in the Great Lakes Region, 1650–1815* (1991).

- Develop in more depth the chapter's key paradox: that Britain's victory over France—which the British colonists officially supported—actually created new sources of tension between Americans and the mother country.

    REFERENCE: Alan Rogers, *Empire and Liberty: American Resistance to British Authority, 1755–1763* (1974).

FOR FURTHER INTEREST: ADDITIONAL CLASS TOPICS

- Compare the image of the "typical" early French colonizer (the fur-trading *voyageur* or Jesuit priest) with the image of the typical Spanish colonizer (the *conquistador*) or English colonizer (the Puritan or tobacco planter). Consider how these images reflect the nature of each nation's colonial effort.

- Approach several of the chapter's issues from a Canadian viewpoint—especially that of a French-Canadian. Point out how the survival and growth of the aggrieved French-Canadian community reflects the losing side of the struggle for North America and discuss whether English-speaking North Americans might have ended up in the same condition had France won the French and Indian War.

- Focus on the "Indian factor" in the French empire and the French and Indian War. Examine French relations with the Indians compared with British (and perhaps Spanish), and consider why most Indians supported France against Britain.

- Use the activities of the young George Washington to illustrate the double role of the colonists as both "British subjects" and "Americans." Discuss how Washington's status as a colonial underling clashed with his status as a young Virginia aristocrat—and reflected all the colonists' frustrations with their subordinate role.

CHARACTER SKETCHES

Samuel de Champlain (1567–1635)

Before founding New France, Champlain had served as a captain in the Spanish navy in the Caribbean and had written a book containing the first proposal for a canal across the Isthmus of Panama. His first French colony was established in Acadia (Nova Scotia). When the struggling colonists there became depressed during the harsh winter, Champlain organized an "Order of Good Cheer" that required the settlers to provide food and entertainment for each other several nights a week.

The Acadia settlement was abandoned in 1607, and a year later Champlain established Quebec. The new colony numbered only about one hundred people during its first twenty years, despite the fact that Champlain constantly lobbied the French government for stronger support. Finally, Cardinal Richelieu helped reorganize the colony and the fur trade. After 1627 about three hundred settlers a year immigrated to New France.

Quote: "It was impossible to know this country without having wintered here, for on arriving in summer everything is very pleasant owing to the woods, the fair landscape, the good fishing…but winter in this country lasts six months!" (1610)

REFERENCE: William Jay Jacobs, *Champlain* (1994).

Robert La Salle (1643–1687)

Born to a wealthy French family, La Salle, who became the greatest of the French-Canadian explorers, immigrated to New France at age twenty-three. Learning of the Ohio River from the Indians, he became convinced that it led to China. Subsequently, so often did he talk about going to China that his neighbors called his estate *Le Chine* ("China").

Selling his estate to get funds for an expedition south from New France, La Salle next enlisted the support of King Louis XIV. After La Salle's venture bogged down on the Illinois River he walked the thousand miles back to Canada to get new supplies and start over. He discovered the mouth of the Mississippi in 1682.

In 1684 Louis XIV sent La Salle back across the Atlantic to drive out the Spanish and establish a permanent settlement. But despite months of searching, he could not find the mouth of the river again. His desperate party landed instead in Texas, where La Salle was murdered by his mutinous men.

Quote: "I have chosen a life more suited to my solitary disposition, which nevertheless does not make me harsh to my people; though joined to a life among savages, it makes me, perhaps, less polished and compliant than the atmosphere of Paris requires." (Letter to France, 1683)

REFERENCE: Robert Weddle, et al., eds., *La Salle, the Mississippi, and the Gulf* (2000).

George Washington (1732–1799)

Before he became the commanding general in the America Revolution and the first U.S. president, Washington was a young Virginia gentleman, surveyor, and militia officer who played an important part in the French and Indian War. We examine here only his early career (up to 1763).

Washington's father died when George was eleven, and almost nothing is known of their relationship. Washington grew up with various Virginia-gentry relatives, including his half-brother Lawrence, whose estate was at Mount Vernon. Lawrence also provided him with what little formal education he received. He learned mathematics and surveying and knew the Bible and some English literature, including contemporary novels like *Tom Jones* and *Humphrey Clinker*. He traveled with Lawrence to Barbados, where he contracted a mild case of smallpox.

During his difficult mission into the Ohio country, he was shot at by Indians, nearly drowned crossing a river, and almost froze from exposure. After his service with Braddock, he married Martha Custis, a wealthy widow, and returned to managing their plantations as a twenty-seven-year-old "patriarch." Solemn, soft-spoken, and extremely dignified in manner, he had a strong liking for fox hunts, fishing, cards, theatrical events, horse racing, billiards, and dancing.

Quote: "The Virginia Companies behaved like men and died like soldiers; for I believe out of the three companies that were there that day scarce thirty were left alive....The English soldiers exposed all those who were inclined to do their duty to almost certain death; and at length, despite every effort to the contrary, [they] broke and ran as sheep before the hounds." (Letter to Governor Dinwiddie on the Battle of Fort Duquense, 1755)

REFERENCE: James Thomas Flexner, *George Washington: The Forge of Experience, 1732–1775* (1965).

QUESTIONS FOR CLASS DISCUSSION

1. Why was the French empire ultimately so much less successful than either the Spanish or the British empires?

2. If France instead of Britain had won the "duel for North America," would the thirteen colonies ever have become independent of Britain, or would they have been forced to stay within the empire for protection against France? Would Detroit, St. Louis, and New Orleans now be cities in "Canada" rather than in the United States?

3. How did the treatment of Americans by British officers and military during the war contribute to simmering resentment against the "mother country"? Do the attitudes and behavior of the colonists during the war suggest that Americans felt less real patriotic loyalty to Britain, and that the ties had become largely practical ones?

4. Should the French and Indian War be considered one of the major causes of the American Revolution? Why or why not?

MAKERS OF AMERICA: THE FRENCH

Questions for Class Discussion

1. How did the eighteenth-century British conquest of New France permanently affect the French experience in America?

2. What differences and similarities exist between the two main concentrations of Franco-Americans: the Cajuns of Louisiana and the migrants from Quebec in New England?

Suggested Student Exercises

- Use maps of the Missouri–Mississippi River system and their tributaries to find French or Cajun place names and identify patterns of French exploration or settlement within the present United States. Consider the long-term effects of the early French empire on later American communities. (Louisiana is a particularly good focus for such examination, but other places such as Detroit, St. Louis, or Vincennes, Indiana might also be studied.)

- Investigate the contemporary descendants of the French settlers in Quebec and elsewhere in Canada. Consider the importance of French as one of Canada's two official languages, and the tensions that still remain between English and French-speaking Canadians. Trace the migration of French Canadians into New England and elsewhere since the late nineteenth century.

7

The Road to Revolution, 1763–1775

CHAPTER THEMES

Theme: The American Revolution occurred because the American colonists, who had long been developing a strong sense of autonomy and self-government, furiously resisted British attempts to impose tighter imperial controls and higher taxes after the end of the French and Indian War in 1763. The sustained conflict over political authority and taxation, enhanced by American agitators and British bungling, gradually moved Americans from asserting rights within the British Empire to openly warring with the mother country.

CHAPTER SUMMARY

The American War of Independence was a military conflict fought from 1775 to 1783, but the American Revolution was a deeper transformation of thought and loyalty that began when the first settlers arrived in America and finally led to the colonies' political separation from Britain.

One source of long-term conflict was the tension between the considerable freedom and self-government the colonists enjoyed in the American wilderness and their participation in the British Empire's mercantile system. While British mercantilism actually provided economic benefits to the colonies along with certain liabilities, its limits on freedom and patronizing goal of keeping America in a state of perpetual economic adolescence stirred growing resentment.

The short-term movement toward the War of Independence began with British attempts to impose higher taxes and tighter imperial controls after the French and Indian War. To the British these were reasonable measures, under which the colonists would simply bear a fair share of the costs of the empire. To the colonists, however, the measures constituted attacks on fundamental rights.

Through well-orchestrated agitation and boycotts, the colonists forced repeal of the Stamp Act of 1765 as well as the Townshend Acts that replaced it, except for the symbolic tax on tea. A temporary lull in conflict between 1770 and 1773 ended with the Boston Tea Party, conducted by a network of Boston agitators reacting to the Massachusetts governor's attempt to enforce the law.

In response to the Tea Party, the British imposed the harsh Intolerable Acts, coincidentally passing the Quebec Act at the same time. These twin actions aroused ferocious American resistance throughout the colonies, and led directly to the calling of the First Continental Congress and the clash of arms at Lexington and Concord.

As the two sides prepared for war, the British enjoyed the advantages of a larger population, a professionally trained militia, and much greater economic strength. The greatest American asset was the deep commitment of those Patriots who were ready to sacrifice for their rights.

DEVELOPING THE CHAPTER: SUGGESTED LECTURE OR DISCUSSION TOPICS

- Explain how the colonists had gradually developed very strong ideas of "rights" and "liberty" that differed considerably from the meaning of those terms within the context of the eighteenth-century British Empire. Show how, as a result, actions that the British considered moderate and reasonable were seen by the colonists as evidence of a vast conspiracy by a corrupt aristocracy to deprive them of their basic freedoms.

    REFERENCE: Bernard Bailyn, *Ideological Origins of the American Revolution* (1967).

- Examine the crucial issues in the conflict, perhaps focusing on the colonial cry of "No taxation without representation." Point out that this slogan actually revealed how strong a sense of self-government the colonists had already developed, since they did not really *want* representation in the British Parliament (even had it been offered). The same goes for the tricky distinction between "internal" and "external" taxation.

    REFERENCE: Robert Middlekauff, *The Glorious Cause: The American Revolution, 1763–1789* (1982).

- Explain more fully how patriotic groups like the Sons and Daughters of Liberty used boycotts, agitation, propaganda, and sometimes violence or near-violence to keep the Revolutionary movement alive, even in periods of seemingly improved relations. The focus might be on the constant spiral of action and reaction that gradually moved the conflict from an ideological and political debate to open violence and warfare.

    REFERENCES: Pauline Maier, *From Resistance to Revolution* (1972); Edward Countryman, *The American Revolution* (1987).

- Develop an appreciation of the relative strengths and weaknesses of the two sides by focusing on their typical military representatives: the British redcoats and the American minutemen (militia). Point out how the professional British army came to be seen as a hostile occupying force (for example, in the Boston Massacre), while the strong American preference for the "citizen-soldier" militia reflected a love of liberty and dislike of powerful authority.

    REFERENCES: Robert Gross, *The Minutemen and Their World* (1976); John Sly, *Toward Lexington: The Role of the British Army in the Coming of the American Revolution* (1965).

FOR FURTHER INTEREST: ADDITIONAL CLASS TOPICS

- Focus on the question of the inevitability of the War of Independence by asking whether independence might have come without a war. Use Canada as a counterexample to show that British colonies in America did not *have* to revolt but might have developed autonomy (and eventually independence) peacefully within the empire.

- Examine the issue of whether the Revolution was a true revolution in the political and social order or whether it was instead a conservative movement, in the sense of *defending* a status quo Americans had long ago accepted as their natural birthright. A good way to sharpen this question is to discuss whether the Revolution should be viewed primarily as a change from monarchy to republic, as a fight to *preserve* colonial rights, or as the separation of the colonies from England.

- Focus on one of the dramatic episodes of the early Revolutionary struggle: The Stamp Act crisis, the Boston Massacre, the Boston Tea Party, or Lexington and Concord. Discuss how the particulars of the event (for example, rock throwing at British soldiers, dumping the tea) fit into the larger political context of the movement toward Revolution.

- Discuss the role of African-Americans and Indians in the Revolution, both in support of the Patriot cause and as "Loyalists" drawn to back the British. Consider the tensions and contradictions in the Patriots' language of rights and liberty in relation to their treatment of slaves and others whom they did not consider part of their communities.

- Reexamine the conditions and events leading up to the Revolution from a British perspective, including the system of mercantilism and the imposition of taxes. Discuss why the British might have thought they were being quite generous to the colonists (for example, in defending them from France almost for free) while seeing the Americans as ungrateful and hostile to all authority.

CHARACTER SKETCHES

Samuel Adams (1722–1803)

Samuel Adams was the principal political activist for American liberty and rebellion in the early 1770s. As organizer of the committees of correspondence, he strongly influenced the movement toward American independence.

Adams came from a moderately well off and ambitious clan that included his second cousin, John Adams. Samuel failed badly after taking over his father's brewery and ended up deeply in debt. But he turned out to be as good at politics as he was bad at business. By 1763 he was the leader of the "Whipping Post Club," a political group that had a strong local influence. Adams took the "democratic" side against royal Governor Thomas Hutchinson and his wealthy political allies. While Adams never endorsed mob violence, he proved a master at turning popular passions to the advantage of the radical cause. When the tea crisis began, Adams organized the rousing public meetings at Faneuil Hall that culminated in the Boston Tea Party.

Although he served in both Continental Congresses, Adams possessed the skills of an agitator, not a legislator, and he rapidly lost influence once the war began. His later career was confined to Massachusetts (where he served as governor from 1794 to 1797), and he remained deeply suspicious of all forms of centralized power.

Quote: "Driven from every other corner of the earth, freedom of thought and the right of private judgment in matters of conscience direct their course to this happy country as their last asylum." (1776)

REFERENCE: Pauline Maier, *The Old Revolutionaries: Political Lives in the Age of Samuel Adams* (1980); Dennis Fradin, *Samuel Adams: The Father of American Independence* (1998).

Abigail Adams (1744–1818)

Abigail Adams was one of the most thoughtful and articulate American women of the Revolutionary era and an early advocate of a larger public role for women.

The daughter of a well-known Massachusetts family, she received almost no formal education, like many women of the time, but she taught herself a good deal by reading on her own, including French and English literature. After marrying John Adams at age twenty (he was twenty-nine), she bore five children between 1765 and 1772. During the ten years of revolutionary upheaval (1773 to 1783), she and her husband, though mostly apart, maintained a constant correspondence that shows Abigail to have been astute and strong-minded. During John's absence she also managed the family businesses, including their farm in Braintree, Massachusetts.

After the war, when her husband became president, she defended his policies so actively that some of Adams's political opponents sarcastically called her "Mrs. President."

Quote: "Remember the ladies, and be more generous and favorable to them than your ancestors. Do not put such unlimited power in the hands of the husbands. Remember all men would be tyrants if they could. If particular care and attention is not paid to the ladies, we are determined to foment a rebellion, and will not hold ourselves bound by any laws in which we have not had voice or representation." (Letter to John Adams at the Second Continental Congress, 1776)

REFERENCE: Lynne Withey, *Dearest Friend: A Life of Abigail Adams* (1981).

Gilbert du Motier, Marquis de Lafayette (1757–1834)

Lafayette was the French nobleman who joined the American Revolution and promoted the Franco-American alliance. His strong sympathy for the Revolution made him an international liberal hero, while in America he has symbolized Franco-American friendship and devotion to freedom. His youthful decision to join the American cause was made partly because he was genuinely stirred by the Revolutionary appeal to liberty but also because the American war offered heroic adventure.

In his first combat, at Brandywine, the teenage general Lafayette was shot in the leg. He also commanded one of the divisions at Valley Forge. After persuading the French government to make a substantial commitment to the American cause, he played a crucial role as a commander of the Continental army in Virginia in the months preceding Cornwallis's surrender.

A leader of the early phase of the French Revolution of 1789, Lafayette lost power when the Revolution turned more radical, and he ended up in prison. His status as an honorary American citizen was used to gain his release. In 1824 he returned to America for a triumphant tour, during which huge crowds turned out everywhere and greeted him warmly.

Quote: "The moment I heard of America I loved her. The moment I knew she was fighting for freedom, I burned with a desire of bleeding for her; and the moment I shall be able to serve her, at any time or in any part of the world, will be the happiest one of my life."

REFERENCE: Jean Fritz, *Why Not, Lafayette?* (1999).

Paul Revere (1735–1818)

Paul Revere, remembered especially for his "midnight ride" in April 1775 to warn that "the British are coming," was a notable American artisan as well as an active patriot in the Revolutionary cause.

Revere's father was a French Huguenot refugee, and Paul took up his father's trade as a highly skilled silversmith. Revere fought in the French and Indian War, and afterward became active in many patriotic groups such as the Sons of Liberty and the North End caucus. He became well known for his anti-British cartoons and engravings, including one of the Boston Massacre. He was one of the leaders of the "Indians" who carried out the Boston Tea Party.

On their famous ride, Revere and William Dawes successfully roused the colonial militia and alerted John Hancock and Samuel Adams to go into hiding to avoid arrest. Revere and Dawes were finally stopped by British patrols just before they got to Concord, but were released. Revere later designed and printed the first Continental money, and achieved the rank of lieutenant colonel in the Revolutionary army.

Quote: (To a British officer) "You're too late. I've alarmed the country all the way up. We should have five hundred men at Lexington soon."

REFERENCE: JoAnn Grote, *Paul Revere: American Patriot* (2000); David Hackett Fischer, *Paul Revere's Ride* (1994).

QUESTIONS FOR CLASS DISCUSSION

1. Was the American Revolution inevitable? Could America have gradually and peacefully developed independence within the British Commonwealth, as Canada later did, rather than engaging in a violent revolt?

2. Were all the American grievances really justified, or were the British actually being more reasonable than most Americans have traditionally believed?

3. What was the Revolutionary movement at its core really all about? The *amount* of taxation? The *right* of Parliament to tax? The political corruption of Britain and the virtue of America? The right of a king to govern America? The colonies' growing sense of national identity apart from Britain? Was the Revolution truly a radical overturning of government and society—the usual definition of a "revolution"—or something far more limited or even "conservative" in its defense of traditional rights?

4. In 1775 which side would a neutral observer have expected to win—Britain or the colonies? Why?

Suggested Student Exercises

- Examine the biographies of some of the better-known Loyalists, and consider why they remained loyal to Britain while others in similar positions did not. Governor Thomas Hutchinson of Massachusetts and Benjamin Franklin's son William, governor of New Jersey, are good examples. (Even General Benedict Arnold came to be considered a "belated Loyalist.")

- Trace the history and continuing influence of the Loyalists who migrated to Canada after the Revolution. Examine their impact on subsequent Canadian history and political theory.

EXPANDING THE "VARYING VIEWPOINTS"

- Carl L. Becker, *Beginnings of the American People* (1915).

    A "progressive" view of the Revolution as the product of social conflict among colonial groups:

    "It was the opposition of interests in America that chiefly made men extremists on either side....Those men who wished to take a safe middle ground, who wished neither to renounce their country nor to mark themselves as rebels, could no longer hold together."

- Bernard Bailyn, *The Ideological Origins of the American Revolution* (1967).

    An "ideological" view of the Revolution as resulting from the colonists' ideas about liberty and power:

    "The colonists believed they saw emerging from the welter of events during the decade after the Stamp Act a pattern whose meaning was unmistakable....They saw about them, with increasing clarity, not merely mistaken, or even evil, policies violating the principles upon which freedom rested, but what appeared to be evidence of nothing less than a deliberate assault launched surreptitiously by plotters against liberty both in England and in America....This belief transformed the meaning of the colonists' struggle, and it added an inner accelerator to the movement of opposition....It was this...that was signaled to the colonists after 1763, and it was this above all else that in the end propelled them to Revolution."

QUESTIONS ABOUT THE "VARYING VIEWPOINTS"

1. According to each of these viewpoints, what provided the fuel that drove the colonists from particular political disagreements to Revolutionary assertion of independence?

2. How would each of these historians interpret the common view of the American Revolution as a fight for liberty?

3. How would the sequence of events leading up to the Revolution (for example, the Stamp Act and the Boston Tea Party) be treated according to each of these perspectives?

8

America Secedes from the Empire, 1775–1783

CHAPTER THEMES

Theme: When hostilities began in 1775, the colonists were still fighting for their rights as British citizens within the empire, but in 1776 they declared their independence, based on a proclamation of universal, "self-evident" truths. Inspired by revolutionary idealism, they also fought for an end to monarchy and the establishment of a free republic.

Theme: A combination of Washington's generalship and British bungling in 1776–1777 prevented a quick British victory and brought French assistance, which enabled the Patriots to achieve victory after several more years of struggle.

CHAPTER SUMMARY

Even after Lexington and Concord, the Second Continental Congress did not at first pursue independence. The Congress's most important action was selecting George Washington as military commander.

After further armed clashes, George III formally proclaimed the colonists in rebellion, and Thomas Paine's *Common Sense* finally persuaded Americans to fight for independence as well as liberty. Paine and other leaders promoted the Revolution as an opportunity for self-government by the people, though more conservative republicans wanted to retain political hierarchy without monarchy. Jefferson's Declaration of Independence deepened the meaning of the struggle by proclaiming its foundation in self-evident and universal human rights.

The committed Patriots, only a minority of the American population, had to fight both Loyalist Americans and the British. Loyalists were strongest among conservatives, city-dwellers, and Anglicans (except in Virginia), while Patriots were strongest in New England and among Presbyterians and Congregationalists.

In the first phase of the war, Washington stalemated the British, who botched their plan to quash the rebellion quickly at Saratoga. When the French and others then aided the Americans, the Revolutionary War became a world war.

American fortunes fell badly in 1780–1781, but the colonial army in the South held on until Cornwallis stumbled into a French-American trap at Yorktown. Lord North's ministry collapsed in Britain, and American negotiators achieved an extremely generous settlement from the Whigs.

DEVELOPING THE CHAPTER: SUGGESTED LECTURE OR DISCUSSION TOPICS

- Show how *Common Sense* and the Declaration of Independence changed the *meaning* of the fighting. Explain why even Patriots were at first reluctant to proclaim independence and how they eventually came to link their struggle for rights with the break from Britain.

  REFERENCE: Pauline Maier, *American Scripture* (1997).

- Show how Washington and his generals essentially pursued a "defensive" strategy in the early phase of the war, while the British had to try for a quick victory. Explain why the Battle of Saratoga was so crucial politically as well as militarily.

    REFERENCE: Bernard Bailyn, *Faces of Revolution: Personalities and Themes in the Struggle for American Independence* (1990); Piers Mackesy, *The War for America, 1775–1783* (1993).

- Consider the political dimensions of the war, particularly the civil war between Patriots and Loyalists and the politics of the French alliance. The focus might be on the role of the American military effort in swinging the neutral population to the Patriot cause.

    REFERENCE: John Shy, *A People Numerous and Armed: Reflections on the Military Struggle for American Independence* (1976).

- Consider how the Revolution has been viewed and celebrated in various periods of American history (e.g., on Independence Day).

    REFERENCE: Michael Kammen, *A Season of Youth: the American Revolution and the Historical Imagination* (1988).

FOR FURTHER INTEREST: ADDITIONAL CLASS TOPICS

- Focus on Washington's dual role as practical military strategist and heroic symbol of the Patriot cause.

- Examine the Declaration of Independence as both historical document and Revolutionary propaganda. Discuss the short-term and long-term historical significance of the grand rhetoric in the first part and the specific indictment in the second part.

- Consider the role of women in the American Revolution, including both their part in revolutionary events and the new understandings that began to develop regarding their public role as "daughters of liberty" and the questions that raised.

- Compare the American Revolution to other major national revolutions. Comparisons with revolutions and struggles for independence in "new nations" like Mexico, India, and Iran, might be especially illuminating.

CHARACTER SKETCHES

Thomas Paine (1737–1809)

Paine's Revolutionary propaganda in *Common Sense* and the *Crisis* played a critical role in arousing American patriotism. Because of his later role in the French Revolution, and especially his attacks on Christianity in *The Age of Reason*, Paine has long been the most controversial of the Revolutionary heroes. Theodore Roosevelt, for instance, once called him a "dirty little atheist."

After the American Revolution Paine traveled to Britain and France to promote his iron-bridge invention. He became a French citizen and was elected to the Revolutionary Convention. His stirring work, *The Rights of Man*, a reply to Edmund Burke's *Reflections on the Revolution in France,* sold hundreds of thousands of copies and made him a wanted man in Britain.

Following his return to America in 1801, even his influential friends, like Jefferson, avoided him, and he ended his life in poverty. After his death a British admirer dug up his bones and shipped them to Britain, where they were lost.

Quote: "One of the strongest natural proofs of the folly of hereditary right in kings is that nature disapproves it, otherwise she would not so frequently turn it into ridicule by giving mankind an Ass for a Lion....But where, some say, is the King of America? I'll tell you, friend, He reigns above, and doth not make havoc of mankind like the Royal Brute of Great Britain." (*Common Sense,* 1776)

REFERENCE: Eric Foner, *Tom Paine and Revolutionary America* (1976).

Richard Henry Lee (1732–1794)

Richard Henry Lee, the most eloquent Revolutionary orator besides Patrick Henry, was the author of the resolution declaring independence in June of 1776.

Lee came from the wealthy and influential Virginia Lee clan. Along with Henry, he gained political influence with his speeches attacking the Stamp Act and British economic domination of the colonies. He was a commanding presence at the Philadelphia Congress; John Adams was awed by him and called him a "masterly man." His brother, Francis Lightfoot Lee, also signed the Declaration of Independence.

His career declined after the Revolution, and like Henry, he was an Anti-Federalist in the fight over the Constitution. Tall and slender, Lee had receding red hair and a musical voice.

Quote: "Why then do we longer delay? Why still deliberate? Let this most happy day give birth to the American republic. Let her arise, not to devastate and conquer, but to re-establish the reign of peace and law." (Speech to Second Continental Congress, 1776)

REFERENCE: Oliver Perry Chitwood, *Richard Henry Lee: Statesman of the Revolution* (1967).

John Paul Jones (1742–1792)

A naval hero of the American Revolution, Jones is known as the founder of the United States Navy. Although he professed deep commitment to America, he was a Scottish immigrant who actually spent little time in the United States, preferring to live abroad after the Revolution.

His original name was John Paul. He added the "Jones" in 1773, evidently to conceal his identity after being accused of killing a mutineer aboard a British merchant ship he was commanding. He then came to Virginia, made influential friends like Robert Morris, and received authorization to begin a navy. The heroic fight when he lashed the *Serapis* to his *Bonhomme Richard* made him an international hero, although in Britain he was considered a pirate because of his raids on coastal towns.

An extremely complex personality, Jones has puzzled historians and has often been the subject of novels, plays, and poems. Despite his service to America's republican cause, he was devoted to King Louis XIV of France and near the end of his life became an officer in the navy of the despotic czarina of Russia, Catherine II.

Quote: "America has been the country of my fond election, from the age of thirteen, when I first saw it. I had the honor to hoist, with my hands, the flag of freedom, the first time it was displayed on the River Delaware; and I have attended it, with veneration, ever since on the ocean." (1779)

REFERENCE: Samuel Eliot Morison, *John Paul Jones* (1959).

Copyright © Houghton Mifflin Company. All rights reserved.

George Rogers Clark (1752–1818)

Clark was the American frontiersman whose daring exploits won the trans-Appalachian west for the new United States.

Born in Virginia, Clark went west at age nineteen to work as a surveyor along the Ohio River. Clark became a leader of the frontier settlers, who deeply resented the British authorities' connections with Indians. Clark returned to Virginia in 1776 to receive a militia commission to attack British forts. He hoped to raise at least 500 men, but only 175 joined him.

After his great successes in the Illinois campaign and the capture of Vincennes, he attempted to capture the British fort at Detroit in 1779, but failed. Besides his skill at frontier warfare, he proved especially adept at persuading many Indians to abandon the British and support the French and Americans, or at least to remain neutral.

He had little success after the war. Jefferson initially offered him command of the expedition to explore Louisiana, but the position went instead to his brother William.

Quote: (Speech to Indians) "The Great Spirit has caused your old Father the French King and other nations to join the big Knife (Washington) and fight with them, so that the English have become like a deer in the woods."

REFERENCE: Lowell H. Harrison, *George Rogers Clark and the War in the West* (1969).

MAKERS OF AMERICA: THE LOYALISTS

Questions for Class Discussion
1. Why have the Loyalists been largely forgotten in American historical memory? Do they deserve to be better known? Do you agree with the text that they were often "tragic" figures?

2. Did the Loyalists act primarily out of conviction and feelings of patriotism toward Britain, or out of self-interest?

3. If you had been an African-American, free or slave, in 1776, would you have tried to back the Patriot cause or the Loyalist cause? Why?

QUESTIONS FOR CLASS DISCUSSION

1. What was radical and new in the Declaration of Independence, and what was old and traditional? What did statements like "all men are created equal" mean in their historical context, and what did they come to mean later?

2. Was military strategy or politics the key to American victory in the war? How did the two coincide?

3. Did the Loyalists deserve to be persecuted and driven out of the country? What difference does it make to understand the Revolution as a civil war *between* Americans as well as a war against the British?

4. What has the Revolution meant to later generations of Americans, including our own? Do we still think of the United States as a revolutionary nation? Why or why not?

9

The Confederation and the Constitution, 1776–1790

CHAPTER THEMES

Theme: The American Revolution was not a radical transformation like the French or Russian revolutions, but it did produce political innovations and some social change in the direction of greater equality and democracy.

Theme: The federal Constitution represented a moderately conservative reaction against the democratic and decentralizing effects of the Revolution and the Articles of Confederation. In effect, it embedded the revolutionary ideals of liberty and popular government within a strong framework designed to advance national identity and interests against the dangers of fragmentation and disorder.

CHAPTER SUMMARY

The American Revolution did not overturn the social order, but it did produce substantial changes in social customs, political institutions, and ideas about society and government. Among the changes were the separation of church and state in some places, the abolition of slavery in the North, written political constitutions, and a shift in political power from the eastern seaboard toward the frontier.

The first weak national government, the Articles of Confederation, was unable to exercise real authority, although it did successfully deal with the western lands issue. The Confederation's weaknesses in handling foreign policy, commerce and the Shays rebellion spurred the movement to alter the Articles.

Instead of revising the Articles, the well-off delegates to the Constitutional Convention created a permanent charter for a whole new government. In a series of compromises, the convention produced a plan that provided for a vigorous central government, a strong executive, and protection for property, while still upholding republican principles and states' rights. The pro-Constitution Federalists, generally representing wealthier and more commercial forces, frightened other groups who feared that the new government would undermine their rights and their interests.

The Federalists met their strongest opposition from Anti-Federalists in Virginia and New York, but through effective organization and argument, as well as promises to incorporate a bill of rights into the document, they succeeded in getting the Constitution ratified. By establishing the new national government, the Federalists checked the Revolutionary movement, but their conservative regime embraced the central Revolutionary values of popular republican government and liberty.

DEVELOPING THE CHAPTER: SUGGESTED LECTURE OR DISCUSSION TOPICS

- Consider the social changes brought about by the Revolution. Consider specific changes such as church-state separation in Virginia and the abolition of slavery in the North in relation to the Revolution's larger social significance.

    REFERENCE: Gordon Wood, *The Radicalism of the American Revolution* (1991).

- Analyze the structure and workings of the Articles of Confederation government, perhaps using the table on text page 181. Emphasis might be placed on the achievements of the Articles government, such as the western lands issue, as well as its obvious weaknesses.

    REFERENCE: Jack N. Rakove, *The Beginnings of National Politics* (1979).

- Address directly the "Beard interpretation" of the Constitution as a conservative counterrevolution by the propertied elite. Explain the elements of the pro-Constitution movement that support such a view as well as its limits.

    REFERENCES: Charles Beard, *An Economic Interpretation of the Constitution* (1913); Robert Brown, *Charles Beard and the Constitution* (1956); Edmund S. Morgan, *Inventing the People* (1988).

- Describe the ratification struggle as both a hard-fought political contest and a great political debate about the nature of humanity and the purposes of government. Consider particularly the key arguments of the Anti-Federalists, and what might or might not have been legitimate concerns of these historical "losers" (while remembering that the Bill of Rights is in effect a part of their legacy.)

    REFERENCE: Herbert J. Storing, *What the Anti-Federalists Were For* (1981).

FOR FURTHER INTEREST: ADDITIONAL CLASS TOPICS

- Discuss the question of how revolutionary the Revolution was, measured by the social changes it caused. One issue might be why Americans have tended to think of the Revolution more in terms of liberty and political ideas than in terms of social change.

- Compare the difficulties of establishing a stable government in post-Revolutionary America with similar situations in other "new nations" of the modern world.

- Consider how America and American government would be different if the Articles of Confederation had remained the national government. One focus might be the extent to which the concept of "the United States government" is identified with the government of the Constitution.

- Discuss the reverence accorded the Constitution and the Founding Fathers in relation to the actual historical events of 1787. Examine particular provisions of the Constitution, and discuss whether they might have meant something different in the eighteenth century than they do today.

- Examine the treatment of race and slavery in the Constitutional Convention (including how and why it was mostly but not completely avoided in the actual text). Consider the question of whether directly addressing the slavery question would have made the creation of a federal union impossible—and perhaps even led to the creation of a separate pro-slavery confederation in 1787.

CHARACTER SKETCHES

Daniel Shays (1747–1825)

Shays was the Massachusetts Revolutionary War veteran whose rebellion in 1786 spurred the movement for a new Constitution.

A militiaman at both Lexington and Bunker Hill, Shays was typical of the ordinary Revolutionary-era Americans who left their farms to fight in the War for Independence. He rose to captain and after the war was elected to various local offices.

Shays emerged as the leader of the revolt by indebted farmers when eight hundred armed men prevented a Springfield court from hearing foreclosure cases. He continually insisted that the farmers wanted only redress of grievances, not violence, but by early 1787 he was preparing to attack a state arsenal. The attack failed, and Shays fled to Vermont. He was condemned to death but pardoned the next year, and eventually he returned to Massachusetts to live out his days in peace.

Quote: "The people assembled in arms…return for answer that, however unjustifiable the measure may be which the people have adopted in recourse to arms, various circumstances have induced them thereto.…That virtue which truly characterizes the citizens of a republican government hath hitherto marked our plans with a degree of innocence, and we wish and trust it will still be the case." (Reply to Gen. Benjamin Lincoln's demand for surrender, 1787)

REFERENCE: David Szatmoy, *Shays's Rebellion* (1980).

James Madison (1750–1836)

Madison, the "Father of the Constitution," is generally considered the most original political thinker among the Founding Fathers. The only failure during his long career of public service was his term as president, which included the near-disastrous War of 1812.

Madison attended Princeton and considered entering the ministry. He strongly disliked religious intolerance, and his first political activities were on behalf of religious disestablishment in Virginia.

Throughout his life he kept extensive journals, and his notes on the proceedings of the secret Constitutional Convention provide the only detailed record of the arguments there.

Madison's marriage to Dolley Payne Todd was a long and happy one. Since Jefferson was a widower, the Madisons' home was the social center of Washington during both the Jefferson and the Madison administrations. Although quiet, bookish, and introspective, Madison was personally warm and engaging, especially in intimate settings.

Quote: "Hearken not to the unnatural voice which tells you that the people of America, knit together as they are by so many cords of affection, can no longer…be fellow-citizens of one great, respectable, and flourishing empire, Hearken not to the voice which petulantly tells you that the form of government recommended for your adoption is a novelty in the political world.…If novelties are to be shunned, believe me, the most alarming of all novelties, the most wild of all projects, the most rash of all attempts, is that of rending us in pieces, in order to preserve our liberties and promote our happiness." (*Federalist* No. 14, 1788)

REFERENCE: Irving Brant, *The Fourth President: A Life of James Madison* (1970).

Patrick Henry (1736–1799)

Henry was the famous Revolutionary orator and five-term Virginia governor who later became the leading Anti-Federalist opponent of the Constitution.

He came from a plain frontier background rather than from the planter aristocracy. When his uncle took him to hear Samuel Davies, a famous Great Awakening preacher, young Patrick fell in love with the art of persuasive speaking.

Henry's eloquent defenses of Virginia liberty at the time of the Stamp Act made him the youthful leader of the radical party in that state. He made his "give me liberty or give me death!" speech during the debate over whether the Virginia assembly should take steps toward independence.

Henry's young protégé Thomas Jefferson succeeded him as governor during the Revolution, but Henry later demanded an investigation of Jefferson's conduct in office that caused a bitter and lasting feud between the two. In his later years Henry was plagued with financial troubles and became increasingly conservative.

Quote: "It is now confessed that this is a national government....The means, says the gentleman, must be commensurate to the end. How does this apply? All things in common are left with this government. There being an infinitude in the government, there must be an infinitude of means to carry it out." (Virginia debate on the Constitution, 1788)

REFERENCE: Richard R. Beeman, *Patrick Henry* (1974).

GREAT DEBATES IN AMERICAN HISTORY

GREAT DEBATE (1787–1789): The Constitution: Should the United States adopt the new Constitution to replace the Articles of Confederation?

For: The Federalists—led by Washington, Hamilton, Madison, Jay, and Marshall; including most commercial, seacoast, urban, and upper-class groups.

Against: The Anti-Federalists—led by Patrick Henry, Samuel Adams, Richard Henry Lee, George Mason, and George Clinton; including many noncommercial, western, agrarian, and state-oriented interests.

ISSUE #1: Need for change. Does the government of the Articles need to be replaced?

Yes: Federalist Alexander Hamilton: "The faith, the reputation, the peace of the whole Union are thus continually at the mercy, the prejudices, the passions, and the interests of every member of which it is composed. Is it possible that foreign nations can either respect or confide in such a government? Is it possible that the people of America will longer consent to trust their honor, their happiness, their safety, on so precarious a foundation?...The Confederation...is a system so radically vicious and unsound, as to admit not of amendment but by an entire change in its leading features and characters."

No: Anti-Federalist Patrick Henry: "The honorable gentleman said that great danger would ensue if the Convention rose without adopting this system. I ask, where is that danger? I see none. Other gentlemen have told us, within these walls, that the union is gone, or that the union will be gone....Till they tell us the grounds of their fears, I will consider them as imaginary....Where is the danger? If, sir, there was any, I would recur to the American spirit which has enabled us to surmount the greatest difficulties."

The Confederation and the Constitution, 1776–1790

ISSUE #2: Can a republic govern a large territory and a diverse population?

Yes: Federalist James Madison: "Extend the sphere, and you take in a greater variety of parties and interests; you make it less probable that the majority of the whole will have a common motive to invade the rights of other citizens.…Hence, it clearly appears that the same advantage which a republic has over a democracy, in controlling the effects of faction, is enjoyed by a large over a small republic.…"

No: Anti-Federalist James Winthrop of Massachusetts: "It is the opinion of the ablest writers on the subject, that no extensive empire can be governed on republican principles, and that such a government will degenerate to a despotism.…No instance can be found of any free government of any considerable extent.…Large and consolidated empires may indeed dazzle the eyes of a distant spectator with their splendour, but if examined more nearly are always found to be full of misery."

ISSUE #3: Will the new constitutional government create an aristocratic power in the presidency?

No: Federalist Alexander Hamilton: "There is no comparison between the intended power of the President and the actual power of the British sovereign.…The President of the United States would be an officer elected by the people for four years; the king of Great Britain is a perpetual and hereditary prince.…What answer shall we give to those who would persuade us that things so unlike resemble each other? The same that ought to be given to those who tell us that a government, the whole power of which would be in the hands of the elective and periodical servants of the people, is an aristocracy, a monarchy and a despotism."

Yes: Anti-Federalist George Clinton of New York: "Wherein does this president, invested with his powers and prerogatives, essentially differ from the king of Great Britain (save as to the name, the creation of nobility and some immaterial incidents…)? The safety of the people in a republic depends on the share or proportion they have in the government; but experience ought to teach you, that when a man is at the head of an elective government invested with great powers, and interested in his reelection…appointments will be made by which means an imperfect aristocracy bordering on monarchy may be established."

ISSUE #4: Does the proposed Constitution protect the people's liberty?

Yes: Federalist Alexander Hamilton: "Here, in strictness, the people surrender nothing; and as they retain everything they have no need of particular reservations.…Bills of rights, in the sense and to the extent in which they are contended for, are not only unnecessary in the proposed Constitution, but would even be dangerous.…Why declare that things not be done which there is no power to do?…the truth is…that the Constitution is itself, in every rational sense, and to every useful purpose, a BILL OF RIGHTS."

No: Anti-Federalist George Mason of Virginia: "There is no declaration of rights: and the laws of the general government being paramount to the laws and constitutions of the several states, the declarations of rights, in the separate states, are no security. Nor are the people secured even in the enjoyment of the benefit of the common law, which stands here upon no other foundations than its having been adopted by the respective acts forming the constitutions of the several states."

Copyright © Houghton Mifflin Company. All rights reserved.

REFERENCES: Gordon Wood, *The Creation of the American Republic, 1776–1787* (1969); Thorton Anderson, *Creating the Constitution* (1993).

QUESTIONS FOR CLASS DISCUSSION

1. Which of the social changes brought about by the Revolution was the most significant? Could the Revolution have gone further toward the principle that "all men are created equal" by ending slavery or granting women's rights?

2. Was the United States in a crisis under the Articles of Confederation, or was the "crisis" exaggerated by the Federalists to justify their movement? Could the United States have survived if the Articles had stayed in effect?

3. Should the Founding Fathers' general elitism and indifference to the rights of people, women, African-Americans, and Indians be held against them? Or should they be viewed with more understanding in their historical context?

4. What was really at stake in the debate between Federalists and Anti-Federalists? Did the Federalists win primarily because of their superior political skills or because they had a clearer view of the meaning of the Revolution and the future of the United States?

EXPANDING THE "VARYING VIEWPOINTS"

- Charles Beard, *An Economic Interpretation of the Constitution* (1913).

    A view of the Constitution as a conservative "counterrevolution":

    "The concept of the Constitution as a piece of abstract legislation reflecting no group interests and recognizing no economic antagonisms is entirely false. It was an economic document drawn with superb skill by men whose property interests were immediately at stake; and as such it appealed directly and unerringly to identical interests in the country at large."

- Gordon Wood, *The Creation of the American Republic* (1969).

    A view of the Constitution as the extension of republican political theory:

    "Because new ideas had grown often imperceptibly out of the familiar, the arguments the federalists used in 1787–88 never really seemed disruptive or discontinuous. Americans had been prepared for a mighty transformation of political thought by a century and half of political experience telescoped into the rapid intellectual changes that had taken place in the three decades of the Revolutionary era....Americans had destroyed the age-old conception of mixed government and had found new explanations for their policies created in 1776, explanations that rested on their expansion of the principle of representation. America had not discovered the idea of representation, said Madison, but it could 'claim the merit of making the discovery the basis of unmixed and extensive republics.'"

QUESTIONS ABOUT THE "VARYING VIEWPOINTS"

1. Why was Beard's view of the Constitution and the Founding Fathers so shocking when it first appeared? What would be the implications if Beard were correct?

2. Does Wood's view fit Beard's critique of those who see the Constitution as "a piece of abstract legislation reflecting no group interests"? What would Wood see as the "interests" of the Founding Fathers?

3. How would the holder of each of these views understand the relationship between the Revolution and the Constitution? How would each of them interpret the Anti-Federalists?

10

Launching the New Ship of State, 1789–1800

CHAPTER THEMES

Theme: Led by Washington and Hamilton, the first administration under the Constitution overcame various difficulties and firmly established the political and economic foundations of the new federal government.

Theme: The cabinet debate over Hamilton's financial measure expanded into a wider political conflict between Hamiltonian Federalists and Jeffersonian Republicans—the first political parties in America.

Theme: The French Revolution created a severe ideological and political division over foreign policy between Federalists and Republicans. The foreign-policy crisis coincided with domestic political divisions that culminated in the bitter election of 1800, but in the end power passed peacefully from Federalists to Republicans.

CHAPTER SUMMARY

The fledgling government faced considerable difficulties and skepticism about its durability, especially since traditional political theory held that large-scale republics were bound to fail. But President Washington brought credibility to the new government, while his cabinet, led by Alexander Hamilton, strengthened its political and economic foundations.

The government's first achievements were the Bill of Rights and Hamilton's financial system. Through effective leadership, Hamilton carried out his program of funding the national debt, assuming state debts, imposing customs and excise taxes, and establishing a Bank of the United States.

The bank was the most controversial part of Hamilton's program because it raised basic constitutional issues. Opposition to the bank from Jefferson and his followers reflected more fundamental political disagreements about republicanism, economics, federal power, and foreign policy. As the French Revolution evolved from moderation to radicalism, it intensified the ideological divisions between the pro-French Jeffersonians and the pro-British Hamiltonians.

Washington's Neutrality Proclamation angered Republicans, who wanted America to aid Revolutionary France. Washington's policy was sorely tested by the British, who routinely violated American neutrality. In order to avoid war, Washington endorsed the conciliatory Jay's Treaty, further outraging the Republicans and France.

After the humiliating XYZ affair, the United States came to the brink of war with France, but Adams sacrificed his political popularity and divided his party by negotiating peace.

These foreign-policy disagreements embittered domestic politics: Federalists passed the Alien and Sedition Acts, to which Jefferson and Madison responded with the Virginia and Kentucky resolutions.

DEVELOPING THE CHAPTER: SUGGESTED LECTURE OR DISCUSSION TOPICS

- Elaborate on the reasons for skepticism about the new government, particularly the view that factionalism would eventually destroy a republican government that extended over such a large territory. Show how Washington deliberately acted to assert the durability of the new regime.

    REFERENCE: Stanley Elkins and Eric McKitrick, *The Age of Federalism: The Early American Republic, 1788–1800* (1993).

- Explain why the French Revolution was such a dangerously divisive world event, even in America. Point out that part of the disagreement in America was over whether the French were only carrying out the principles of the American Revolution or whether they were advocating a more radical doctrine of class conflict.

    REFERENCE: Daniel Lang, *Foreign Policy in the Early Republic* (1985).

- Show how the Federalist-Republican conflict over foreign policy embittered domestic politics, since it raised charges of "disloyalty" on both sides. The Genêt affair, Jay's Treaty, the quasi-war with France, and the Alien and Sedition Acts might all be viewed in this light.

    REFERENCE: Leonard Levy, *Legacy of Suppression* (1960).

- Consider the Adams-Jefferson contest of 1796 in relation to both foreign and domestic-policy disagreements. The focus might be on how, despite the depth of the conflict over issues, the Federalists and Republicans finally kept their contest within the bounds of peaceful electoral politics and the shared value of republicanism.

    REFERENCE: Lance Banning, ed., *After the Constitution: Party Conflict in the New Republic* (1989).

FOR FURTHER INTEREST: ADDITIONAL CLASS TOPICS

- Focus on the components of Washington's image as the central symbol of republican government and virtue: heroism, integrity, nonpartisanship, reluctance to hold power.

- Compare the American political dilemmas presented by the French Revolution with those in the twentieth century caused by the Russian, Chinese, and Iranian revolutions.

- Discuss the Alien and Sedition Acts as threats to liberty. Consider especially their relation to the new, fragile Bill of Rights.

- Consider whether the Hamilton-Jefferson conflict was just a "normal" political disagreement like those between later American political parties or whether it was a more profound ideological disagreement that really threatened to destroy the new government.

CHARACTER SKETCHES

George Washington (1732–1799)

As both military leader of the Revolution and first president under the Constitution, Washington symbolized the republican ideal of Cincinnatus, the Roman citizen-soldier who only reluctantly abandoned private life to serve his country.

The only serious challenge to Washington's leadership during the Revolution came in 1777 from the "Conway cabal," a group of disgruntled officers, encouraged by some members of Congress, who plotted futilely to oust Washington from command.

In 1782 some Continental army officers proposed making Washington king of America; he was outraged when he heard of it and refused to allow anyone to mention the idea in his presence.

During his "retirement" from 1783 to 1787, his greatest interest was in linking the Potomac and Ohio rivers by road, and he traveled on horseback 650 miles to examine possible routes.

Quote: "My movements to the chair of government will be accompanied by feelings not unlike those of a culprit who is going to his place of execution." (1788)

REFERENCE: Garry Wills, *Cincinnatus* (1984).

Alexander Hamilton (1757–1804)

Hamilton was the political and financial genius of the early Republic whose heroic postures, personal ambition, and taste for aristocratic government made many of his contemporaries fear him, even though everyone recognized his great talents.

Born on the British West Indian island of Nevis, Hamilton came to New York at age fourteen to begin his education. The unfair attacks on him as a "bastard" arose because his mother had not obtained a legal divorce from her previous husband before establishing her union with Hamilton's father.

He became Washington's aide-de-camp in the Revolution and rose to lieutenant colonel. Extremely hot-tempered and sometimes vindictive, Hamilton denounced Washington behind his back and resigned from his staff after Washington once rebuked him for lateness.

He feuded with Aaron Burr for years in New York and helped block him from the governorship and, possibly, the presidency. He tried to avoid Burr's demand for a duel, but when Burr made Hamilton's refusal a matter of public honor, Hamilton reluctantly accepted.

Quote: "The love of fame, the ruling passion of the noblest minds, prompts a man to plan and undertake extensive and arduous enterprises for the public benefit, requiring considerable time to mature and perfect them." (*Federalist* No. 72, 1788)

REFERENCE: Gerald Stourzh, *Alexander Hamilton and the Idea of Republican Government* (1970).

John Jay (1754–1829)

Jay was one of the authors (with Madison and Hamilton) of the *Federalist Papers*. His negotiation of Jay's Treaty with Great Britain in 1795 made him a hero to Federalists and a hated symbol of American humiliation to Jeffersonian Republicans.

Although somewhat humorless and vain, Jay had a very high sense of honor. At King's College (Columbia) he was once temporarily suspended for refusing to reveal the name of a fellow student who had committed vandalism.

Washington offered him his choice of any position in the new government, and Jay chose chief justice of the United States. He carefully cultivated influential British citizens during the negotiation of the commercial treaty with Britain in order to obtain the most favorable terms, but to the Republicans who burned him in effigy, these contacts were proof that he had sold out American interests.

Quote: "Further concessions on the part of Great Britain cannot, in my opinion, be attained. If this treaty fails, I despair of another....If I entirely escape censure, I shall be agreeably disappointed." (Letter, 1795)

REFERENCE: Richard B. Morris, *John Jay* (1975).

John Adams (1735–1826)

Adams was the Massachusetts Revolutionary and Federalist president whose public appeal never matched his political and intellectual talents.

He originally considered becoming a minister, but "frigid John Calvin" repelled him, and he turned to law. During his frequent missions abroad, he lived very frugally and constantly complained of the "extravagance" of his fellow diplomats like Franklin and Jay.

He thought that Hamilton maneuvered to get him elected to the vice presidency, which he called "the most insignificant office that ever the invention of man contrived or the mind of man conceived." Although he was prickly and cold in most situations, his diaries and letters to his wife Abigail show his warm, anxious, and generous side.

He renewed his friendship with Jefferson after both left office, and they exchanged numerous letters until they died within a few hours of each other on July 4, 1826. Adams's last words were "Thomas Jefferson still lives."

Quote: "My reputation has been so much the sport of the public, for fifty years, and will be with posterity, that I hold it a bubble, a gossamer, that idles in the wanton summer air." (Letter to Jefferson, 1813)

REFERENCE: Peter Shaw, *The Character of John Adams* (1976).

Aaron Burr (1756–1836)

Burr was the vice president of the United States who killed Alexander Hamilton in a duel and then organized a mysterious conspiracy to separate parts of the West from the United States.

A grandson of Jonathan Edwards, the Great Awakening preacher, Burr was charming and eloquent but always loved adventure and intrigue. He nearly joined the Conway cabal against Washington and helped organize the Tammany Hall political club in New York.

After killing Hamilton in the duel on July 11, 1804, he first fled but then returned to preside as vice president over the impeachment trial of Samuel Chase before embarking on his western conspiracy.

Burr's plotting was so complicated and confusing that it is still uncertain whether he wanted to set up a new western nation under himself or to form a private army to invade Mexico. Although technically acquitted in his treason trial, he was completely disgraced. He fled to France, where he lived in poverty and tried to get Napoleon to endorse his schemes for an invasion of America.

Quote: "Political opposition can never absolve gentlemen from a rigid adherence to the laws of honor....You have indulged in the use of language derogatory to my honor as a gentleman....To this I expect a definite reply which must lead to an accommodation, or the only alternative which the circumstances of the case will justify." (Dueling challenge to Alexander Hamilton, 1804)

Copyright © Houghton Mifflin Company. All rights reserved.

REFERENCE: Herbert S. Parmet and Marie B. Hecht, *Aaron Burr: Portrait of an Ambitious Man* (1967).

GREAT DEBATES IN AMERICAN HISTORY

GREAT DEBATE (1791–1801): Whose political theories and programs are more conducive to creating a strong, free Republic: Hamilton's or Jefferson's?

For Hamilton: The Federalists—led by Hamilton, Adams, Jay, Marshall, and Pickering; including merchants, urban upper classes and conservative clergy.

For Jefferson: The Republicans—led by Jefferson, Madison, Monroe, and Burr; including farmers, westerners, and urban craft workers and tradespeople.

ISSUE #1: Loose or strict construction. Should the Constitution be interpreted loosely to grant implied powers to the federal government?

Yes: Federalist Hamilton: "The means by which national exigencies are to be provided for, national inconveniences obviated, national prosperity promoted are of such infinite variety, extent, and complexity, that there must of necessity be great latitude of discretion in the selection and application of these means. If the *end* be clearly comprehended within any of the specified powers, and if the measure have an obvious relation to the *end,* and it is not forbidden by any particular provision of the constitution, it may safely be deemed to come within the compass of the national authority."

No: Republican Jefferson: "I consider the foundation of the Constitution as laid on this ground—that *all powers not delegated to the United States by the Constitution, nor prohibited by it to the states, are reserved to the states, or to the people.* To take a single step beyond the boundaries thus specifically drawn around the powers of congress is to take possession of a boundless field of power, no longer susceptible of any definition."

ISSUE #2: Manufacturing versus agriculture. Should urban commerce and manufacturing be promoted as much as agriculture?

Yes: Federalist Hamilton: "The spirit of enterprise, useful and prolific as it is, must necessarily be contracted or expanded, in proportion to the simplicity or variety of the occupations and productions which are to be found in a society. It must be less in a nation of mere cultivators, than in a nation of cultivators and merchants; less in a nation of cultivators and merchants, than in a nation of cultivators, artificers, and merchants."

No: Republican Jefferson: "Those who labour in the earth are the chosen people of God, if ever he had a chosen people, whose breasts he has made his peculiar deposit for substantial and genuine virtue....Corruption of morals in the mass of cultivators is a phenomenon of which no age nor nation has furnished an example....Generally speaking the proportion which the aggregate of the other classes of citizens bears in any state to that of its husbandmen, is the proportion of its unsound to its healthy parts....The mobs of great cities add just so much to the support of pure government, as sores do to the strength of the human body."

ISSUE #3: Should the common people be trusted with government?

No: Federalist Hamilton: "All communities divide themselves into the few and the many. The first are the rich and well born; the other, the mass of the people. The voice of the people has been said to be the voice of God; and however generally this maxim has been quoted and believed, it is not true in fact. The people are turbulent and changing; they seldom judge or determine right. Give therefore to the first class a distinct, permanent share in the government. They will check the unsteadiness of the second; and as they cannot receive any advantage by a change, they therefore will ever maintain good government."

Yes: Republican Jefferson: "Whenever the people are well-informed, they can be trusted with their own government; wherever things get so far wrong as to attract their notice, they may be relied on to set them right.

"I am not among those who fear the people. They, and not the rich, are our dependence for continued freedom.

"The mass of mankind has not been born with saddles on their backs, nor a favored few booted and spurred ready to ride them legitimately, by the grace of God."

ISSUE #4: The French Revolution. Should the United States view the French Revolution with sympathy and approval?

No: Federalist Hamilton: "The cause of France is compared with that of America during its late revolution. Would to heaven that the comparison were just. Would to heaven that we could discern in the mirror of French affairs the same humanity, the same decorum, the same gravity, the same order, the same dignity, the same solemnity, which distinguished the cause of the American Revolution. Clouds and darkness would not then rest upon the issue as they now do. I own I do not like the comparison."

Yes: Republican Jefferson: "I still hope the French Revolution will end happily. I feel that the permanence of our own leans in some degree on that; and that a failure there would be a powerful argument to prove there must be a failure here.

"My own affections have been deeply wounded by some of the martyrs to this cause, but rather than it should have failed, I would have seen half the earth desolated; were there but an Adam and Eve left in every country, and left free, it would be better than it now is."

REFERENCES: Richard Buel, Jr., *Securing the Revolution: Ideology in American Politics*, 1789–1815 (1972); Daniel Lang, *Foreign Policy in the New Republic* (1985).

QUESTIONS FOR CLASS DISCUSSION

1. Why did Hamilton move so rapidly to create large financial commitments by the federal government? Since we normally think of the "federal debt" as something bad, why did Hamilton think of it as something good and necessary for the national welfare?

2. How sympathetic should Revolutionary Americans have been to the king-killing French Revolution?

3. Why were political parties viewed as so dangerous by the Founding Fathers? Why did parties come into being at all, and why did they come to be accepted as legitimate ways to express political disagreement?

Copyright © Houghton Mifflin Company. All rights reserved.

4. Contrast the Hamiltonian Federalist belief that the "wealthy and well educated" ought to run the government with the Jeffersonian Republican belief that the common person, if educated, could be trusted to manage public affairs. Was Jefferson's faith in the ordinary white farmers too much linked to his support of slavery?

EXPANDING THE "VARYING VIEWPOINTS"

- John Fiske, *Essays Historical and Literary* (1902).

    A view of the Hamiltonian-Jeffersonian conflict as fundamentally philosophical:

    "It may be said that in American politics all men must be disciples either of Jefferson or of Hamilton. These two statesmen represented principles that go beyond American history, principles that have found their application in the history of all countries and will continue to do so....The question always is how much authority shall the governing portion of the community be allowed to exercise, to how great an extent shall it be permitted to interfere with private affairs, to take people's money in the shape of taxes, whether direct or indirect, and in other ways to curb or restrict the freedom of individuals....Now if we compare parties in America with parties in England, unquestionably the Jeffersonians correspond to the Liberals and Hamiltonians to the Tories. It is, on the whole, the latter who wish to enlarge the powers of government."

- Charles Beard, *Economic Origins of Jeffersonian Democracy* (1915).

    A view of the Hamilton-Jefferson dispute as fundamentally economic:

    "The spokesmen of the Federalist and Republican parties, Hamilton and Jefferson, were respectively the spokesmen of capitalistic and agrarian interests....The party of opposition to the administration charged the Federalists with building up an aristocracy of wealth by the measures of government and appealed to the mass of the people, that is, the farmers, to resist the exactions of a 'moneyed aristocracy.' By the ten years' campaign against the ruling class, they were able to arouse the vast mass of the hitherto indifferent voters and in the end swamp the compact minority which had dominated the country."

QUESTIONS ABOUT THE "VARYING VIEWPOINTS"

1. What does each of these views see as the basic issue between the Hamiltonians and Jeffersonians?

2. How does each of them explain the extension of the Hamilton-Jefferson dispute into a sustained party conflict?

3. How would each of them explain the conflict over Hamilton's Bank and governmental support for business?

11

The Triumphs and Travails of Jeffersonian Democracy, 1800–1812

CHAPTER THEMES

Theme: Jefferson's effective, pragmatic policies strengthened the principles of two-party republican government, even though the Jeffersonian "revolution" caused sharp partisan battles between Federalists and Republicans over particular issues.

Theme: Despite his intentions, Jefferson became deeply entangled in the foreign-policy conflicts of the Napoleonic era, leading to a highly unpopular and failed embargo that revived the moribund Federalist Party.

Theme: James Madison fell into an international trap, set by Napoleon, that Jefferson had avoided. Western War Hawks' enthusiasm for a war with Britain was matched by New Englanders' hostility.

CHAPTER SUMMARY

The ideological conflicts of the early Republic culminated in the bitter election of 1800 between Adams and Jefferson. Despite the fierce rhetoric of the campaign, the "Revolution of 1800" demonstrated that the infant Republic could peacefully transfer power from one party to another. The election of 1800 also signaled the decline of the conservative Federalist Party, which proved unable to adjust to the democratic future of American politics.

Jefferson the political theorist came to Washington determined to restore what he saw as the original American revolutionary ideals and to implement his Republican principles of limited and frugal government, strict construction, and an antimilitarist foreign policy. But Jefferson the practical politician had to compromise many of these goals, thereby moderating the Republican-Federalist ideological conflict.

The sharpest political conflicts occurred over the judiciary, where John Marshall worked effectively to enshrine the principles of judicial review and a strong federal government. Against his original intentions, Jefferson himself also enhanced federal power by waging war against the Barbary pirates and by his dramatic purchase of Louisiana from Napoleon. The Louisiana Purchase was Jefferson's greatest success, increasing national unity and pointing to America's long-term future in the West. But in the short term the vast geographical expansion fostered schemes like Aaron Burr's to break the west away from the United States.

Nevertheless, Jefferson became increasingly entangled in the horrific European wars between Napoleonic France and Britain, as both great powers obstructed American trade and violated freedom of the seas. Jefferson attempted to avoid war through his embargo policy, which damaged the American economy and stirred bitter opposition in New England.

Jefferson's successor, James Madison, soon stumbled into a diplomatic trap set by Napoleon, and western "War Hawks" hoping to acquire Canada whooped the United States into a war with Britain in 1812. The nation went to war totally unprepared, bitterly divided, and devoid of any coherent strategy.

DEVELOPING THE CHAPTER: SUGGESTED LECTURE OR DISCUSSION TOPICS

- Focus on the rivalry between John Adams and Jefferson, examining their genuine and deeply held differences of principle regarding power, liberty, and the meaning of the new American experiment. Trace the evolution of their relationship, as it eventually revealed (in their letters) the even deeper commitments to American values that they shared.

    REFERENCE: Joseph Ellis, *Founding Brothers* (2001).

- Consider the close connection between politics and law in the early history of the Supreme Court, with Federalist Marshall contending with Republican Jefferson. Show the importance of Marshall's bold new principle that the Supreme Court has the final power to interpret the Constitution.

    REFERENCE: G. Edward White, *The Marshall Court and Cultural Change* (1988).

- Analyze the causes and consequences of the Louisiana Purchase, particularly its long-term implications for the Federalist-Republican conflict. Consider the expansion into Louisiana in relation to Americans' increasing fascination with the West, spurred in part by the Lewis and Clark expedition.

    REFERENCE: Donald Jackson, *Thomas Jefferson and the Stony Mountain* (1981).

- Consider the puzzling problem of the causes of the War of 1812, and particularly the issue of maritime causes versus the Western War Hawks' frontier concerns. Examine the question of whether declaring war against Britain was essentially an emotional and irrational outburst, or whether it involved a defense of central American interests and principles.

    REFERENCE: Donald R. Hickey, *The War of 1812: A Forgotten Conflict* (1989); J.C.A. Stagg, *Mr. Madison's War: Politics, Warfare, and Diplomacy in the Early American Republic* (1983).

FOR FURTHER INTEREST: ADDITIONAL CLASS TOPICS

- Focus on Jefferson as political philosopher, practical political leader, and enduring symbol of American democracy. Examine the elements of Jefferson's political ideals, and compare them with his actual performance in office.

- Consider the role of the Supreme Court and judicial review in the American political system in Jefferson's time and after. Discuss particularly its apparently "antidemocratic" character.

- Focus on the causes and consequences of the Louisiana Purchase, particularly on its implications for the future westward movement of the United States. Examine the Lewis and Clark Expedition as both an enterprise of geographical and scientific inquiry and as a political maneuver to put an American imprint on the North American continent. (Note that Lewis and Clark traveled far beyond the Purchase territory proper, implying even further expansion.)

- Examine the background and ambitions of the young western "War Hawks" of 1812, including people like Congressman Henry Clay. Consider the important place of Canada in the thinking of those who pushed for war against Britain.

CHARACTER SKETCHES

Thomas Jefferson (1743–1826)

Jefferson was, after Washington and Franklin, the most celebrated of the Founding Fathers, and the one who most completely combined intellectual genius in many fields with practical political skill.

In his youth Jefferson was a lighthearted socialite, horseman, and violinist, but he became more serious and philosophical after an unhappy love affair, and especially after the death of his young wife in 1782.

A poor public speaker, Jefferson nevertheless excelled at legislative and political work behind the scenes. His literary skill led Franklin, Adams, and the other members of the drafting committee to assign him to write the Declaration of Independence. His original version included an attack on slavery, but this was removed.

Soft-spoken and informal in manner, Jefferson liked to receive visitors at Monticello or the White House in slippers and casual clothes and drape himself across furniture as he spoke. The charge that he fathered children by one of his slaves, Sally Hemings, grew out of contemporary rumors and was published by a hostile journalist in 1802. Although Jefferson's paternity was accepted as fact within the black Hemings clan, Jefferson's admirers contended over the years that Jefferson's nephew was the father. In the late 1990s, DNA tests of Jefferson's acknowledged white descendants and descendants of Hemings confirmed the very high likelihood that Jefferson did have a liaison with Hemings. On his tombstone Jefferson listed his three great achievements as being the author of the Declaration of Independence and the Virginia Statute for Religious Freedom and the founder of the University of Virginia.

Quote: "A government regulating itself by what is just and wise for the many, uninfluenced by the local and selfish interests of the few who direct their affairs, has not been seen, perhaps, on earth. . . . Still, I believe it does exist here in a greater degree than anywhere else, and for its growth and continuance I offer sincere prayers." (Letter to John Adams, 1813)

REFERENCE: Noble Cunningham, *In Pursuit of Reason: The Life of Thomas Jefferson* (1987); Joseph Ellis, *American Sphinx: The Character of Thomas Jefferson* (1997).

Meriwether Lewis (1774–1809)

Lewis was Jefferson's private secretary and leader of the expedition that explored the Louisiana Purchase territory.

He grew up as Jefferson's neighbor and friend. As Jefferson's presidential secretary, he supervised White House social life as well as official correspondence.

Jefferson and Lewis had planned an expedition to the west coast even before the Louisiana Purchase. William Clark was the geographer and manager of the expedition, while the better-educated Lewis carried out the scientific and cultural side of the mission. On the return trip from Oregon, Lewis was accidentally wounded by one his men, who mistook him for a deer.

Shortly after being made governor of Louisiana, Lewis was shot to death in a remote Tennessee inn. Some people claimed he was murdered, but Jefferson said Lewis was subject to frequent bouts of depression and believed he had committed suicide.

Quote: "We were now about to penetrate a country at least two thousand miles in width, on which the foot of civilized man has not trodden; the good or evil it had in store for us was an experiment yet to determine....Entertaining, as I do, the most confident hope of succeeding in a voyage which has formed a project of mine for the last ten years, I could but esteem this moment of departure as among the most happy of my life." (Journal, Fort Mandan, 1805)

Copyright © Houghton Mifflin Company. All rights reserved.

REFERENCE: Stephen Ambrose, *Undaunted Courage* (1996).

Sacajawea (1787?–1812?)

Sacajawea was the Shoshone Indian who served as translator and negotiator on the Lewis and Clark expedition.

The daughter of a chief, she was married, along with another Indian woman, to Toussaint Charbonneau, a French-Canadian *voyageur* who lived with the Indians. Charbonneau became an interpreter for Lewis and Clark at Fort Mandan in Dakota, and Sacajawea joined the expedition even though she had given birth two months before to a son, John Baptiste.

Contrary to legend, Sacajawea did little guiding, but she did translate. When the expedition reached her own people along the Snake River, she was overjoyed and learned that her brother had become chief.

Clark became attached to her son and offered to raise him. After initially refusing, she and Charbonneau joined Clark in St. Louis, left their son with him, and returned to Dakota.

Controversy surrounds whether Sacajawea died shortly thereafter at Fort Mandan or lived to old age on the Wind River reservation in Wyoming. Because she was taken up as a heroine by American suffragists, there are more monuments to her than to any other American woman.

REFERENCE: Ella Clark and Margot Edmonds, *Sacajawea of the Lewis and Clark Expedition* (1979).

Henry Clay (1777–1852)

Clay was a Kentucky congressman and senator who, along with Webster and Calhoun, dominated congressional politics in the early nineteenth century. Beginning his career as a spokesman for the new West, he spent most of it as a Border State moderate trying to mediate between North and South.

Clay moved from Virginia to Lexington, Kentucky, in 1797 and became the state's most renowned criminal lawyer. Although initially sympathetic to Aaron Burr's schemes, he was eventually convinced by Jefferson of Burr's treasonous intentions.

Eloquent and impetuous, Clay displayed a hot western temper. His lifelong feud with Jackson began when he criticized Jackson's invasion of Florida in 1819. He maneuvered during his whole political life for the presidency but never attained it. His statement "I would rather be right than be President" can be taken with a grain of salt, since he frequently modified positions for political advantage, notably in the presidential campaign of 1844.

Like other westerners of the time, he loved horse racing, cards, liquor, and dueling—though he finally gave up the last practice.

Quote: "An honorable cause is attainable by an efficient war.... In such a cause, with the aid of Providence, we must come out crowned with success. But if we fail, let us fail like men, lash ourselves to our gallant tars, and expire together in one common struggle, fighting for Free Trade and Seamen's Rights." (Congressional speech, 1811)

REFERENCE: Robert Remini, *Henry Clay: Statesman for the Union* (1991).

Tecumseh (1768–1813)

Tecumseh was a Shawnee warrior who organized a major Indian confederacy against the United States just before the War of 1812.

His father, a Shawnee chief, was killed in battle with whites in 1774. Between 1805 and 1810 Tecumseh worked to organize his own people and also became well known among the Potawatomies and Kickapoos in Ohio and Indiana.

He was at first subordinate to his brother Tenskwatawa—commonly called the Prophet—a Shawnee shaman, or medicine man, who preached a revival of traditional Indian religion. In 1810–1811 Tecumseh expanded his influence across the whole Northwest, persuading each of the tribes not to sell land to whites without the consent of all.

Ignoring Tecumseh's advice, his brother launched a premature battle against General Harrison at Tippecanoe and was killed. Tecumseh and his remaining warriors joined the British side in the War of 1812, but Tecumseh, too, was killed at the battle of the Thames, ending the last Indian attempt at a united front against white advance.

Quote: "The Great Spirit...gave this great island to his red children. He placed the whites on the other side of the big water. They were not content with their own, but came to take ours from us. They have driven us from the sea to the lakes. We can go no farther. They have taken upon themselves to say this tract belongs to the Miami, this to the Delawares, and so on. But the Great Spirit intended it to be the common property of all the tribes, nor can it be sold without the consent of all." (Speech, 1810)

REFERENCE: R. David Edmunds, *Tecumseh and the Quest for Indian Leadership* (1984).

QUESTIONS FOR CLASS DISCUSSION

1. In what sense, if any, is the idea of a "Revolution of 1800" justified? (Note that Jefferson himself always considered that his election represented a genuine "revolution"—but what did he really mean or understand by that term in this context?)

2. How did Jefferson's Louisiana Purchase transform America's understanding of itself and its future? Was it inevitable that the west would become part of a much greater United States, or was their real danger in efforts like Aaron Burr's to break those areas off from the country?

3. How does the period 1800–1812 look if viewed through American Indian eyes? Could the attempt of Tecumseh and the Prophet to unite western Indians against American expansion have created a different dynamic in white-Indian relations?

4. Was there any merit at all in Jefferson's embargo policy? Could some other policy have succeeded? Was Madison's ill-prepared stumble into war any better than the embargo, or was the United States simply stuck in an impossible position between Britain and France?

12

The Second War for Independence and the Upsurge of Nationalism, 1812–1824

CHAPTER THEMES

Theme: The American effort in the War of 1812 was plagued by poor strategy, political divisions, and increasingly aggressive British power. Nevertheless, the United States escaped with a stalemated peace settlement, and soon turned its isolationist back to the Atlantic European world.

Theme: The aftermath of the War of 1812 produced a strong surge of American nationalism that was reflected in economics, law, and foreign policy. The rising nationalistic spirit and sense of political unity was, however, threatened by the first severe sectional dispute over slavery.

CHAPTER SUMMARY

Americans began the War of 1812 with high hopes of conquering Canada. But their strategy and efforts were badly flawed, and before long British and Canadian forces had thrown the United States on the defensive. The Americans fared somewhat better in naval warfare, but by 1814 the British had burned Washington and were threatening New Orleans. The Treaty of Ghent ended the war in a stalemate that solved none of the original issues. But Americans counted the war a success and increasingly turned away from European affairs and toward isolationism.

Despite some secessionist talk by New Englanders at the Hartford Convention, the ironic outcome of the divisive war was a strong surge of American nationalism and unity. Political conflict virtually disappeared during the "Era of Good Feelings" under President Madison. A fervent new nationalism appeared in diverse areas of culture, economics and foreign policy.

The Era of Good Feelings was soon threatened by the Panic of 1819, caused largely by excessive land speculation and unstable banks. An even more serious threat came from the first major sectional dispute over slavery, which was postponed but not really resolved by the Missouri Compromise of 1820.

Under Chief Justice John Marshall, the Supreme Court further enhanced its role as the major force upholding a powerful national government and conservative defense of property rights. Marshall's rulings partially checked the general movement toward states' rights and popular democracy.

Nationalism also led to a more assertive American foreign policy. Andrew Jackson's military adventures in Spanish Florida resulted in the cession of that territory to the U.S. American fears of European intervention in Latin America encouraged Monroe and J. Q. Adams to lay down the Monroe Doctrine.

DEVELOPING THE CHAPTER: SUGGESTED LECTURE OR DISCUSSION TOPICS

- Examine the military stalemate of the war, particularly the American failure to conquer Canada and the relative success of American naval forces on the Great Lakes.

REFERENCE: Donald R. Hickey, *The War of 1812* (1989).

- Examine Madison's largely unsuccessful role as wartime president, in contrast with his genius as political theorist, constitution-maker, and legislative leader. Indicate the various international and domestic divisions that he proved unable to navigate in the White House.

    REFERENCE: Jack N. Rakove, *James Madison and the Creation of the American Republic* (1990).

- Explain the conflict of 1819–1820 about Missouri as the first clear indication of a deep-seated sectional division over slavery. Emphasize the two essential principles of sectional balance enshrined in the compromise: equal Senate representation of the 36° 30' line as the northern boundary of slavery.

    REFERENCE: Glover Moore, *The Missouri Controversy, 1819–1821* (1953).

- Consider the causes and consequences of the Monroe Doctrine. The emphasis might be on the difference between the doctrine's original context (the monarchist threat to the new Latin American republics) and the controversial ways in which the doctrine has sometimes been invoked in American history. Explain the relationship of the doctrine to the permanent issue of the United States' interactions with its Latin American neighbors.

    REFERENCE: James E. Lewis, *The American Union and the Problem of Neighborhood* (1998).

FOR FURTHER INTEREST: ADDITIONAL CLASS TOPICS

- Consider the War of 1812 in relation to American nationalism. Discuss the way that Andrew Jackson's victory in a battle fought *after* the peace treaty had been signed enabled Americans to emerge with flag-waving patriotism after a bungled and divisive war.

- Analyze the Federalist opposition and the Hartford Convention. Consider whether the charge of treason was justified.

- Discuss the war in relation to Canada. Consider how it might look from a Canadian perspective.

- Analyze one or more of Marshall's rulings—for example, *McCulloch v. Maryland*—in order to show how he strengthened conservative federal power against the democratizing tendencies of states' rights.

- Discuss the mixed motives behind the Monroe Doctrine and the ambiguous meanings that could be attached to it. Consider whether its primary purpose was to thwart Britain and the Old World powers, to protect the Latin American republics, or assert American security interests.

CHARACTER SKETCHES

Francis Scott Key (1779–1843)

Key was the author of "The Star-Spangled Banner" during the War of 1812.

The scion of a well-off Maryland family, he was an influential young Washington attorney at the time of the war. Having been sent aboard a British ship to negotiate the release of an American doctor captured during the British attack on Washington, Key spent the night there when the ship began bombarding Fort McHenry. The following morning he was thrilled to see the American flag.

He wrote the poem rapidly on an envelope. A few days later it was printed in the *Baltimore American* and was soon being sung in taverns and theaters in Baltimore and elsewhere in the country to the tune of the English drinking song "To Anacreon in Heaven." Key may have had the tune in mind when he composed the poem.

He wrote only a few other light verses in his life. He later became the U.S. district attorney for the District of Columbia and carried out negotiations with southwestern Indians.

Quote: "Oh, thus be it ever, when free men shall stand
Between their loved homes, and the war's desolation
Blessed with vict'ry and peace, may the heaven-rescued land
Praise the power that hath made and preserved us a nation.
Then conquer we must, when our cause it is just
And this be our motto, 'In God is our trust.'
And the Star-Spangled Banner in triumph shall wave
O'er the land of the free and the home of the brave."
(Last verse of "The Star-Spangled Banner," 1814)

REFERENCE: George Suejda, *History of the Star-Spangled Banner from 1814 to the Present* (1969).

James Monroe (1758–1831)

Monroe was the last of the "Virginia dynasty" of presidents who presided over the "Era of Good Feelings."

He owed much of his political rise to Jefferson and in 1788 purchased a new plantation in order to live closer to Monticello.

Although not present at the Constitutional Convention, Monroe was a delegate to the Virginia ratifying convention, where he opposed the Constitution. He was thus the only Anti-Federalist elected president.

As minister to France in 1794, Monroe was sharply criticized for his excessively friendly remarks to the Revolutionary National Convention. He maneuvered for the presidency as early as 1809 but backed down when Madison became the clear favorite.

He was diligent, persevering, efficient, but rather unimaginative and colorless, especially compared with the other Virginia presidents.

Quote: "The Missouri question absorbs, by its importance, and the excitement it has produced, every other....I have never known a question so menacing to the tranquillity and even the continuance of our Union as the present one. All other subjects have given way to it and appear to be almost forgotten." (Letter to Jefferson, 1820)

REFERENCE: Harry Ammon, *James Monroe: The Quest for National Identity* (1971).

John C. Calhoun (1782–1850)

Calhoun was Monroe's secretary of war, senatorial spokesman for the South, and a brilliant political theorist and defender of slavery.

He was among Clay's young "war hawks" who advocated the War of 1812 and an ardent nationalist in the years following the war. After seeking the presidency in 1824, he settled for the vice presidency under Adams and then under Jackson.

His extended feud with Jackson began when Jackson learned that Calhoun had opposed Jackson's invasion of Florida in cabinet discussions. It reached fever pitch when Calhoun's socially conscious wife snubbed Peggy Eaton, forcing Calhoun's resignation from the vice presidency.

Once he became a purely sectional figure, Calhoun spent much time writing political theory, including his doctrine of the "concurrent majority." He also proposed the creation of a dual presidency, with a northern president and a southern president each having mutual veto power.

He died shortly after his last speech was read for him in the Senate during the debate over the Compromise of 1850. His last words were, "The South, the poor South."

Quote: "Our fate as a people is bound up in the question of preserving slavery. If we yield, we will be extirpated; but if we successfully resist we will be the greatest and most flourishing people of modern time. It is the best substratum of population in the world; and one on which great and flourishing commonwealths may be most easily and safely reared." (Speech, 1838)

REFERENCE: John Niven, *John C. Calhoun and the Price of Union* (1988).

John Marshall (1755–1835)

Marshall was the chief justice who originated judicial review and established the Supreme Court as an influential branch of government.

Born in a log cabin on the frontier, he was taught primarily by his father. He fought in many Revolutionary battles and served at Valley Forge, remarking that the Revolution made him "confirmed in the habit of considering America as my country and Congress as my government."

Although he moved in aristocratic Federalist circles in Washington, Marshall was the most democratic of men. He liked to drink whiskey in taverns with ordinary country people, do his own marketing, and play quoits and horseshoes with farmers. When not in his judicial robes, he wore dirty, shabby clothes, and even his casual cousin Jefferson considered his appearance unkempt.

Quote: "There, Brother Story, that's the law. Now you find the precedents." (Comment to Justice Joseph Story, c. 1820)

REFERENCE: Leonard Baker, *John Marshall: A Life in Law* (1974).

QUESTIONS FOR CLASS DISCUSSION

1. Is it valid to call the War of 1812 "America's worst-fought war"? Was the cause of the failure essentially military, or was it an inevitable result of the political disunity over the war's purposes? (One might compare the War of 1812 to other politically divisive conflicts like the Mexican War and the Vietnam War.)

2. What was significant about the strong spirit of nationalism that appeared in America from 1815 to 1824? What were its accomplishments?

3. Did the Missouri Compromise effectively deal with the sectional conflict over slavery or merely shove it out of view?

4. Was the Monroe Doctrine a valuable assertion of the principles of liberty and self-determination in the Americas against potential European and monarchical intrusion, or was it in effect an early

manifestation of a patronizing and potentially imperialistic attitude by the United States toward Latin America?

MAKERS OF AMERICA: SETTLERS OF THE OLD NORTHWEST

Questions for Class Discussion

1. What historical factors worked to make the Old Northwest (today's Midwest) a distinctive region with its own identity? What perspectives divided the region's settlers?

2. Was it inevitable that the Old Northwest would eventually align itself with the Northeast in the struggles that led up to the Civil War? Why did even settlers originally from the South tend to dislike the southern plantation elite?

Suggested Student Exercises

- Trace the patterns of settlement and institution-building across both the "southern" and "northern" tier of the states of Ohio, Indiana, and Illinois. Perhaps contrast the "Western Reserve" area of northern Ohio, heavily settled by Yankees, with the Ohio River counties of southern Ohio, heavily settled by pioneers from Virginia and Kentucky.

- Use a current religious atlas of the United States to discover how persistent the original patterns of religious settlement remain in the Old Northwest states; e.g., are Methodists, Baptists, and Disciples of Christ still more prominent in the southern tier, and Presbyterians and Congregationalists (United Church of Christ) still stronger in the northern tier? The patterns of denominational sponsorship of colleges in the region might also be examined.

13

The Rise of a Mass Democracy, 1824–1840

CHAPTER THEME

Theme: The election to the presidency of the frontier aristocrat and common person's hero, Andrew Jackson, signalled the end of the older elitist political leadership represented by John Quincy Adams. A new spirit of mass democracy and popular involvement swept through American society, bringing new energy as well as conflict and corruption to public life.

Theme: Jackson successfully mobilized the techniques of the New Democracy and presidential power to win a series of dramatic political battles against his enemies. But by the late 1830s, his Whig opponents had learned to use the same popular political weapons against the Democrats, signaling the emergence of the second American party system.

Theme: Amidst the whirl of democratic politics, issues of tariffs, financial instability, Indian policy, and possible expansion in Texas indicated that difficult sectional and economic problems were festering beneath the surface and not being very successfully addressed.

CHAPTER SUMMARY

Beginning in the 1820s, a powerful movement celebrating the common person and promoting the "New Democracy" transformed the earlier elitist character of American politics. The controversial election of the Yankee sophisticate John Quincy Adams in 1824 angered the followers of Andrew Jackson.

Jackson's sweeping presidential victory in 1828 represented the political triumph of the New Democracy, including the spoils-rich political machines that thrived in the new environment. Jackson's simple, popular ideas and rough-hewn style reinforced the growing belief that any ordinary person could hold public office. The "Tariff of Abominations" and the nullification crisis with South Carolina revealed a growing sectionalism and anxiety about slavery that ran up against Jackson's fierce nationalism.

Jackson exercised the powers of the presidency against his opponents, particularly Calhoun and Clay. He made the Bank of the United States a symbol of evil financial power and killed it after a bitter political fight. Destroying the bank reinforced Jacksonians' hostility to concentrated and elite-dominated financial power, but also left the United States without any effective financial system.

Jackson's presidency also focused on issues of westward expansion. Pursuing paths of "civilization," Native Americans of the Southeast engaged in extensive agricultural and educational development. But pressure from white settlers and from the state governments proved overwhelming, and Jackson finally supported the forced removal of all southeastern Indians to Oklahoma along the "Trail of Tears."

In Texas, American settlers successfully rebelled against Mexico and declared their independence. Jackson recognized the Texas Republic but, because of the slavery controversy, he refused its application for annexation to the United States.

Jackson's political foes soon formed themselves into the Whig party, but in 1836 they lost to his handpicked successor, Van Buren. Jackson's ill-considered economic policies came home to roost under the unlucky Van Buren, as the country plunged into a serious depression following the panic of 1837.

The Whigs used these economic troubles and the political hoopla of the new mass democratic process to elect their own hero in 1840, following the path of making a western aristocrat into a democratic symbol.

The Whig victory signaled the emergence of a new two-party system, in which the two parties' genuine philosophical differences and somewhat different constituencies proved less important than their widespread popularity and shared roots in the new American democratic spirit.

DEVELOPING THE CHAPTER: SUGGESTED LECTURE OR DISCUSSION TOPICS

- Analyze the rise of mass politics and popular democracy. Focus on the increasing democratic American celebration of "the people" in opposition to entrenched elites, as well as specific political innovations: the end of property qualifications, political conventions, political machines, and the spoils system.

    REFERENCE: Harry L. Watson, *Liberty and Power: The Politics of Jacksonian America* (1990).

- Contrast Adams and Jackson as symbols of the old and new politics. Show how the Jacksonians used the "elitist" and "corrupt" election of 1824 to arouse popular feelings for their sweeping democratic victory in 1828.

    REFERENCES: Samuel Bemis, *John Quincy Adams and the Union* (1956); Robert V. Remini, *Andrew Jackson and the Course of American Freedom* (1981).

- Develop the theme of rising sectionalism in the late 1820s and 1830s. Show how the assertion of states' rights and nullification in the tariff controversies reflected growing southern fears of northern political and economic power.

    REFERENCE: William J. Cooper, *The South and the Politics of Slavery, 1828–1856* (1978).

- Connect Jackson's political battles with the emergence of the second two-party system. Show how Jackson especially appealed to plain people who distrusted eastern bankers and capitalists, while the Whigs grew out of the various groups that disliked Jackson and the Democrats.

    REFERENCE: Robert V. Remini, *Andrew Jackson and the Course of American Democracy, 1833–1845* (1984).

- Explain both the Indian removal and the Texas rebellion as products of the expansionism and "land hunger" of the time. The emphasis might be on how, in both cases, the U.S. government essentially reacted to local political developments.

    REFERENCES: Michael Green, *The Politics of Indian Removal* (1982); Anthony Wallace, *The Long, Bitter Trail: Andrew Jackson and the Indians* (1993).

- Show how the Whigs turned the Democrats' own political techniques against them in the "log-cabin and hard-cider" campaign of 1840.

    REFERENCE: Robert G. Gunderson, *The Log-Cabin Campaign* (1957).

FOR FURTHER INTEREST: ADDITIONAL CLASS TOPICS

- Contrast the earlier elitist method of selecting presidents (reflected in the four-way election of 1824) with the new, more democratic political methods, including national conventions and noisy popular campaigns.

- Discuss the political machines and the spoils system. Consider the advantages and disadvantages of Jackson's democratic belief that any citizen could hold public office without special qualifications.

- Focus on Jackson's personality, particularly his fierce animosities against his enemies, and the secrets of his appeal as a symbol of democracy and the common person.

- Provide more material on the "five civilized tribes," particularly the Cherokees, and discuss their fate during and after the "Trail of Tears."

- Examine the dramatic events of the Texas revolution, such as the Alamo and San Jacinto, in relation to the broad historical context of the Texas revolt. Explain the reasons so many northerners regarded the Texas revolt as a slaveholders' conspiracy. Consider how the Texas developments might have looked from a Mexican perspective.

- Reflect on the ways in which the Maysville Road Veto (1830) brought up issues of federal-state relationships and the role of government in society.

   REFERENCE: David M. Kennedy and Thomas A. Bailey, *The American Spirit*, Tenth Edition, p. 266
   (provided for the classroom by the publisher)

CHARACTER SKETCHES

David ("Davy") Crockett (1786–1836)

Davy Crockett, the frontier congressman and hero who died at the Alamo, has remained a half-legendary symbol of western democracy and humor.

Crockett's father was an Irish immigrant and Revolutionary soldier who frequently beat his son, causing him to run away from home on several occasions. The young Crockett attended school for six months in order to please a girlfriend but left when she jilted him and never returned to school.

He became a legendary hunter in frontier Tennessee, once killing 105 bears in nine months. Crockett also served with Jackson in the Indian wars and became a justice of the peace, though barely able to read and write. He considered spelling and grammar "contrary to nature."

The suggestion that he run for Congress was first made as a joke, but he was so popular with his pioneer neighbors that he was elected to three terms. A Whig who strongly opposed Jackson and defended the Indians in the Cherokee removal, he became a national hero during his "tour of the North" from 1834 to 1835, when he regaled big-city audiences with his frontier anecdotes. He headed for frontier Texas and the Alamo because of disappointment over his defeat in a bid for reelection to Congress.

Quote: "What a miserable place a city is….I sometimes wonder they don't clear out to a new country where every skin hangs by its own tail." (Comment during his tour of the North, 1835)

REFERENCE: Walter Blair, *Davy Crockett* (1955).

John Quincy Adams (1767–1848)

Adams was the secretary of state who proposed the Monroe Doctrine, the sixth president, and a noted opponent of slavery in the House of Representatives.

He grew up at his father's side and early on began keeping detailed diaries that form a memorable record of his thoughts and experiences. In 1794 he became minister to the Netherlands, the first of his numerous diplomatic assignments.

Regarded as a traitor by Federalists for supporting Jefferson's embargo, he also aroused Jackson's hatred, even though he was Old Hickory's only cabinet supporter in the Monroe administration.

After leaving the presidency, he planned to retire to write history but was elected to Congress and returned for eight successive terms. "Old Man Eloquent" was contentious and sarcastic in his speeches against the "gag rule." In 1841 he won the famous *Amistad* court case on behalf of black slaves who had revolted and taken command of a slave ship.

Quote: "When I came to the Presidency the principle of internal improvement was swelling the tide of public prosperity....The great object of my life therefore as applied to the administration of the government of the United States has failed. The American Union as a moral person in the family of nations is to live from hand to mouth, to cast away instead of using for the improvement of its own condition, the bounties of Providence, and to raise to the summit of power a succession of Presidents the consummation of whose glory will be to growl and snarl with impotent fury against a money broker's shop, to rivet into perpetuity the clanking chain of the slave, and to waste in boundless bribery to the West the invaluable inheritance of the public lands." (Letter, 1837)

REFERENCE: Samuel Bemis, *John Quincy Adams and the Union* (1956).

Daniel Webster (1782–1852)

Webster, a Massachusetts senator and U.S. secretary of state, was considered the greatest orator and lawyer of his time.

In childhood, fragile health compelled him to stay indoors and read much of the time. When he attended Dartmouth, "Black Dan" was frequently thought to be an Indian because of his swarthy appearance.

Not only was Webster's law practice lucrative, often bringing in $65,000 a year or more, but he was also liberally subsidized by Massachusetts textile-mill owners. He lived in splendor and entertained lavishly at his estate at Marshfield, Massachusetts.

The debate with Robert Hayne came one month after Webster's second marriage, to New York socialite Caroline LeRoy. His eloquence was so renowned that huge crowds gathered for even minor occasions, and generations of schoolchildren memorized his most famous utterances.

Quote: "When my eyes shall be turned to behold for the last time the sun in heaven, may I not see him shining on the broken and dishonored fragments of a once glorious Union; on states dissevered, discordant, belligerent; on a land rent with civil feuds, or drenched, it may be, in fraternal blood! Let their last feeble and lingering glance rather behold the glorious ensign of the republic, now known and honored throughout the earth, still full high advanced, its arms and trophies streaming in their original luster, not a stripe erased or polluted, nor a single star obscured...." (Webster-Hayne debate speech, 1831)

REFERENCE: Irving Bartlett, *Daniel Webster* (1978).

Nicholas Biddle (1786–1844)

Biddle was the wealthy, learned financier who fought and lost the Bank War with President Jackson.

He graduated from Princeton as valedictorian in 1801, with honors in the classics. Although he became a lawyer, Biddle spent most of his time on literary endeavors, including writing a history of the Lewis and Clark expedition and composing poetry.

Having left the scholarly life for government service in 1819 at the request of his friend President Monroe, in 1822 he became president of the Second Bank of the United States. The charges of "corruption" against him arose partly because he represented the interests of the bank's private stockholders as well as the government.

After losing the bank battle, he retired to Andalusia, his Delaware estate, and pursued his interest in classical Greece. He also wrote works on economics, in which he advocated such progressive policies as shorter hours and higher wages for workers.

Quote: "My own course is decided—all the other Banks and all the merchants may break, but the Bank of the United States shall not break." (1834)

REFERENCE: Thomas P. Govan, *Nicholas Biddle* (1959).

Black Hawk (1767–1838)

Black Hawk was the Sauk chief who led his people to defeat in Black Hawk's War of 1832.

His bitterness toward Americans developed when William Henry Harrison obtained a treaty ceding the Indians' land along the Mississippi by getting two lesser Sauk chiefs drunk. Black Hawk fought beside Tecumseh in the War of 1812 and after the war continued to seek British aid against Americans.

In 1831 he formed a war alliance with a Winnebago shaman, White Cloud, but when U.S. troops were called up, Black Hawk withdrew to Iowa. After his attempted recrossing of the Mississippi ended in disaster, he was imprisoned and taken to meet President Jackson. Those who saw them together claimed that the two old chieftains resembled each other.

While in federal custody Black Hawk dictated his life story to an interpreter. A journalist wrote it up, and it became a minor classic.

Quote: "I surveyed the country that had caused us so much trouble, anxiety, and blood, and that now caused me to be a prisoner of war. I reflected upon the ingratitude of the whites, when I saw their fine houses, rich harvests…and recollected that this land had been ours, for which I and my people had never received a dollar, and that the whites were not satisfied until they took our villages and our grave yards from us and removed us across the Mississippi." (Autobiography, 1835)

REFERENCE: Donald Jackson, ed., *Black Hawk: An Autobiography* (1964); Cecil Eby, *"That Disgraceful Affair": The Black Hawk War* (1973).

Sam Houston (1793–1863)

Houston was the military hero of Texas independence and later president of the Texas Republic.

He grew up with his widowed mother near Cherokee country in Tennessee, learning the Cherokee customs and language as a boy. Throughout his life he had a strong sympathy for Indians.

In 1827 he became governor of Tennessee. In 1829 he married, but his bride returned to her parents after three months, and the subsequent scandal and divorce ruined his political career.

Houston first headed to Indian territory, where he became an Indian trader and married an Indian woman. In 1835 he moved to Texas and became commander of the tiny Texas army. Only 6 of his 783 men were killed in the decisive Battle of San Jacinto; Houston was badly wounded in the leg.

As U.S. senator from 1846 to 1860, he was almost the only southerner to support sectional compromise, even on slavery. As governor in 1861, he refused to recognize the authority of the secession convention or to swear allegiance to the Confederacy; he was therefore forced to resign the office.

Quote: "While an enemy to your independence remains in Texas the work is incomplete; but when liberty is firmly established by your patience and valor, it will be fame enough to say, 'I was a member of the army of San Jacinto.' " (Message to Texas army, 1836)

REFERENCE: John Hoyt Williams, *Sam Houston* (1993).

Martin Van Buren (1782–1862)

Van Buren was the New York politician who helped engineer Jackson's presidential victories in 1828 and 1832, before being elected to his own unsuccessful term as president.

A tavern keeper's son, Van Buren rose to power amid the fiercely competitive factional politics of New York. His own political machine, the "Albany Regency," eventually achieved dominance by perfecting the techniques of patronage and spoils.

Van Buren was Jackson's most intimate political associate and the only cabinet member to back him completely in the Peggy Eaton affair. In 1830 Jackson suggested that if Van Buren would become his vice president, he, Jackson, would resign and let Van Buren become president.

Although badly beaten in 1840 after his unsuccessful presidency, Van Buren probably could have been renominated in 1844 if he had not come out against annexing Texas. In 1847 he and other "Barnburner" New York antislavery Democrats broke away from the proslavery "Hunkers" who controlled the party. In 1848 he accepted the nomination of the Free Soil party for president.

Quote: "Why the deuce is it that they have such an itching for abusing me? I try to be harmless and positively good-natured, and a most decided friend of peace." (Comment on newspapers, 1822)

REFERENCE: John Niven, *Martin Van Buren and the Romantic Age of American Politics* (1983).

QUESTIONS FOR CLASS DISCUSSION

1. What were the advantages and disadvantages of the new politics of mass democracy? Were such things as the spoils system, party machines, and hoopla-driven campaigns inevitable accompaniments of popular democracy, or could "the people" have been mobilized by a more open and less partisan system?

2. Did John Quincy Adams's cold personality make him a less competent president than popular hero Andrew Jackson? Why did Americans come to expect their presidents to be charismatic "men of the people" as well as skilled political leaders or administrators? What American presidents fit well into the Jackson mold?

3. How was Jackson able to make the "Bank War" such an effective symbol of democracy and of his presidency? Why were his opponents, like Clay and Biddle, unable to counter his appeals, even when their arguments appeared to have economics and stability on their side?

4. What were the causes and consequences of the Texas revolt? Why did Texas remain for a time an independent nation rather than become a state of the Union?

5. How did the "log-cabin and hard-cider" campaign of 1840 demonstrate the nature of the two-party system in the New Democracy?

MAKERS OF AMERICA: MEXICAN OR TEXICAN?

Questions for Class Discussion

1. In what ways were the original Texas settlers like other westward-moving American pioneers, and in what ways were they different?

2. How have its unique beginnings made Texas different from most other American states?

Suggested Student Exercises

- Examine a map of Texas for Hispanic place names. Find the parts of the state where such names are common and where they appear less often.

- The text notes that many of the Texas pioneers were originally Scots-Irish. Consider which of their qualities may have derived from their Scots-Irish ancestry. (See "Makers of America: The Scots-Irish," Chapter 5.)

EXPANDING THE "VARYING VIEWPOINTS"

- Arthur M. Schlesinger, Jr., *The Age of Jackson* (1945).

  A view of Jacksonian democracy as a product of class conflict:

  "During the Bank War, laboring men began slowly to turn to Jackson as their leader, and his party as their party....This conversion of the working classes to the hard-money policy injected new strength and determination into the hard-money party....From it would come the impetus to carry through the second stage in the national struggles of Jacksonian democracy."

- Lee Benson, *The Concept of Jacksonian Democracy: New York as a Test Case* (1961).

  A view of Jacksonian democracy as a product of ethnic and cultural conflict:

  "A composition portrait of their [Whigs' and Democrats'] social and economic backgrounds reveals striking similarities. Their most significant difference is that several Democratic leaders claimed Dutch or German ancestry, while the Whigs invariably claimed British ancestry (mostly by way of New England)."

QUESTIONS ABOUT THE "VARYING VIEWPOINTS"

1. What does each of these historians see as the fundamental difference between the two major parties of the Jacksonian era?

2. Why would Schlesinger think of the political conflicts of the day as "real" and critical to the national future, while Benson would tend to regard them as largely "symbolic"?

3. How would each of these historians approach an event like Andrew Jackson's attack on the Bank of the United States?

14

Forging the National Economy, 1790–1860

CHAPTER THEMES

Theme: In the era of Jacksonian democracy, the American population grew rapidly and changed in character. More people lived in the raw West and in the expanding cities, and immigrant groups like the Irish and Germans added their labor power to America's economy, sometimes arousing hostility from native-born Americans in the process.

Theme: In the early nineteenth century, the American economy developed the beginnings of industrialization. The greatest advances occurred in transportation, as canals and railroads bound the Union together into a continental economy with strong regional specialization.

CHAPTER SUMMARY

The youthful American republic expanded dramatically on the frontier in the early nineteenth century. Frontier life was often crude and hard on the pioneers, especially women.

Westward-moving pioneers often ruthlessly exploited the environment, exhausting the soil and exterminating wildlife. Yet the wild beauty of the West was also valued as a symbol of American national identity, and eventually environmentalists would create a national park system to preserve pieces of the wilderness.

Other changes altered the character of American society and its workforce. Old cities expanded, and new cities sprang up in the wilderness. Irish and German immigrants poured into the country in the 1830s and 1840s, and the Irish in particular aroused nativist hostility because of their Roman Catholic faith.

Inventions and business innovations like free incorporation laws spurred economic growth. Women and children were the most exploited early factory laborers. Male workers made some gains in wages and hours but generally failed in unionization attempts.

The most far-reaching economic advances before the Civil War occurred in agriculture and transportation. The early railroads, despite many obstacles, gradually spread their tentacles across the country. Foreign trade remained only a small part of the American economy, but changing technology gradually created growing economic links to Europe. By the early 1860s the telegraph, railroad, and steamship had gone far toward replacing older means of travel and communication like the canals, clipper ships, stagecoach, and pony express.

The new means of transportation and distribution laid the foundations for a continental market economy. The new national economy created a pattern of sectional specialization and altered the traditional economic functions of the family. There was growing concern over the class differences spawned by industrialization, especially in the cities. But the general growth of opportunities and the increased standard of living made America a magnetic "land of opportunity" to many people at home and abroad.

DEVELOPING THE CHAPTER: SUGGESTED LECTURE OR DISCUSSION TOPICS

- Focus on the Irish and German immigrants and the nativist reaction to them. Show why nativists thought that immigrant poverty and Catholicism posed a threat to American democracy. Consider the important role that the Catholic Church played in the lives of Irish and German Catholic immigrants, despite the opposition of nativists.

    REFERENCES: Kerby Miller, *Emigrants and Exiles: Ireland and the Irish Exodus to North America* (1985); Jay P. Dolan, *The Immigrant Church* (1975).

- Examine the effects of early industrial development on labor and society. Show how the change from a subsistence to a market economy affected workers, farmers and especially women.

    REFERENCES: Herbert Gutman, *Work, Culture, and Society in Industrializing America* (1976); Mary Blevitt, *Men, Women, and Work* (1988).

- Consider the various stages of the market and transportation revolutions. Focus on the particular significance of the steamboat and the canal, and their gradual replacement by the railroad.

    REFERENCE: Charles Sellers, *The Market Revolution: Jacksonian America, 1815–1846* (1992).

- Analyze the relation between the growing national economy and the regional economic specialization of the Northeast, South, and Midwest. Point out the paradoxical way in which economic development both united and divided the sections.

    REFERENCE: W. Elliot Brownlee, *Dynamics of Ascent* (1974).

FOR FURTHER INTEREST: ADDITIONAL CLASS TOPICS

- Discuss the roots of Irish immigration to America. Consider the changing historical "image" of Irish-Americans and their culture from the nineteenth century to the present, and the relationship between popular stereotypes (Irish police, St. Patrick's Day) and the actual experience of Irish-Americans.

- Discuss one or more of the early inventions and their relation to economic growth, e.g., the cotton gin, the sewing machine, the mechanical reaper, the telegraph. Consider how much technological progress depends on the proper social and economic conditions.

- Compare the early-nineteenth-century American economy with those of developing Third World countries today. Discuss the absolutely crucial role that developing a basic "infrastructure"—particularly transportation and communication facilities—play in the early stages of industrial development.

- Focus on the lives of early factory workers, perhaps using the female textile workers of Lowell, Massachusetts, as a case study.

CHARACTER SKETCHES

Eli Whitney (1765–1825)

Whitney was the American inventor whose two major innovations—the cotton gin and the system of interchangeable parts—revolutionized the American economy.

He did not care for school, preferring to spend his time making and fixing things in his father's shop. Whitney once took his father's watch completely apart and reassembled it without his father discovering the deed. For a time he supported himself by manufacturing nails and hatpins.

He earned money to attend Yale by fixing things around the college. One campus carpenter allegedly said, "There was a good mechanic spoiled when you went to college."

He built the first cotton gin in ten days and a larger model in a year. The original machine was stolen, and imitations were produced; it took Whitney many years of legal battles to gain the sole patent for the device.

Quote: "There were a number of very respectable Gentlemen at Mrs. Greene's who all agreed that if a machine could be invented which would clean the cotton with expedition, it would be a great thing both to the country and to the inventor....I concluded to relinquish my school and turn my attention to perfecting the Machine. I made one before I came away which required the labor of one man to turn it and with which one man will clean ten times as much cotton as he can in any other way before known...." (Letter to his father, 1793)

REFERENCE: Constance M. Green, *Eli Whitney and the Birth of American Technology* (1956).

Robert Fulton (1765–1815)

Fulton is best known in America for his development of the steamboat, but he was also a successful artist and an inventor of the submarine and the torpedo.

As a boy, Fulton became a skilled gunsmith, and in school he made his own pencils. He liked to fish but hated to row boats, so at fourteen he devised a paddle wheel to move the boat by foot.

A talented artist, he studied in London under Benjamin West and was earning a successful living by painting before he turned to mechanics and engineering.

He first worked in Britain on iron aqueducts and bridges, then went to France, where he built a "diving boat," the *Nautilus*, which could stay underwater for four hours. But Napoleon lost interest in the device when it proved unable to sink British shipping.

His first steamboat sank on the Seine, but a second model, built in 1803, was successful. This became the prototype for the *Clermont*.

Quote: "When [the *Clermont*] came so near that the noise of the machine and paddles were heard...some prostrated themselves and besought Providence to protect them from the approach of the horrible monster which was marching on the wave and lighting its path by spitting fire." (Newspaper account of the *Clermont*'s first voyage, 1807)

REFERENCE: Kirkpatrick Sale, *Fire of His Genius: Robert Fulton and the American Dream* (2001).

Samuel F. B. Morse (1791–1872)

Morse, the inventor of the telegraph, was also a superb American painter and was for a time a leader of nativist agitation.

He studied painting in England, with some of his work winning prizes in the Royal Academy competitions. He returned to Boston in 1815 but discovered that he could earn a living only by painting portraits. After Congress rejected his plan to paint the Capitol rotunda, he reluctantly abandoned art and turned to inventing.

From his time in Europe he had developed a strong dislike of Catholicism, and in the 1830s he was a leader of American anti-Catholic agitation.

He developed the first ideas for the telegraph from hearing lectures on electricity. But it took several years of experimentation to perfect the sending and receiving devices and to develop his "Morse code" for communicating messages by short and long signals. He was in continual poverty and was nearly at the point of abandoning the project when Congress finally authorized funds for the successful Baltimore-to-Washington line.

Quote: "If the presence of electricity can be made visible in any part of an electric circuit closed by an electromagnet, I see no reason why intelligence may not be transmitted instantaneously by electricity." (1832)

REFERENCE: Carleton Mabee, *American Leonardo: A Life of Samuel F. B. Morse* (1943).

QUESTIONS FOR CLASS DISCUSSION

1. How does the image of the frontier compare with the reality of pioneer life as described in the chapter?

2. Why was transportation—particularly the canals and the railroads—so important in the early stages of industrialization?

3. Which technological innovation was most important for early-nineteenth-century economic development?

4. What effects did the movement from a subsistence to a market economy have on American society, including farmers, laborers, and women? What were the advantages and disadvantages of the change?

MAKERS OF AMERICA: THE IRISH

Questions for Class Discussion

1. In what ways were the Irish similar to other immigrants from the British Isles, such as the English (Chapter 3) and the Scots-Irish (Chapter 5), and in what ways were they different?

2. How did the Irish particularly shape the history of American politics, urban life, and religion? What factors contributed to their success in America, and what made it difficult for them to get ahead?

Suggested Student Exercises

- Use your local yellow pages to find the names of Irish businesses or professions.

- Examine some well-known Irish-Americans (e.g., John F. Kennedy, Mayor Richard Daley, Eugene O' Neill, Al Smith). Consider why more Irish-Americans have achieved prominence in the twentieth century than in the nineteenth.

MAKERS OF AMERICA: THE GERMANS

Questions for Class Discussion

1. Compare the historical experience of German immigrants, both before and after immigration, with that of the Irish. How did the patterns of German settlement compare with those of the Irish?

2. What elements of American culture have been influenced by the German presence? Is that presence more visible in certain regions of the country than in others?

Suggested Student Exercises

- Use maps of Pennsylvania and Wisconsin, or of cities like Cincinnati or Milwaukee, to identify German place names.

- Consider the rather harsh persecution of German-Americans during World War I as a contrast to their generally benign experience in America. (See Chapter 33 in the text.)

15

The Ferment of Reform and Culture, 1790–1860

CHAPTER THEMES

Theme: The spectacular religious revivals of the Second Great Awakening reversed a trend toward secular rationalism in American culture, and helped to fuel a spirit of social reform. In the process, religion was increasingly "feminized," while women in turn took the lead in movements of reform, including those designed to improve their own condition.

Theme: The attempt to improve Americans' faith, morals, and character affected nearly all areas of American life and culture, including education, the family, literature, and the arts—culminating in the great crusade against slavery.

CHAPTER SUMMARY

In early nineteenth century America, movements of moral and religious reform accompanied the democratization of politics and the creation of a national market economy. After a period of growing rationalism in religion, a new wave of revivals beginning about 1800 swept out of the West and effected great change not only in religious life but also in other areas of society. Existing religious groups were further fragmented, and new groups like the Mormons emerged. Women were especially prominent in these developments, becoming a major presence in the churches and discovering in reform movements an outlet for energies that were often stifled in masculinized political and economic life.

Among the first areas to benefit from the reform impulse was education. The public elementary school movement gained strength, while a few women made their way into still tradition-bound colleges. Women were also prominent in movements for improved treatment of the mentally ill, peace, temperance, and other causes. By the 1840s some women also began to agitate for their own rights, including suffrage. The movement for women's rights, closely linked to the antislavery crusade, gained adherents even while it met strong obstacles and vehement opposition.

While many reformers worked to improve society as a whole, others created utopian experiments to model their religious and social ideals. Some of these groups promoted radical sexual and economic doctrines, while others appealed to high-minded intellectuals and artists.

American culture was still quite weak in theoretical sciences and the fine arts, but a vigorous national literature blossomed after the War of 1812. In New England the literary renaissance was closely linked to the philosophy of transcendentalism promoted by Emerson and others. Many of the great American writers like Walt Whitman reflected the national spirit of utopian optimism, but a few dissenters like Hawthorne and Melville explored the darker side of life and of their own society.

DEVELOPING THE CHAPTER: SUGGESTED LECTURE OR DISCUSSION TOPICS

- Explain the revivals of the Second Great Awakening and their broad cultural implications. Emphasize how the spirit of social reform grew out of individual conversion, and how religious change was linked to the wider democratic movements in American society.

REFERENCES: Nathan Hatch, *The Democratization of American Christianity* (1989); Robert Abzug, *Cosmos Crumbling: American Reform and the Religious Imagination* (1994).

- Examine the nature of the nineteenth-century family and its relation to society, stressing particularly how the "cult of domesticity" and women's "separate sphere" gave women a specially defined role in society. Examine how some female reformers began to advocate their own rights as well as the betterment of others.

    REFERENCE: Carl Degler, *At Odds: Women and the Family in America from the Revolution to the Present* (1980).

- Examine the early women's movement as one of the most important reforms and explain the obstacles it faced. Show the relationship between women's growing activism and the broader reforms of the antebellum era.

    REFERENCE: Lori Ginzburg, *Women and the Work of Benevolence* (1990).

- Explore the "perfectionist" and "utopian" quality of early American culture, as revealed in both the utopian communal experiments and philosophical movements like transcendentalism. Point out the involvement of many writers in reform movements and experiments like Brook Farm.

    REFERENCE: Anne C. Rose, *Transcendentalism as a Social Movement, 1830–1850* (1981).

FOR FURTHER INTEREST: ADDITIONAL CLASS TOPICS

- Examine the general American perception of Irish immigration to America and the historical "image" of Irish-Americans and their culture from the nineteenth century to the present. Consider particularly the relationship between popular stereotypes (Irish police, St. Patrick's Day, etc.) and the actual experience of Irish-American immigrants over several generations.

- Use popular contemporary texts like *McGuffey's Readers* or *Godey's Lady's Book* to illuminate early American character and values. Discuss how the "messages" that were especially aimed at children or women reveal prevalent social attitudes, as well as the nature and purposes of nineteenth-century education.

- Compare the early nineteenth-century American economy with those of one or more important Third World countries today (e.g., Brazil or Nigeria). Discuss the absolutely crucial role that basic "infrastructure"—particularly transportation, communication, and water/sanitation facilities—play as a foundation in the early stages of industrial development.

- Analyze one or more of the utopian communities, such as the Shaker communes, New Harmony, Oneida, or Brook Farm. Consider how the success or failure of such efforts should be judged.

CHARACTER SKETCHES

Charles G. Finney (1792–1875)

Finney was the most influential revivalist of the Second Great Awakening and a president of Oberlin College, a center of abolitionism and reform.

Although he was a successful attorney before turning to preaching, Finney never attended college or law school. Despite his dislike of conventional churches, he underwent a total conversion to religion after reading the Bible on his own. He then abandoned his law practice entirely, saying that he had a "retainer from the Lord to plead His cause."

Finney was ordained by the Presbyterians but was often at odds with them and conducted revivals completely on his own. Besides the "anxious bench," some of his other "new methods" included praying by name for the conversion of sinners in the community, holding extended nightly meetings for a week or more, and encouraging women to pray and speak publicly. He also used theatrical gestures, movement, and emotional rhetoric to rouse his listeners.

Quote: "A revival is not a miracle, or dependent on a miracle in any sense. It is a purely philosophical result of the right use of the constituted means." (*Lectures on Revivalism,* 1835)

REFERENCE: William G. McLoughlin, *Modern Revivalism: Charles Grandison Finney to Billy Graham* (1959).

Joseph Smith (1805–1844)

Smith was the founder and original prophet of the Mormon church.

The poor New York frontier family in which he grew up frequently moved during his childhood. He experienced his first vision of the angel Moroni in 1820, followed by subsequent encounters that led to the discovery of the Book of Mormon. The Book of Mormon recounts the coming of Old Testament people to America and the battles of the good Nephites with the evil Lamanites (American Indians).

The Mormon church was organized very hierarchically, with Smith as "Seer, Translator, Prophet, Apostle of Jesus Christ, and Elder of the Church." He gave numerous new revelations before his martyrdom in Carthage, Illinois. The most famous was that allowing polygamy; Smith himself had twenty-seven wives at the time of his death. He had also announced his plan to run for president of the United States in 1844.

A magnetic personality, Smith was down-to-earth, clever, physically vigorous, and virile.

Quote: "We believe in the literal gathering of Israel and in the restoration of the Ten Tribes; that Zion will be built upon this continent; that Christ will reign personally upon the earth; and that the earth will be renewed and receive its paradisaical glory." (statement of faith, 1843)

REFERENCE: Richard Bushman, *Joseph Smith and the Beginnings of Mormonism* (1984).

Catharine Beecher (1800–1878)

Beecher was a prominent women's educator and writer and a member of the famous Evangelical family.

Catharine, the oldest of four Beecher daughters, was very close to her father, and when her mother died, sixteen-year-old Catharine took over much of the responsibility for managing the household and the younger children.

Her plans to marry an unchurched man in 1822 came to naught when he died four months after their engagement, and she took the death as a divine judgment on her. The following year she opened the first of her female seminaries.

Beecher insisted that the young ladies in her schools take up physical exercise and attacked the confining clothing and social norms that restricted women. But she opposed higher education for women and attacked women's involvement in abolitionism and other social reforms. Her popular *Treatise on Domestic Economy,* written with her sister Harriet Beecher Stowe, contained practical tips on child-rearing, cooking, family health, and other matters that would enable women to run their homes effectively.

Quote: "Any activity that throws woman into the attitude of a combatant, either for herself or others, lies outside her appropriate sphere." (*An Essay on Slavery and Abolitionism,* 1837)

REFERENCE: Kathryn Kish Sklar, *Catharine Beecher: A Study in American Domesticity* (1973).

Elizabeth Cady Stanton (1815–1902)

Stanton, the cofounder (with Lucretia Mott) of the Seneca Falls Convention, was the most influential nineteenth-century American feminist.

Her father was a lawyer, and she took great interest in his work. When he said to her, "Oh, my daughter, I wish you were a boy," she set out to show him that girls were as good as boys.

She wrote the "Declaration of Sentiments" for the Seneca Falls Convention and pushed through the demand for woman suffrage. For a few years she wore Amelia Bloomer–style pants outfits in protest against women's confining clothing.

After 1851 she worked in close collaboration with Susan B. Anthony. Anthony was the traveler and organizer who focused almost exclusively on suffrage, while Stanton was the writer and theorist who advocated a broader feminism and many other radical causes. She was lively, humorous, well read, and a very popular speaker.

Quote: "I should feel exceedingly diffident to appear before you at this time, having never before spoken in public, were I not nerved by a sense of sacred right and duty [and]…did I not believe that woman herself must do this work; for woman alone can understand the height, the depth, the length and the breadth of her degradation." (Speech to the Seneca Falls Convention, 1848)

REFERENCE: Alma Lutz, *Created Equal: A Biography of Elizabeth Cady Stanton* (1973).

Mary Lyon (1797–1849)

Lyon was a pioneering women's educator and the founder of Mt. Holyoke Seminary (later Mt. Holyoke College).

One of her male schoolteachers told her that the general belief in women's mental inferiority was wrong and the girls could absorb as much advanced learning as they had an opportunity to obtain. She opened her first girls' school in 1824 but spent much time pursuing knowledge on her own by attending lectures at all-male Amherst College.

She raised the first thousand dollars for Mt. Holyoke on her own and took no salary until the venture was under way. The original name for the school was to be Pangynaskean (Greek for "whole-woman-making"), but this was dropped after press ridicule. Mt. Holyoke was unique among female seminaries because the young ladies were taught the same academic subjects as men and because the students managed their own cooking, housekeeping, and laundry.

A very religious woman, Lyon often encouraged campus revivals. She was hardworking, friendly, and very popular with students and faculty. So indifferent was she to dress that her students bought her stylish hats to replace the unfashionable ones she usually wore.

Quote: "During the past year my heart has so yearned over the female youth…that it has sometimes seemed as if there was a fire shut up in my bones." (1834)

REFERENCE: Anne Rose, *Voices of the Marketplace: American Thought and Culture* (1995).

Henry David Thoreau (1817–1862)

Thoreau was the writer and friend of Emerson whose works on nature and civil disobedience have had a continuing influence on American culture.

He was born in Concord, Massachusetts. The death of his older brother John at a young age deeply affected Henry and contributed to the lonely and tragic side of his character.

After resigning from schoolteaching after a few weeks because he refused to discipline the children, he later organized a "progressive" school, where classes were held outdoors and children were encouraged to develop their own interests.

Emerson agreed to allow Thoreau to build his cabin on Emerson's property at Walden Pond if Thoreau would clear the land and put in a garden. Thoreau moved there on the Fourth of July, 1845, and stayed two years and two months. During that time he wrote his two masterpieces, *Walden* and *A Week on the Concord and Merrimack Rivers*.

Quote: On his deathbed Thoreau was asked if he had made his peace with God. He replied, "I did not know that we had ever quarreled."

REFERENCE: Robert D. Richardson, *Thoreau: A Life of the Mind* (1986).

Ralph Waldo Emerson (1803–1882)

Emerson was the most famous American writer and philosopher of the early nineteenth century, whose transcendentalist theories shaped the golden age of New England literature.

He came from a long line of New England clergymen but eventually abandoned both the pulpit and conventional religion. His speech to the Harvard Divinity School in 1838, which questioned the value of historical Christianity, aroused ministerial opposition and prevented his returning to Harvard until 1865.

Emerson was popular in the local community of Concord, where he was once elected Hogreeve (the town official in charge of rounding up stray pigs). After his "American Scholar" lecture, he was in great demand as a speaker and traveled thousands of miles to deliver his addresses—which he repeated many times. His booming platform voice belied his generally quiet and mild-mannered demeanor.

Quote: "Books are for the scholar's idle times. When he can read God directly, the hour is too precious to be wasted in other men's transcripts of their readings." ("American Scholar" address, 1837)

REFERENCES: Joel Porte, *Representative Man: Emerson in His Time* (1979); Robert D. Richardson, *Emerson: The Mind on Fire* (1995).

QUESTIONS FOR CLASS DISCUSSION

1. What particular qualities did Evangelical religion give to the early American culture? Why did so many of its energies move toward the reform of society? Were there elements of American religion that resisted the reform impulse?

2. Were the "cult of domesticity" and the rise of the child-centered family signs of an improvement or a restriction in women's status and condition? Was the "new family" a progressive reflection of American democratic ideals, or a restriction on them?

3. Why did America produce so many reform and utopian movements? What did they contribute to American culture?

4. What made women such prominent leaders in the religious and reform movements? How did the women's rights movement compare with the other movements of the period? What obstacles did women reformers face? Why did women often have more difficulty working on their own behalf than they did advocating other causes?

MAKERS OF AMERICA: THE ONEIDA COMMUNITY

Questions for Class Discussion

1. What were the fundamental human and social problems that Noyes' radical ideas attempted to address? Why was he able to put them into practice in antebellum America?

2. Was the Oneida experiment doomed to "failure" from the start? Or should its nearly thirty years of existence be considered a rather remarkable "success," especially in its challenge to traditional Victorian patterns of marriage gender relations, considering the very short life-span of most utopian communes?

Suggested Student Exercises

- Locate Putney, Vermont, and Oneida, New York on maps. Compare the pattern of Noyes' communal migrations with those of other utopian groups that challenged conventional patterns of monogamous marriage—especially Joseph Smith's Mormons and Mother Ann Lee's Shakers. Consider why such groups frequently migrated toward the frontier.

- Examine some of Noyes' own statements and writings. Consider whether his sexual and communal experimentation was really a movement toward "freedom," or whether it really represented a kind of "cult-like" control by the founder himself that was resented by the younger generation reared in the commune.

EXPANDING THE "VARYING VIEWPOINTS"

- David Donald, *Lincoln Reconsidered* (1956).

    A view of reformers as motivated by cultural anxiety:

    "In these plebeian days they could not be successful in politics; family tradition and education prohibited idleness; and agitation allowed the only chance for personal and social self-fulfillment....What they did question, and what they did rue, was the transfer of leadership to the wrong groups in society, and their appeal for reform was a strident call for their own class to re-exert its former social dominance....Leadership of humanitarian reform may have been influenced by revivalism or by British precedent, but its true origin lay in the drastic dislocation of Northern society."

- Nancy Cott, *The Bonds of Womanhood: "Women's Sphere" in New England, 1780–1835* (1977).

A view of social reform as a reflection of women's social ties:

"Women who joined maternal associations thus asserted their formative power over their children's lives, took up evangelical goals, and complemented the private job of child rearing by approaching their occupation cooperatively with their peers. Women joined moral reform societies to accomplish different immediate aims, but with similar reasoning....Like maternal associations, moral reform societies focused women's energies on the family arena in order to solve social problems."

QUESTIONS ABOUT THE "VARYING VIEWPOINTS"

1. How do the proponents of these two viewpoints each explain the relationship between the reformers' backgrounds and their reform activities?

2. How might these different views of reformers' motives affect our judgments about the value of social reform?

3. How might each of these historians interpret the temperance movement or the career of Dorothea Dix?

16

The South and the Slavery Controversy, 1793–1860

CHAPTER THEMES

Theme: The explosion of cotton production fastened the slave system deeply upon the South, creating a complex, hierarchical racial and social order that deeply affected whites as well as blacks.

Theme: The emergence of a small but energetic radical abolitionist movement caused a fierce proslavery backlash in the South and a slow but steady growth of moderate antislavery sentiment in the North.

CHAPTER SUMMARY

Whitney's cotton gin made cotton production enormously profitable, and created an ever-increasing demand for slave labor. The South's dependence on cotton production tied it economically to the plantation system and racially to white supremacy. The cultural gentility and political domination of the relatively small plantation aristocracy concealed slavery's great social and economic costs for whites as well as blacks.

Most slaves were held by a few large planters. But most slaveowners had few slaves, and most southern whites had no slaves at all. Nevertheless, except for a few mountain whites, the majority of southern whites strongly supported slavery and racial supremacy because they cherished the hope of becoming slaveowners themselves, and because white racial identity gave them a sense of superiority to the blacks.

The treatment of the economically valuable slaves varied considerably. Within the bounds of the cruel system, slaves yearned for freedom and struggled to maintain their humanity, including family life.

The older black colonization movement was largely replaced in the 1830s by a radical Garrisonian abolitionism demanding an immediate end to slavery. Abolitionism and the Nat Turner rebellion caused a strong backlash in the South, which increasingly defended slavery as a positive good and turned its back on many of the liberal political and social ideas gaining strength in the North.

Most northerners were hostile to radical abolitionism, and respected the Constitution's evident protection of slavery where it existed. But many also gradually came to see the South as a land of oppression, and any attempt to extend slavery as a threat to free society.

DEVELOPING THE CHAPTER: SUGGESTED LECTURE OR DISCUSSION TOPICS

- Analyze the complex relations among the different elements of southern society: planter-aristocrats, small planters, poor whites, slaves, and free blacks. Contrast the dominant slaveholding elite with the mass of poorer whites who nevertheless supported slavery.

    REFERENCES: Bruce Collins, *White Society in the Antebellum South* (1985); Ira Berlin, *Slaves Without Masters* (1975).

- Examine the nature of slavery. Explain how slavery was both an economic institution and a social system that shaped whites and blacks alike, including their social and family life.

  REFERENCE: Brenda Stevenson, *Life in Black and White: Family and Community in the Slave South* (1996).

- Describe the lives of blacks under slavery. Show both the burdens of the system and the slaves' struggles to survive and maintain their humanity.

  REFERENCE: Eugene Genovese, *Roll, Jordan, Roll* (1976).

- Explain the various responses to slavery, from radical abolitionism to the defense of slavery as a positive good, and why the abolitionists had such a great impact even though they were an unpopular minority.

  REFERENCE: Lewis Perry and Michael Fellman, *Antislavery Reconsidered* (1979).

FOR FURTHER INTEREST: ADDITIONAL CLASS TOPICS

- Describe the operation of a typical large plantation or the working life of a typical large-plantation owner, including relations with overseers and slaves.

- Examine the black family and black religion. Consider how slavery affected both white and black views of women, family, and sexuality.

- Examine the paradox that slavery often involved intimate and personal relationships between individual whites and blacks (exemplified by the photo of the slave nurse with white child on p. 359), even while it maintained a strict and often violent system of control over the slaves as a group. Ask why this "paternalistic" element of American slaveholding was so important to southerners' self-justification of slavery.

- Discuss the northern debate over the *means* of ending slavery by contrasting Garrison's radical abolitionism with the moderate "no-expansion" position of a politician like Lincoln.

CHARACTER SKETCHES

Theodore Dwight Weld (1803–1895)

Weld was the leader of the abolitionist "Lane rebels," the West's most influential antislavery preacher, and the author of *American Slavery As It Is,* the most important abolitionist propaganda book besides *Uncle Tom's Cabin.*

He was converted by Charles Finney and joined Finney's "holy band" of young men who wanted to "convert the world." Weld's first causes were temperance and manual labor, but the English abolitionist Charles Stuart converted him to antislavery.

He and his fellow antislavery Lane Seminary students worked in the poverty-stricken black community of "Little Africa" in Cincinnati. After he led the "Lane rebels" out of the seminary, he traveled and lectured constantly on behalf of the antislavery cause.

In 1838 he married Angelina Grimké, who with her sister Sarah had left South Carolina to become a prominent abolitionist. Angelina helped Weld write *American Slavery As It Is,* but they both eventually "retired" from active crusading to raise their family and organize a school in New Jersey.

Quote: "Slavery, with its robbing of body and soul from birth to death, its exactions of toil unrecompensed, its sunderings from kindred, its frantic orgies of lust, its intellect levelled with dust, its baptisms of blood, and its legacy of damning horrors to the eternity of the spirit—slavery in this land of liberty, and light, and revivals of millenial glory—its days are numbered and well-nigh finished....The nation is shaking off its slumbers to sleep no more." (1934)

REFERENCE: Robert Abzug, *Passionate Liberator: Theodore Dwight Weld and the Dilemma of Reform* (1980).

William Lloyd Garrison (1805–1879)

Garrison was the most famous American abolitionist, an advocate of "nonresistance," and editor of *The Liberator*.

His father, a Canadian sea captain who drank heavily, deserted the family when Garrison was a child. Garrison received little education and practiced a number of trades before becoming a printer in Maryland.

He first crusaded for nationalism and temperance, then for moderate abolition, before being converted to radical abolition. Besides attacking slavery, *The Liberator* promoted many other causes, including peace, women's rights, temperance, and abolition of capital punishment.

Garrison eventually denounced the northern churches and the Constitution for their "compromises" with slavery. He was often threatened by antiabolitionist mobs, and several southern states offered rewards for his arrest. Despite his pacifism, he supported the Civil War as a means to end slavery.

Quote: "I am earnest—I will not equivocate—I will not excuse—I will not retreat a single inch—and *I will be heard.*" (*The Liberator,* 1831)

REFERENCE: Henry Mayer, *All on Fire: William Lloyd Garrison and the Abolition of Slavery* (2000).

Frederick Douglass (1817–1895)

Douglass was a former slave who became the leading pre-Civil War black abolitionist and the most influential African-American of the nineteenth century.

Douglass's original name was Frederick Bailey. His father was white and his mother a black slave from whom he was separated at an early age. His first escape attempt failed, and he landed in jail. He was trained as a ship caulker in Baltimore and escaped to New York in 1838 by disguising himself as a sailor.

He moved to Boston, changed his name to Douglass to avoid capture, and worked as a common laborer for three years. After a speech before an antislavery meeting, he became an abolitionist agent. He eventually split with Garrison and formed his own paper, *The North Star.* After the Civil War he was prominent in Republican politics and served in various federal positions, such as minister to Haiti from 1889 to 1891.

Quote: "I have been frequently asked how I felt when I found myself in a free state....It was a moment of the highest excitement I ever experienced....This state of mind, however, very soon subsided; and I was again seized with a feeling of great insecurity and loneliness. I was yet liable to be taken back, and subjected to all the tortures of slavery. This in itself was enough to damp the ardor of my enthusiasm." (*Narrative of the Life of Frederick Douglass,* 1845)

REFERENCE: William McFeely, *Frederick Douglass* (1990).

Martin Delany (1812–1885)

Delany was the pioneering black nationalist and author who advocated that African-Americans leave the United States.

He was born a free man in Virginia. His grandfather was said to have been an African chief who was captured and sold to America, and traditions and memories of Africa remained alive in Delany's family.

Delany moved to Pennsylvania, became involved in the black convention movement, and started a black newspaper. For a time he worked with Garrison and Douglass but despaired of abolitionism after the Fugitive Slave Act of 1850 and began working to encourage blacks to leave America.

In 1856 he moved to a fugitive-slave community in Canada. Before his exploratory trip to Africa in 1859–1860, Delany communicated with African-Americans in Liberia. Upon his return to the United States, he served in the army during the Civil War. He later became involved in Republican politics in South Carolina during Reconstruction.

Quote: "I care but little what white men think of what I say, write or do; my sole desire is to benefit the colored people. This being done I am satisfied—the opinion of every white person in the country or the world to the contrary notwithstanding." (Letter to Frederick Douglass, 1852)

REFERENCE: Victor Ullman, *Martin R. Delany: The Beginnings of Black Nationalism* (1971).

GREAT DEBATES IN AMERICAN HISTORY

GREAT DEBATE (1830–1860): Slavery: Is slavery an intolerable institution?

Yes: Antislavery forces: abolitionists, led by Garrison, Weld, and the Grimké sisters; Free Soil and Republican politicians, led by Lincoln, Seward, and Sumner.	*No:* Proslavery forces: white southerns, led by Calhoun, Davis, and Butler; northern moderates, led by Webster, Douglas, and Buchanan.

ISSUE #1: Is slavery a violation of fundamental moral and religious principles?

Yes: Antislavery leader Angelina Grimké: "The great fundamental principle of abolitionists is, that man cannot rightfully hold his fellow man as property....It matters not what *motive* he may give for such a monstrous violation of the laws of God. The claim to him as *property* is an annihilation of his right to himself, which is the foundation upon which all his other rights are built. It is high-handed robbery of Jehovah; for he has declared, 'All souls are mine.' "	*No:* Proslavery Senator Andrew Butler of South Carolina: "Inequality seems to characterize the administration of the providence of God. I will not undertake to invade that sanctuary, but I will say that the abolitionists cannot make those equal whom God has made unequal, in human estimation. That He has made the blacks unequal to the whites, human history...has pronounced its uniform judgment."

ISSUE #2: Is slavery incompatible with the most fundamental American principles?

Yes: Antislavery leader Abraham Lincoln: "There is no reason in the world why the negro is not entitled to all the natural rights enumerated in the Declaration of Independence—the right to life, liberty, and the pursuit of happiness. I hold that he is as much entitled to these as the white man. I agree with Judge Douglas that he is not my equal in many respects....But in the right to eat the bread, without the leave of anybody else, which his own hand earns, he is my equal and the equal of Judge Douglas, and the equal of every living man."

No: Proslavery Senator Stephen A. Douglas: "At the time the Constitution was framed there were thirteen states in the Union, twelve of which were slaveholding states and one a free state....For one, I am opposed to negro citizenship in any and every form. I believe this government was made on the white basis. I believe it was made by white men for the benefit of white men and their posterity forever, and I am in favor of confining citizenship to white men...instead of conferring it upon negroes, Indians, and other inferior races...."

ISSUE #3: Would the attempted abolition of slavery threaten the foundations of the Union?

No: Antislavery leader William Seward: "Hitherto the two systems have existed in different states, but side by side within the American Union. This has happened because the Union is a confederation of states. But in another aspect the United States constitute only one nation....It is an irrepressible conflict between opposing and enduring forces, and it means that the United States must and will, sooner or later, become either entirely a slaveholding nation or entirely a free-labor nation....Our forefathers knew it to be true, and unanimously acted upon it when they framed the constitution of the United States."

Yes: Proslavery Senator Alfred Iversen of Georgia: "Sir, I believe that the time will come when the slave states will be compelled, in vindication of their rights, interests, and honor, to separate from the free states and erect an independent confederacy....At all events, I am satisfied that one of two things is *inevitable;* either that the slave states must surrender their peculiar institutions or separate from the North....No union or no slavery will sooner or later be forced upon the choice of the southern people."

ISSUE #4: Should slavery be allowed to expand into the territories if the people of those territories want it?

No: Antislavery leader Abraham Lincoln: "I believe we shall not have peace upon the question until the opponents of slavery arrest the further spread of it and place it where the public mind shall rest in the belief that it is in the course of ultimate extinction....Now I believe if we could arrest the spread, and place it where Washington and Jefferson and Madison placed it, it would be in the course of ultimate extinction and the public mind would, as for eighty years past, believe that it was in the course of ultimate extinction....The crisis would be past and the institution might be let

Yes: Proslavery Senator Stephen A. Douglas: "Whenever it becomes necessary, in our growth and progress, to acquire more territory, I am in favor of it, without reference to the question of slavery, and, when we have acquired it, I will leave the people free to do as they please, either to make it slave or free territory, as they prefer....If they prohibit slavery, it shall be prohibited. They can form their institutions to please themselves, subject only to the Constitution; and I, for one, stand ready to receive them into the Union."

alone for a hundred years—if it should live so long—in the states where it exists, yet it would be going out of existence in the way best for both the black and the white races."

REFERENCES: Don E. Fehrenbacher, *Prelude to Greatness: Lincoln in the 1850s* (1962); J. Jeffrey Auer, ed., *Antislavery and Disunion, 1858–1861: Studies in the Rhetoric of Compromise and Conflict* (1963).

QUESTIONS FOR CLASS DISCUSSION

1. How did slavery affect whites—those who owned slaves and those who did not?

2. How did blacks respond to the condition of slavery?

3. Why did the South move from viewing slavery as a "necessary evil" to proclaiming it a "positive good"?

4. How effective were the abolitionists in achieving their goals? Did they hasten or delay the end of slavery?

EXPANDING THE "VARYING VIEWPOINTS"

- Stanley Elkins, *Slavery* (1959).

    A view of slavery as a totalitarian system that destroyed blacks' personalities:

    "Both [the Nazi concentration camp and slavery] were closed systems from which all standards based on prior connections had been effectively detached. A working adjustment to either system required a childlike conformity, a limited choice of 'significant others.'...Absolute power for [the master] meant absolute dependency for the slave—the dependency not of the developing child but of the perpetual child....The result would be something resembling 'Sambo.'"

- Eugene Genovese, *Roll, Jordan, Roll* (1972).

    A view of slavery as a paternalistic system within which blacks could maintain their humanity:

    "Thus, the slaves, by accepting a paternalistic ethos and legitimizing class rule, developed their most powerful defense against the dehumanization implicit in slavery. Southern paternalism may have reinforced racism as well as class exploitation, but it also unwittingly invited its victims to fashion their own interpretation of the social order it was intended to justify. And the slaves, drawing on a religion that was supposed to assure their compliance and docility, rejected the essence of slavery by projecting their own rights and value as human beings."

QUESTIONS ABOUT THE "VARYING VIEWPOINTS"

1. How does the holder of each of these viewpoints see the relationship between masters and slaves?

2. How does each of these historians connect the nature of slavery with its effect on blacks?

3. What might each of these historians say about the long-term effects of slavery on African-Americans?

17

Manifest Destiny and Its Legacy, 1841–1848

CHAPTER THEME

Theme: American expansionism gained momentum in the 1840s, leading first to the acquisition of Texas and Oregon, and then to the Mexican War, which added vast southwestern territories to the United States and ignited the slavery question.

CHAPTER SUMMARY

As Tyler assumed the presidency after Harrison's death, the United States became engaged in a series of sharp disputes with Britain. A conflict over the Maine boundary was resolved, but British involvement in Texas revived the movement to annex the Lone Star Republic to the United States.

The Texas and Oregon questions became embroiled in the 1844 campaign, as the Democrats nominated and elected the militantly expansionist Polk. After Texas was added to the Union, conflicts with Mexico over California and the Texas boundary erupted into war in 1846.

American forces quickly conquered California and New Mexico. Winfield Scott's and Zachary Taylor's invasion of Mexico was also successful, and the United States obtained large new territories in the peace treaty.

Besides adding California, New Mexico, and Utah to American territory, the Mexican War trained a new generation of military leaders and aroused long-term Latin American resentment of the United States. Most important, it forced the slavery controversy to the center of national debate, as first indicated by the Wilmot Proviso.

DEVELOPING THE CHAPTER: SUGGESTED LECTURE OR DISCUSSION TOPICS

- Explain the movement toward expansion in relation to the theories of American "Manifest Destiny" and "mission." The focus might be on how the drives to acquire Oregon, Texas, and California arose from the general belief that America should expand across the continent.

  REFERENCE: Ray Billington, *Westward Expansion* (1974).

- Examine the role of women in the westward expansion of the 1840s to Oregon and elsewhere. Compare their outlooks and concerns to those that dominated the "manifest destiny" ideology.

  REFERENCE: Susan Butuille, ed., *Women's Voices from the Oregon Trail* (1994).

- Consider the origins of the Mexican War in relation to Polk's desire for California and the narrow issue of the Texas boundary. Analyze the charges by the war's opponents that Polk's essential aim was to add new slave territory to the United States. Consider the long-term results of the Mexican War.

REFERENCE: Patricia Nelson Limerick, *The Legacy of Conquest* (1987).

- Examine the Mexican War in relation to broader patterns of ethnic and racial conflict in the Southwest.

REFERENCE: Reginald Horsman, *Race and Manifest Destiny* (1981).

FOR FURTHER INTEREST: ADDITIONAL CLASS TOPICS

- Discuss whether the Mexican War would have happened without the annexation of Texas.

- Focus on the Manifest Destiny campaign of 1844. Discuss whether Polk had a "mandate" for expansionism and, if so, whether he successfully fulfilled the American majority's goals in the West.

- Use Lincoln's "spot resolutions" or Thoreau's "Civil Disobedience" essay to highlight the opposition to the war, particularly the charge that Polk had maneuvered to bring on the fighting.

- Consider the Mexican War from a Mexican perspective. Discuss the long-term consequences of acquiring the "Spanish borderlands" for both Mexicans and Americans.

CHARACTER SKETCHES

Thomas Hart Benton (1782–1858)

Benton, the most prominent Jacksonian Democratic senator of the early nineteenth century, was a grand spokesman for national greatness and the common person.

Having grown up on the Tennessee frontier, he moved to St. Louis in 1815 and became editor of the second newspaper printed west of the Mississippi. In his youth he was involved in numerous duels, including one in which he and his brother nearly killed Andrew Jackson. He later became one of Jackson's closest political allies.

Benton was a huge man with great energy and long-winded speaking capacity. When not orating in the Senate, he undertook speaking tours of up to a thousand miles on horseback, and huge crowds gathered to hear him talk for two or three hours. Mark Twain used one of Benton's visits to Hannibal, Missouri, as the basis for an episode in *Tom Sawyer*.

Like most Jacksonians, Benton tried to divert national attention away from the slavery issue, thinking that it would disappear. But he harshly condemned southerners who threatened secession over slavery.

Quote: "I shall not fall on my sword, as Brutus did . . . but I shall save it, and save myself, for another day, and for another use—for the day when the battle of the disunion of these states is to be fought—not with words but with iron—and for the hearts of the traitors who appear in arms against their country." (Senate speech, 1844)

REFERENCE: William Chambers, *Old Bullion Benton: Senator from the New West* (1956).

James K. Polk (1795–1849)

Polk was the dark-horse presidential winner of 1844 who carried out his ambitious program of Manifest Destiny.

The scion of a stern Scots-Irish family, he was very serious and fanatically hardworking, never able to relax or get away from politics.

He was Andrew Jackson's leader in the House of Representatives during the Bank War. Although called a dark-horse nominee in 1844, Polk was actually a very well known Democrat and would probably have been the vice-presidential candidate with Van Buren in 1844 if the former president had not opposed the Texas annexation.

During his presidency Polk operated almost entirely alone, having no personal friends, and his diaries show that he was often secretive and manipulative. He exhausted himself with overwork and died only a few months after leaving office.

Quote: "After repeated menaces, Mexico has passed the boundary of the United States, has invaded our territory, and shed American blood upon American soil. She has proclaimed that hostilities have commenced, and that the two nations are at war….War exists, and notwithstanding all our efforts to avoid it, exists by the act of Mexico herself…." (War Message to Congress, 1846)

REFERENCE: Sam W. Haynes, *James K. Polk and the Expansionist Impulse* (1997).

Antonio López de Santa Anna (1795–1876)

Santa Anna was the Mexican military dictator who lost both the Texas war for independence and the Mexican War.

The uneducated son of a minor Spanish bureaucrat, Santa Anna emerged from the turmoil of the independence movement to dominate Mexican politics. He was an unscrupulous manipulator and opportunist who ruled by granting favors to the army and exploiting the peasant masses. When not at war, Santa Anna spent most his time in cockfighting and gambling. He loved to stage fantastic, expensive public entertainments, which he would attend with his numerous mistresses.

He lost a leg defending Vera Cruz against a French raid in 1838 and used this sacrifice as proof of his patriotism when it was questioned. He was frequently driven into exile in Cuba and Colombia but usually managed to return to power when civilian politicians led the country to chaos.

Quote: "Mexicans! You have a religion—protect it! You have honor—free yourself from infamy! You love your wives, your children—then liberate them from American brutality!" (Appeal to the Mexican populace, 1847)

REFERENCE: Oakah L. Jones, *Santa Anna* (1968).

Winfield Scott (1786–1866)

Scott, the American commander in the Mexican War, was the most important U.S. military leader between the Revolution and the Civil War.

Scott first became a national hero as a young officer in the War of 1812, when he was wounded in the Battle of Lundy's Lane. He fought in several Indian wars in the 1830s before becoming head of the army in 1841. He was called "Old Fuss and Feathers" because of his love for military pomp and detailed regulations. His campaign from the coast at Vera Cruz over the mountains to Mexico City is still considered a military masterpiece. During the year in which he ruled the city under military occupation, he was considered very fair and just by the Mexicans.

Although he had a decent understanding of politics from a military perspective, his Whig candidacy for the presidency in 1852 was doomed by sectional conflict within the party. He was still holding on as the aged commander of the U.S. army at the outbreak of the Civil War, but was shortly replaced.

Quote: "The object of all our dreams and hopes, toils and dangers—once the gorgeous seat of the Montezumas. That splendid city will soon be ours!" (Speech to troops, 1847)

REFERENCE: James McCaffrey, *Army of Manifest Destiny* (1992).

QUESTIONS FOR CLASS DISCUSSION

1. Was American expansion across North America an "inevitable" development? How was the idea of Manifest Destiny used to justify expansionism?

2. Why was the Texas annexation so controversial? What would have happened had Texas remained an independent nation?

3. What caused the Mexican War? Did Polk provoke the Texas-boundary conflict in order to gain California or expand slavery, as war opponents like Lincoln charged?

4. What were the benefits and costs of the Mexican War both immediately and in the longer run of American history?

MAKERS OF AMERICA: THE CALIFORNIOS

Questions for Class Discussion

1. What distinctive features of Spanish and Mexican society and culture affected the early history of settlement in California?

2. In what ways was the Californios' experience of being forcibly incorporated into the United States similar to that of voluntary immigrants, and in what ways was it different?

Suggested Student Exercises

- Use a map of California to discover Spanish place names. Consider why it is misleading to assume that all such names derive from the pre-1848 Californios.

- Compare this early history of California settlement with the later image of California as a golden land of youth and excitement. Consider which features of the Californios' actual historical experience have been incorporated into this romantic vision of California, and which have not.

18

Renewing the Sectional Struggle, 1848–1854

CHAPTER THEMES

Theme: The sectional conflict over the expansion of slavery that erupted after the Mexican War was temporarily quieted by the Compromise of 1850, but Douglas's Kansas-Nebraska Act of 1854 exploded it again.

Theme: In the 1850s American expansionism in the West and the Caribbean was extremely controversial because it was tied to the slavery question.

CHAPTER SUMMARY

The acquisition of territory from Mexico created acute new dilemmas concerning the expansion of slavery, especially for the two major political parties, which had long tried to avoid the issue. The antislavery Free Soil party pushed the issue into the election of 1848. The application of gold-rich California for admission to the Union forced the controversy into the Senate, which engaged in stormy debates over slavery and the Union.

After the timely death of President Taylor, who had blocked a settlement, Congress resolved the crisis by passing the delicate Compromise of 1850. The compromise eased sectional tension for the moment, although the Fugitive Slave Law aroused opposition in the North.

As the Whig party died, the Democratic Pierce administration became the tool of proslavery expansionists. Controversies over Nicaragua, Cuba, and the Gadsden Purchase showed that expansionism was closely linked to the slavery issue.

The desire for a northern railroad route led Stephen Douglas to ram the Kansas-Nebraska Act through Congress in 1854. By repealing the Missouri Compromise and making new territory subject to "popular sovereignty" on slavery, this act aroused the fury of the North, sparked the rise of the Republican party, and set the stage for the Civil War.

DEVELOPING THE CHAPTER: SUGGESTED LECTURE OR DISCUSSION TOPICS

- Discuss the conflicts created by the Mexican War acquisitions and explain how the Compromise of 1850 tried to resolve them. The focus might be on the extreme delicacy of the sectional adjustment.

    REFERENCE: David Potter, *The Impending Crisis, 1848–1861* (1976).

- Assess the breakup of the second two-party system in relation to the slavery controversy. Show how the Whig demise and Democratic divisions paved the way for the Republicans.

    REFERENCE: Bruce Levine, *Half Slave and Half Free: The Roots of the Civil War* (1992).

- Show the connection between the proslavery expansionist schemes, particularly the Cuban affair and the Gadsden Purchase, and the sectional controversy. Emphasize southern hopes and northern fears of potential slavery expansion to the Caribbean or Central America.

    REFERENCE: Robert May, *The Southern Dream of a Caribbean Empire* (1973).

- Examine the Kansas-Nebraska Act and explain why it aroused such wrath in the North. Particular attention might be paid to the railroad-promoting Douglas, with his theory of "popular sovereignty," and to the rise of the "free soil" ideology in the North.

    REFERENCE: Richard Sewell, *A House Divided* (1988).

FOR FURTHER INTEREST: ADDITIONAL CLASS TOPICS

- Consider the characters and drama of the Senate debates over the Compromise of 1850, especially the roles of Webster, Clay, Seward, and Douglas.

- Discuss the Fugitive Slave Law and the Underground Railroad as running sores in the sectional conflict. The life of Harriet Tubman might provide a focus.

- Examine the various "filibustering" efforts in connection with the issues of Cuba and Central America, and relate them to the southern dream of expanding slavery by acquiring new territory to the South.

- Focus on Douglas as a "typical" northern Democrat—one who did not really like slavery but thought it a secondary issue that should not disrupt important matters like railroads.

CHARACTER SKETCHES

Zachary Taylor (1784–1850)

Taylor was the military hero of the Mexican War and the Whig president whose political ineptitude nearly blocked the Compromise of 1850.

He came from a slaveholding Kentucky family and fought in the War of 1812, the Black Hawk War, and the Seminole wars before his performance in the Mexican War made him a national hero.

Using daring and risky troop movements, Taylor defeated Santa Anna's much larger army at Buena Vista. Polk was jealous of Taylor's appeal but failed to stop the public and journalistic celebration of "Old Rough and Ready."

While Taylor had long supported the Whigs, he was so politically ignorant that he nearly ruined his 1848 candidacy by writing blunt letters. At the time of his death, Whig politicians were despairing of Taylor's incompetence and trying to persuade prominent figures to enter the cabinet and keep him under control.

Quote: "I am a Whig, but not an ultra Whig. If elected I would not be the mere President of a party. I would endeavor to act independent of party domination. I should feel bound to administer the government untrammeled by party schemes." (1848)

REFERENCE: K. Jack Bauer, *Zachary Taylor: Soldier, Planter, Statesman of the Old Southwest* (1985).

Harriet Tubman (1821–1913)

Tubman was a fugitive slave and black abolitionist who led many slaves out of the South.

She was born a slave in Maryland, and, as a child, suffered a severe head injury that affected her throughout her life. She worked as a field hand, displaying tremendous physical stamina.

In 1844 her master forced her to marry another slave against her wishes. Five years later she escaped across the Pennsylvania border, traveling only by night.

She began making raids back into the South and eventually led out an estimated three hundred slaves, including her elderly parents. Between trips she worked as a cook and used much of her income to help the fugitives get a start or move to Canada.

Tubman was illiterate but learned to speak before abolitionist groups. During the Civil War she went south with the Union army and worked as a cook, laundress, nurse, and spy.

Quote: "Jes' so long as he [God] wanted to use me, he would take keer of me, an' when he didn't want me no longer, I was ready to go. I always tole him, I'm gwine to hole stiddy on you, an' you've got to see me trou'." (Comment, 1868)

REFERENCE: Sarah Bradford, *Harriet Tubman: The Moses of Her People* (1974).

Stephen A. Douglas (1813–1861)

Douglas was the Democratic senator whose Kansas-Nebraska Act helped bring on the Civil War that ruined his party and dashed his once-high presidential hopes.

Born in Vermont, he made his way to frontier Illinois, where he taught school and learned law. Although only briefly a judge on the state supreme court, he was always called "Judge Douglas." Douglas was first elected to the Illinois legislature in 1836, along with young Abraham Lincoln.

Douglas's first wife inherited a southern plantation with many slaves, and this became a political liability for Douglas. His second wife was related to Dolley Madison and was well connected in Washington high society, where the Douglases were very prominent in the late 1850s.

Once Douglas realized he had no hope of winning the 1860 election, he concentrated on rallying Democratic support for the Union and against secession. Although he and Lincoln had been longtime political rivals, he held Lincoln's hat at his inaugural and publicly defended him in the secession crisis. Douglas died of typhoid fever in 1861.

Quote: "I hold that under the Constitution of the United States each state of this Union has a right to do as it pleases on the subject of slavery. In Illinois we have exercised that right by abolishing slavery....It is none of our business whether slavery exist in Missouri. Hence I do not choose to occupy the time allotted to me in discussing a question that we have no right to act upon." (Lincoln-Douglas debates, 1858)

REFERENCE: Robert W. Johannsen, *Stephen A. Douglas* (1973).

William Walker (1824–1860)

Walker was the American filibusterer and adventurer who attempted to add a Central American slave empire to the American commonwealth before the Civil War.

A graduate of the University of Nashville, Walker earned a medical degree, practiced law, and edited a New Orleans newspaper, but his boredom with ordinary pursuits constantly drove him into exotic and dangerous schemes. He first attempted to set up a republic with himself as president in Lower California (part of Mexico) in 1853, but was arrested and acquitted of violating neutrality laws.

His briefly successful dictatorship in Nicaragua in 1855 began to collapse when he attempted to seize control of overland transit in the country from Cornelius Vanderbilt's company. An angry Vanderbilt helped turn other Central American countries and U.S. authorities against Walker, and his southern friends in the American navy proved unable to save him from capture and execution.

Quote: "That which you ignorantly call 'filibustering' is not the offspring of hasty passion or ill-regulated desire. It is the fruit of the supreme instincts that act in accord with fixed laws as old as creation." (Autobiography, 1860)

REFERENCE: Laurence Greene, *The Filibuster: The Career of William Walker* (1937).

QUESTIONS FOR CLASS DISCUSSION

1. Was the Compromise of 1850 a wise effort to balance sectional differences or a futile attempt to push the slavery issue out of sight?

2. Why did the North so strongly resent the Fugitive Slave Law, and why did the South resent northern resistance to enforcing it?

3. Why was the issue of acquiring Cuba so controversial in the 1850s? Could some of the Caribbean islands or parts of Central America have become incorporated as slave states with the United States?

4. Would the sectional conflict have been reheated had Douglas not pushed through the Kansas-Nebraska Act? Why or why not?

19

Drifting Toward Disunion, 1854–1861

CHAPTER THEME

Theme: A series of major North-South crises in the late 1850s culminated in the election of the antislavery Republican Lincoln to the presidency in 1860. His election caused seven southern states to secede from the union and form the Confederate States of America.

CHAPTER SUMMARY

The 1850s were punctuated by successive confrontations that deepened sectional hostility until it broke out in the Civil War.

Harriet Beecher Stowe's *Uncle Tom's Cabin* fanned northern antislavery feeling. In Kansas, proslavery and antislavery forces fought a bloody little preview of the Civil War. Buchanan's support of the proslavery Lecompton Constitution alienated moderate northern Democrats like Douglas. Congressman Brooks's beating of Senator Sumner aroused passions in both sections.

The 1856 election signaled the rise of the sectionally based Republican party. The Dred Scott case delighted the South, while northern Republicans pledged defiance. The Lincoln-Douglas debates of 1858 deepened the national controversy over slavery. John Brown's raid on Harpers Ferry made him a heroic martyr in the North but caused outraged southerners to fear a slave uprising.

The Democratic party split along sectional lines, allowing Lincoln to win the four-way 1860 election. Seven southern states quickly seceded and organized the Confederate States of America.

As southerners optimistically cast off their ties to the hated North, lame-duck President Buchanan proved unable to act. The last-minute Crittenden Compromise effort failed because of Lincoln's opposition.

DEVELOPING THE CHAPTER: SUGGESTED LECTURE OR DISCUSSION TOPICS

- Explain how the events of the late 1850s developed in a chain reaction, with each crisis deepening sectional hatreds, thus paving the way for another critical event.

    REFERENCE: David M. Potter, *The Impending Crisis, 1848–1861* (1976).

- Analyze the Kansas conflict as a small-scale rehearsal for the Civil War. The focus might be on the way sectional violence fed on itself, producing extremist figures like Brown and the "border ruffians."

    REFERENCE: James A. Rawley, *Race and Politics: "Bleeding Kansas" and the Coming of the Civil War* (1969).

- Use the Lincoln-Douglas debates to explain the rise of Lincoln and the Republican party, and the issues in the northern debate about how to deal with slavery. Focus on Lincoln's rise to national prominence in relation to the slavery issue.

REFERENCE: Don E. Fehrenbacher, *Prelude to Greatness: Lincoln in the 1850s* (1962).

- Examine the 1860 election and its consequences. Emphasize the Democratic split, the sectional character of the voting, and the Deep South's clear determination to secede as soon as Lincoln won, even before he took office.

REFERENCE: Steven A. Channing, *Crisis of Fear* (1970).

FOR FURTHER INTEREST: ADDITIONAL CLASS TOPICS

- Use Stowe's *Uncle Tom's Cabin,* and the southern reaction to it, to demonstrate the growing division of outlook between the sections.

- Focus on John Brown as a crucial character in two of the major events of the decade, bleeding Kansas and Harpers Ferry.

- Trace the rise of Lincoln through the events of the decade, from the Kansas-Nebraska Act to the Lincoln-Douglas debates to the 1860 election.

- Consider the southern decision to secede and the last-minute Crittenden Compromise effort.

CHARACTER SKETCHES

Harriet Beecher Stowe (1811–1896)

A member of the famous Beecher family, Stowe wrote *Uncle Tom's Cabin,* the book that more than anything else deepened northern hostility to slavery.

Stowe was closer to her brother Henry, later a famous preacher, than to her father or her older sister Catharine. She was very fond of her parents' free black servants, particularly one kind woman who may have been a model for characters in *Uncle Tom's Cabin*.

Although she had published a few stories before marrying Calvin Stowe, a professor at her father's seminary, she then gave up writing. For eighteen years she was a housewife who struggled to raise her seven children on a very limited income. She visited slaveholding areas of Kentucky during that time and knew abolitionists at her father's seminary but at first was not very sympathetic to them.

Her brother urged her to write against slavery, and she submitted *Uncle Tom's Cabin* in serial form to a magazine. Although the magazine paid her only $300, the book sold 10,000 copies the first week, 300,000 the first year, and eventually millions in the United States and abroad.

Quote: "As long as the baby sleeps with me nights I can't do much of anything—but I shall *do it at last*. I shall write it if I live...." (Letter to Calvin Stowe, 1850)

REFERENCE: Joan Hedrick, *Harriet Beecher Stowe: A Life* (1994).

John Brown (1800–1859)

Brown was the militant abolitionist whose violent attacks at Osawatomie, Kansas, and Harpers Ferry, Virginia, helped to bring on the Civil War.

An unsuccessful tanner, cattle driver, and sheep raiser, Brown was frequently in financial difficulty. He had twenty children—seven by his first wife and thirteen by his second.

For a time he lived in a black community in New York on land donated by abolitionist Gerrit Smith. After five of his sons migrated to Kansas in 1855, he joined them with a wagonload of guns and ammunition and then hacked five proslavery settlers to death in the Osawatomie massacre.

After Osawatomie he solicited money and supplies from some New England intellectuals and began planning to lead a slave uprising. He rented a farm near Harpers Ferry in the summer of 1859 and gradually accumulated weapons and his little army of twenty-one men. He could have escaped after raiding the armory, but his plans were too confused. Two of his sons died in the fighting.

Quote: "I John Brown am now quite certain that the crimes of this guilty land will never be purged away, but with blood. I had, as I now think, vainly flattered myself that without very much bloodshed it might be done." (Statement before hanging, 1859)

REFERENCE: Stephen B. Oates, *To Purge This Land with Blood: A Biography of John Brown* (1970).

Dred Scott (1795–1858)

Scott was the slave whose attempt to secure his freedom was denied by the Supreme Court, which declared that blacks "have no rights that white men are bound to respect."

Born a slave in Virginia, Scott was later purchased by a U.S. Army doctor who took him for three years to Illinois (a free state) and two years to Wisconsin (a free territory).

After the doctor died, Scott passed into other hands, but his former owner's sons sympathized with him and helped carry his case through the state and federal courts.

After he lost the case, the doctor's sons bought Scott and freed him. Although unskilled and illiterate, he was intelligent and proud of his notoriety. Scott was married, had several children, and ended his days as a janitor in a St. Louis hotel.

Quote: "I have no money to pay anybody at Washington to speak for me....Will nobody speak for me at Washington, even without hope of other reward than the blessings of a poor black man and his family?...I can only pray that some good heart will be moved by pity to do that for me which I cannot do for myself; and that if the right is on my side it may be so declared by the high court to which I have appealed." (Pamphlet containing Scott's appeal for aid, 1854)

REFERENCE: Don E. Fehrenbacher, *The Dred Scott Case* (1978).

QUESTIONS FOR CLASS DISCUSSION

1. How did each of the major crisis events of the 1850s contribute to the advent of the Civil War?

2. How could a fanatical and violent man like John Brown come to be regarded as a hero by millions of northerners?

3. Why did Douglas's "popular sovereignty" approach to the slavery question prove to be unworkable in Kansas and elsewhere?

4. Why was sectional compromise impossible in 1860, when such compromises had previously worked in 1820 and 1850? Since Lincoln had guaranteed to protect slavery in the states where it existed, why did the seven southern states secede as soon as he was elected?

EXPANDING THE "VARYING VIEWPOINTS"

- Charles and Mary Beard, *The Rise of American Civilization* (1927).

    A view of the Civil War as an economic and social revolution:

    "At bottom, the so-called Civil War...was a social war, ending in the unquestioned establishment of a new power in the government, making vast changes in the arrangement of class, in the accumulation and distribution of wealth, in the course of industrial development, and in the Constitution inherited from the Fathers....If the series of acts by which the bourgeois and peasants of France overthrew the king, nobility, and clergy is to be called the French Revolution, then accuracy compels us to characterize by the same term the social cataclysm in which the capitalists, laborers, and farmers of the North and West drove from power in the national government the planting aristocracy of the South....The so-called civil war was in reality a Second American Revolution, and in a strict sense, the First."

- David M. Potter, *The Impending Crisis, 1848–1861* (1976).

    A view of the 1850s as a time of irreconcilable conflict between North and South over the central issue of slavery:

    "Thus slavery suddenly emerged as a transcendent sectional issue in its own right, and as a catalyst of all sectional antagonisms, political, economic, and cultural....The slavery question became the sectional question, the sectional question became the slavery question, and both became the territorial question....From the sultry August night in 1846 when Wilmot caught the chairman's eye, the slavery question steadily widened the sectional rift until an April dawn in 1861 when the batteries along the Charleston waterfront opened fire on Fort Sumter...."

- Michael Holt, *Forging a Majority: The Formation of the Republic Party in Pittsburgh, 1848–1860* (1969).

    A view of the 1850s as a time when many issues besides slavery dominated national politics:

    "Politics did not revolve around [slavery and the South] just as politics today does not revolve around communism, although most people dislike it. Instead, social, ethnic, and religious considerations often determined who voted for whom between 1848 and 1861. Divisions between native-born Americans and immigrants and between Protestants and Catholics, rather than differences of opinion about the tariff or the morality of slavery, distinguished Whigs and Republicans from Democrats....Interpreting the rise of the Republican party in the North solely in terms of hostility to slavery or economic issues is, therefore, too simplified."

QUESTIONS ABOUT THE "VARYING VIEWPOINTS"

1. How does each of these views see the relationship between slavery and sectional feeling?

2. What does each of these views see as the relationship between slavery and other issues in the 1850s?

3. How would each of these historians interpret the decline of the Whigs and the rise of the Republicans in the 1850s?

20

Girding for War: The North and the South, 1861–1865

CHAPTER THEMES

Theme: The North effectively brought to bear its long-term advantages of industrial might and human resources to wage a devastating total war against the South. The war helped organize and modernize northern society, while the South, despite heroic efforts, was economically and socially crushed.

Theme: Lincoln's skillful political leadership helped keep the crucial Border States in the Union and maintain northern morale, while his effective diplomacy kept Britain and France from aiding the Confederacy.

CHAPTER SUMMARY

South Carolina's firing on Fort Sumter aroused the North for war. Lincoln's call for troops to suppress the rebellion drove four upper South states into the Confederacy. Lincoln used an effective combination of political persuasion and force to keep the deeply divided Border States in the Union.

The Confederacy enjoyed initial advantages of upper-class European support, military leadership, and a defensive position on its own soil. The North enjoyed the advantages of lower-class European support, industrial and population resources, and political leadership.

The British upper classes sympathized with the South and abetted Confederate naval efforts. But effective diplomacy and Union military success thwarted those efforts and kept Britain as well as France neutral in the war.

Lincoln's political leadership proved effective in mobilizing the North for war, despite political opposition and resistance to his infringement on civil liberties. The North eventually mobilized its larger troop resources for war and ultimately turned to an unpopular and unfair draft system.

Northern economic and financial strengths enabled it to gain an advantage over the less-industrialized South. The changes in society opened new opportunities for women, who had contributed significantly to the war effort in both the North and South. Since most of the war was waged on Southern soil, the South was left devastated by the war.

DEVELOPING THE CHAPTER: SUGGESTED LECTURE OR DISCUSSION TOPICS

- Analyze the Sumter crisis and the secession of the upper South. The focus might be on Lincoln's success in maneuvering South Carolina into firing the first shot, thereby arousing the North for a war it had previously been reluctant to fight.

REFERENCE: Richard Current, *Lincoln and the First Shot* (1963).

- Explain the various internal political conflicts in the North, focusing on Copperheadism and the 1864 campaign. Point out how crucial it was for Lincoln to achieve military success in order to overcome such opposition, since any political settlement would have meant recognition of the Confederacy.

    REFERENCE: James A. Rawley, *The Politics of Union* (1974).

- Examine Lincoln the wartime leader and Lincoln the martyr and hero. Contrast the many contemporary criticisms of his leadership with those qualities that now constitute his greatness.

    REFERENCE: David H. Donald, *Lincoln* (1995).

- Explain the role of women both on the home front and in such new areas as battlefield nursing. Compare and contrast the situations and ideologies of northern and southern women.

    REFERENCES: Catherine Clinton and Nina Silber, eds., *Divided Houses* (1992); Drew Gilpin Faust, *Mothers of Invention: Women of the Slaveholding South in the American Civil War* (1996).

FOR FURTHER INTEREST: ADDITIONAL CLASS TOPICS

- Focus on the ordinary soldiers, North and South. Point out the differences (for example, in supplies) as well as the similarities in the experiences of Billy Yank and Johnny Reb.

- Discuss different interpretations of the Civil War. Point out how its meaning has varied according to changes in North-South and black-white relations.

- Focus on the "might-have-beens" that could have resulted in a Confederate victory.

- Discuss the effects of the Civil War on the "homefront," North and South, including ways the war affected women.

CHARACTER SKETCHES

Abraham Lincoln (1809–1865)

Born in a log cabin in Kentucky, Lincoln, who would become our sixteenth president, had only vague but fond memories of his mother, Nancy, who died when he was nine. His father was a stocky, heavyset, hard-drinking frontier drifter. Lincoln became estranged from him and did not attend his final illness or funeral, even though he was only seventy miles away at the time.

The story that Lincoln's one true love was the beautiful Ann Rutledge rests solely on the report of his law partner William Herndon following Lincoln's death, thirty years after the supposed romance. Lincoln did know Ann Rutledge, but he never mentioned her, and Mary Todd Lincoln emphatically denied the Herndon story.

His natural melancholy was much deepened by the deaths of his children, especially eleven-year-old Willie in 1862. He thought a good deal about the afterlife, and at his wife's instigation brought spiritualist mediums into the White House and attended séances to communicate with the dead.

Quote: "The dogmas of the quiet past are inadequate to the stormy present....As our case is new, so we must think anew, and act anew. We must disenthrall ourselves, and then we shall save our country." (Message to Congress, 1862)

REFERENCE: David Herbert Donald, *Lincoln* (1995).

Elizabeth Blackwell (1821–1910)

Blackwell was the first American female physician and a pioneer in developing medical knowledge and health care for women and children.

Blackwell was born in Bristol, England, into a family of twelve children. Her father, a charming sugar refiner and social reformer, believed in women's rights and was a great influence on Elizabeth. He died when she was eleven, shortly after the family immigrated to America.

She was turned down by many medical schools before being accepted by Geneva College—though the acceptance was initially considered a joke by the male students.

After graduation from Geneva and further study in England, she opened a clinic on Bleecker Street in New York and began treating poor women. In 1868 she opened her own women's medical college. She later wrote extensively on "the human element in sex," and attempted to combat ignorance and prejudice concerning women's sexuality.

Quote: "The idea of acquiring a doctor's degree gradually assumed the aspect of a great moral struggle, and the moral fight possessed great attraction for me." (Memoir, 1879)

REFERENCE: Dorothy Clarke Wilson, *Lone Woman: The Story of Elizabeth Blackwell* (1970).

Clara Barton (1821–1912)

Barton was the Civil War nurse who founded and led the American Red Cross for twenty-three years.

Born in Massachusetts of old Yankee stock, Barton was close to her family, including her older brother David, whom she nursed through a two-year illness. Shy and lonely, she attempted schoolteaching, but gave it up to become a clerk in the U.S. Patent Office in Washington—one of the first female federal employees.

When she saw the lack of medical facilities after the Battle of Bull Run, she organized her friends to provide first aid, using her own house as a store room. Scorned at first, she eventually won the respect of military officers and men.

She suffered a nervous breakdown after the war and went to Europe for relief, where she learned of the newly formed Red Cross in Switzerland. She returned to the United States and waged a long, difficult campaign to found the American branch of the organization in 1881.

Quote: "The paths of charity are over the roadways of ashes, and he who would tread them must be prepared to meet opposition, misconstruction, jealousy, and calumny. Let his work be that of angels, still it will not satisfy all." (Speech, 1887)

REFERENCE: Stephen B. Oates, *A Woman of Valor: Clara Barton and the Civil War* (1995).

Copyright © Houghton Mifflin Company. All rights reserved.

QUESTIONS FOR CLASS DISCUSSION

1. How justified were Lincoln's wartime abridgments of civil liberties and his treatment of the Copperheads?

2. How was the impact of the Civil War different for the soldiers and civilians of the North and South?

3. Did the results of the Civil War justify its cost? Does the answer to that question depend partly on whether you are a Northerner or a Southerner, black or white?

4. What made Lincoln a great president? Was it primarily his political leadership, or his personal qualities and character?

21

The Furnace of Civil War, 1861–1865

CHAPTER THEMES

Theme: The Civil War, begun as a limited struggle over the Union, eventually became a total war to end slavery and transform the nation.

Theme: After several years of seesaw struggle, the Union armies under Ulysses Grant finally wore down the Southern forces under Robert E. Lee and ended the Confederate bid for independence as well as the institution of slavery.

CHAPTER SUMMARY

The Union defeat at Bull Run ended Northern complacency about a quick victory. George McClellan and other early Union generals proved unable to defeat the tactically brilliant Confederate armies under Lee. The Union naval blockade put a slow but devastating economic noose around the South.

The political and diplomatic dimensions of the war quickly became critical. In order to retain the border states, Lincoln first de-emphasized any intention to destroy slavery. But the Battle of Antietam in 1862 enabled Lincoln to prevent foreign intervention and turn the struggle into a war against slavery. Blacks and abolitionists joined enthusiastically in a war for emancipation, but white resentment in part of the North created political problems for Lincoln.

The Union victories at Vicksburg in the West and Gettysburg in the East finally turned the military tide against the South. Southern resistance remained strong, but the Union victories at Atlanta and Mobile assured Lincoln's success in the election of 1864 and ended the last Confederate hopes. The war ended the issues of disunion and slavery, but at a tremendous cost to both North and South.

DEVELOPING THE CHAPTER: SUGGESTED LECTURE OR DISCUSSION TOPICS

- Examine how the different political and military perspectives and respective advantages that the North and the South (see Chapter 20) brought to the war affected their respective strategies. Show why the failure of McClellan's "Peninsular Campaign" almost guaranteed a long and bloody struggle.

  REFERENCE: James M. McPherson, *Battle Cry of Freedom* (1988).

- Explain why the North won the Civil War and why the South lost. The factors of military strategy, political leadership, and economic resources might be related to key turning points of the war, such as Vicksburg and Gettysburg.

  REFERENCES: Herman Hattaway and Archer Jones, *How the North Won* (1983); Richard E.

Beringer, Herman Hattaway, Archer Jones, and William N. Still, Jr., *Why the South Lost the Civil War* (1986).

- Examine the politics of the war, especially the way Lincoln gradually turned it from being strictly a "war to preserve the Union" into a war for black emancipation. Show how Lincoln first kept the war aims limited to appease the Border States but later used the Emancipation Proclamation to strengthen the North's moral position.

    REFERENCE: James M. McPherson, *Ordeal by Fire: The Civil War and Reconstruction* (1982).

- Consider the role of slavery and the "race question" in the changing politics of the Civil War. The career of Frederick Douglass provides a good window on the racial question during the war.

    REFERENCE: David W. Blight, *Frederick Douglass' Civil War* (1989).

FOR FURTHER INTEREST: ADDITIONAL CLASS TOPICS

- Consider the various crucial "What Ifs?" of the Civil War (see p. 441) in relation to the possibilities of a) a Confederate victory or negotiated settlement and b) a war that might have preserved the Union but not ended slavery. Critically analyze the text's assertion that even though Vicksburg and Gettysburg were the decisive military battles of the war, Antietam was probably the political and diplomatic turning point.

- Compare Grant and Lee as military leaders. The focus might be on Lee as the greatest of the "traditional" strategists, whereas Grant represents the new age of total war.

- Use Lincoln's First Inaugural Address, Gettysburg Address, Emancipation Proclamation, and Second Inaugural Address to examine the changing interpretations that he gave to secession, the Union, and the issue of slavery.

- Examine the effects of the use of black soldiers on the Union military effort and on public opinion. (The film *Glory* might be used as a resource and starting point for discussion.)

CHARACTER SKETCHES

Clement Vallandigham (1820–1871)

Vallandigham was the Copperhead Democratic politician who was convicted of treason and exiled by Lincoln, only to return and continue his peace agitation.

Vallandigham's family originally came from Virginia, and they romanticized the South as a land of noble social ideals and order. As an Ohio politician and congressman, he was a bitter foe of Republicans and abolitionists. In 1859 he interviewed John Brown in prison and came away convinced that there was a widespread abolitionist conspiracy to bring about a civil war.

He was given direct military orders to stop his calls for resistance to the war before he was arrested, convicted, and exiled to the South. He used a disguise with a false mustache and a pillow to sneak back across the border from Canada in 1864. The government decided not to rearrest him, and he helped push through the peace plank at the 1864 Democratic convention.

Quote: "Yes, it is amazing that our people—Americans, proud, boastful, free—should have submitted to usurpation and despotism….I am a Democrat—for the Constitution, for law, for the Union, for liberty—this is my only crime." (1863)

REFERENCE: Frank Clement, *Copperheads in the Middle West* (1972).

Robert E. Lee (1807–1870)

Lee was the son of "Light-Horse Harry" Lee, a cavalry hero of the revolution and a member of the great Lee family of Virginia. When Robert was still a boy, his father sank into debtor's prison and disgrace, and eventually left the family.

An 1829 graduate of West Point, where he was a distinguished student, the younger Lee married Mary Custis, a great-granddaughter of Martha Washington, and became master of the Custis estate at Arlington. Lee became a military hero in the Mexican War, and later commanded the soldiers who captured John Brown at Harpers Ferry in 1859.

Politically a strong Whig, Lee was initially very unsympathetic to secession. He always said, however, that he would follow the decision of his home state regarding secession. When offered the field command of the Union Army, he turned it down, and instead assumed command of Confederate forces.

Lee had only 7,800 fully armed troops left with him when he surrendered at Appomattox. Most of them wept when he rode by them on his horse Traveler to say farewell. After the war he served as president of Washington College, which was later renamed "Washington and Lee College."

Quote: "After four years of arduous service, marked by unsurpassing courage and fortitude, the Army of Northern Virginia has been compelled to yield to overwhelming numbers and resources….Feeling that valor and devotion could accomplish nothing that could compensate for the loss that would have attended the continuation of the contest, I have determined to avoid the useless sacrifice of those whose past services have endeared them to their countrymen." (Farewell Speech to Confederate Troops, 1865)

REFERENCE: Emory Thomas, *Robert E. Lee: A Biography* (1995); George W. Gallagher, *Lee the Soldier* (1996).

Ulysses S. Grant (1822–1885)

Grant was a national hero as the commanding Union general in the Civil War, but his reputation suffered badly from his two unfortunate terms as president.

Born in a log cabin in Ohio, Grant inherited his mother's strong, silent, fiercely determined character but not her marked religious bent. Although officially "Hiram Ulysses," he changed his name to "Ulysses Hiram" at West Point because he was afraid he would be laughed at for his initials "HUG." Later a military error substituted "Simpson" for "Hiram," and he left it that way.

Grant's drinking bouts in California were partly caused by his having served a horrendous tour of duty in Panama and by his separation from his family. He was totally devoted to his wife, Julia, who often advised him during his years in politics.

After leaving the presidency, he took a grand tour of Europe for two years and lived so lavishly that he was soon poverty-stricken. He completed his memoirs, which are still greatly admired, while dying of cancer of the throat.

Quote: "I saw an open field…so covered with dead that it would have been possible to walk across the clearing, in any direction, stepping on dead bodies, without touching a foot on the ground." (After the Battle of Shiloh, 1862)

Copyright © Houghton Mifflin Company. All rights reserved.

REFERENCE: William McFeely, *Grant* (1981).

Salmon P. Chase (1808–1873)

Chase was Lincoln's politically ambitious secretary of the treasury.

He made his career as an antislavery lawyer in Ohio. Although he aided many fugitive slaves as Ohio attorney general, Chase was actually fearful of large black migrations to the North and hoped that emancipation would keep blacks in the South.

In the 1860 Republican convention, Chase had forty-nine votes before throwing them to Lincoln. He always considered Lincoln a weak leader and in December 1862 conspired with some radical Republicans in Congress to try to take control of the cabinet. But Lincoln invited the conspirators into a cabinet meeting, where Chase was forced to express his support of the president.

He wanted the nomination in 1864 but ran the other way when the movement collapsed. After being extremely unhappy as chief justice of the United States, in 1868 he maneuvered for the Democratic nomination. Chase was self-righteous, opinionated, and difficult to get along with.

Quote: "I think a man of different qualities from those the President has will be needed for the next four years. I am not anxious to be regarded as that man. I am quite willing to leave [the choice] to the decision of those who think some such man should be chosen." (Diary, 1864)

REFERENCE: John Niven, *Salmon P. Chase: A Biography* (1995); David Donald, ed., *Inside Lincoln's Cabinet: The Civil War Diaries of Salmon P. Chase* (1954).

John Wilkes Booth (1838–1865)

Booth was the prominent Shakespearean actor who assassinated Abraham Lincoln.

Booth's father was Junius Brutus Booth, one of the most famous actors of his time. Junius Booth eventually went insane, and John Wilkes was always high-strung, moody, and emotionally unstable. Although probably not actually insane, he did experience periods of wild fantasy and irrationality. He would sometimes go into a rage at the sight of cats and occasionally killed them.

The younger Booth was dark, handsome, and always wore a long black cloak. He was especially popular with women and was said to have had numerous affairs. His favorite roles were Hamlet and Macbeth, but he also played popular melodramas.

He had planned to abduct Lincoln as early as 1864. Several of those he gathered for the assassination plot were feebleminded. He visited Lincoln's box the afternoon before the performance to arrange the assassination. The barn where he hid after fleeing was set on fire by Union soldiers, and Booth then evidently shot himself.

Quote: "I am not a murderer. I have done nothing that a soldier on the battlefield would not do. I do not regret what I have done." (Statement to physician aiding him, April 15, 1865)

REFERENCE: Albert Furstwangler, *Assassin on Stage* (1991).

QUESTIONS FOR CLASS DISCUSSION

1. Why did the North win the Civil War? How might the South have won?

2. Should the Civil War be seen primarily as a war to save the Union or as a war to free the slaves? Why? What name would you give to the conflict?

3. What role did race and racism play in the Civil War? How did the war itself reflect and affect American attitudes toward race? Why were the black Union soldiers so critical in this regard?

4. How does the popular image of the Civil War compare with the historical reality? Discuss the different perceptions and memories of the war in the North and South (for example, the popular images of Lee or Sherman in the two sections).

EXPANDING THE "VARYING VIEWPOINTS"

- T. Harry Williams, *Lincoln and His Generals* (1952).

    A view of Northern victory focused on military leadership:

    "Fundamentally Grant was superior to Lee because in a modern total war he had a modern mind, and Lee did not. Lee looked to the past in war as the Confederacy did in spirit….What was realism to Grant was barbarism to Lee. Lee thought of war in the old way as a conflict between armies and refused to view it for what it had become—a struggle between societies. To him, economic war was needless cruelty to civilians. Lee was the last of the great old-fashioned generals, Grant the first of the great moderns."

- Allan Nevins, *The War for the Union* (1971).

    A view of Northern victory focused on political leadership:

    "One cardinal deficiency of the Confederacy…lay in the lack of a chief national executive possessing some of the energy, foresight, and firm decision exhibited by those other leaders of a newborn republic at war, Washington, Cromwell, or Masaryk. It is impossible for a student of the great rebellion to avoid comparing the character, talents, and sagacity of Lincoln with the parallel gifts of Jefferson Davis, greatly to the disadvantage of the latter. This broad subject…must always be kept in mind as an essential element of the war."

- Thomas C. Cochran, "Did the Civil War Retard Industrialization?" *Mississippi Valley Historical Review* (1961).

    A view of the Civil War actually slowed capitalist economic transformation:

    "Collectively these statistical estimates support a conclusion that the Civil War retarded American industrial growth….Economically the effects of war and emancipation over the period 1840 to 1880 were negative….If factory industry and mechanized transportation be taken as the chief indexes of early industrialism, its spread in the United States was continuous and rapid during the entire nineteenth century….Few economists would see a major stimulation to economic growth in the events of the Civil War."

- James McPherson, *Battle Cry of Freedom* (1988).

    A view of the Civil War as expanding national power and Northern economic dominance:

"The old federal republic in which the national government had rarely touched the average citizen except through the post-office gave way to a more centralized polity that taxed the people directly and created an internal revenue bureau to collect these taxes, drafted men into the army, expanded the jurisdiction of the federal courts, created a national currency and a national banking system, and established the first national agency for social welfare—the Freedmen's Bureau....These changes in the federal balance paralleled a radical shift of political power from South to North....The accession to power of the Republican party, with its ideology of competitive, egalitarian, free-labor capitalism, was a signal to the South that the northern majority had turned irrevocably toward this frightening, revolutionary future. Union victory in the war destroyed the southern vision of America and ensured that the northern vision would become the American vision."

QUESTIONS ABOUT THE "VARYING VIEWPOINTS"

1. How does Williams alter the usual judgment concerning Lee's superior military leadership? Does his definition of military leadership differ from the common one?

2. Are the political failings that Nevins sees in Davis similar to the military failings that Williams sees in Lee?

3. How might each of these historians interpret such turning points of the war as the Emancipation Proclamation, Vicksburg, and Gettysburg?

22

The Ordeal of Reconstruction, 1865–1877

CHAPTER THEME

Theme: Johnson's political blunders and Southern white recalcitrance led to the imposition of congressional military Reconstruction on the South. Reconstruction did address difficult issues of reform and racial justice in the South and achieved some successes, such as the Fourteenth (citizenship and equal protection of the laws) and Fifteenth (black voting rights) Amendments. But its ultimate abandonment meant those provisions remained unfulfilled promises, while Reconstruction left behind a deep legacy of racial and sectional bitterness.

CHAPTER SUMMARY

With the Civil War over, the nation faced the difficult problems of rebuilding the South, assisting the freed slaves, reintegrating the Southern states into the Union, and deciding who would direct the Reconstruction process.

The South was economically devastated and socially revolutionized by emancipation. As slaveowners reluctantly confronted the end of slave labor, blacks took their first steps in freedom. Black churches and freedmen's schools helped the former slaves begin to shape their own destiny.

The new President Andrew Johnson was politically inept and personally contentious. His attempt to implement a moderate plan of Reconstruction, along the lines originally suggested by Lincoln, fell victim to Southern whites' severe treatment of blacks and his own political blunders.

Republicans imposed harsh military Reconstruction on the South after their gains in the 1866 congressional elections. The Southern states reentered the Union with new radical governments, which rested partly on the newly enfranchised blacks, but also had support from some sectors of southern society. These regimes were sometimes corrupt but also implemented important reforms. The divisions between moderate and radical Republicans meant that Reconstruction's aims were often limited and confused, despite the important Fourteenth and Fifteenth Amendments.

Embittered whites hated the radical governments and mobilized reactionary terrorist organizations like the Ku Klux Klan to restore white supremacy. Congress impeached Johnson but failed narrowly to convict him. In the end, the poorly conceived Reconstruction policy failed disastrously.

DEVELOPING THE CHAPTER: SUGGESTED LECTURE OR DISCUSSION TOPICS

- Analyze in more detail the condition of the South at the end of the Civil War, particularly the economic and social revolution caused by the end of slavery. The focus might be on the great difficulty of working out a new system of racial relations, and on blacks' efforts to make their own way under harsh conditions.

    REFERENCE: Leon Litwack, *Been in the Storm So Long* (1979).

- Compare the mild presidential Reconstruction plans of Lincoln and Johnson with the harsher congressional Reconstruction, perhaps emphasizing how Johnson's blunders and severe treatment of blacks in the South handed the radical Republicans their chance.

    REFERENCE: James McPherson, *Ordeal by Fire: The Civil War and Reconstruction* (1982).

- Explain the actual impact of Reconstruction in the South. Particular consideration might be given to the limitations of the Republican governments and the Freedmen's Bureau, especially in altering fundamental economic and social conditions.

    REFERENCE: Eric Foner, *Reconstruction: America's Unfinished Revolution, 1863–1877* (1988).

- Examine the impeachment and acquittal of Johnson in relation to the overreaching of the radical Republicans and the declining support for military Reconstruction in the North.

    REFERENCE: Michael Les Benedict, *Impeachment and Trial of Andrew Johnson* (1973); Hans Trefousse, *The Impeachment of a President* (1975).

FOR FURTHER INTEREST: ADDITIONAL CLASS TOPICS

- Discuss the new circumstances and experiences of the ordinary freed African-Americans. Consider such developments as the westward-migrating "Exodusters" and the newly powerful black churches.

- Look at the Ku Klux Klan in relation to its historical significance in the 1870s and its enduring presence as a symbol of white racism and illegal violence.

- Focus on the character of Andrew Johnson, and particularly his difficulty as a "poor Southern white" in the White House during Republican Reconstruction. Perhaps contrast him with his great enemy Thaddeus Stevens.

- Compare the enormous gap between the still widely held popular image of Reconstruction and the more complicated historical reality described in the text. The D. W. Griffith film *Birth of a Nation* would be a good starting point, since it helped to fix the general image of the period more than any other work.

CHARACTER SKETCHES

Andrew Johnson (1808–1875)

Even after Johnson's wife taught him to read as an adult, he frequently misspelled words. He once said, "It is a man of small imagination that cannot spell his own name in more than one way."

As a representative of poor mountain whites, he hated slaveholders, blacks, and abolitionists. Even though he hated slavery, he opposed emancipation because, he said: "What will you do with two million Negroes in our midst? Blood, rape, and rapine will be our portion."

The attacks on Johnson during his "swing around the circle" were partly orchestrated by Republican newspapers, which played up his vulgar language and behavior. Once they discovered that Johnson would go out of control, radical hecklers baited him at every stop.

Johnson remained a political hero to the plain whites of Tennessee following his departure from the presidency. After several tries he was reelected to the Senate in 1875 but attended only one session before he died.

Quote: (In reply to hecklers' shouts of "Judas!"): "There was a Judas, and he was one of the twelve apostles....If I have played Judas, who has been my Christ that I have played Judas with? Was it Thad Stevens? Was it Wendell Phillips? Was it Charles Sumner?" (Swing around the circle, 1866)

REFERENCE: Hans Trefousse, *Andrew Johnson: A Biography* (1989).

Oliver O. Howard (1830–1909)

Howard was the Civil War general who became head of the Freedmen's Bureau during Reconstruction.

In the Battle of Fair Oaks, Howard lost his right arm. His Civil War record was somewhat mixed: he bungled several operations and once refused to obey an order from General Hooker. Considered a "Christian officer," he was shocked by the destruction inflicted on Georgia by Sherman's army, even though he justified it as militarily necessary.

After leaving the Freedmen's Bureau, he founded Howard University in Washington, D.C., and served as its president from 1869 to 1874. He caused a split in his church in Washington by demanding the admission of black members.

Howard later returned to active military duty and commanded the 1877 expedition against the Nez Percé Indians in the West. He wrote frequently for newspapers and magazines and was a popular lecturer.

Quote: "A brief experience showed us that the negro people were capable of education, with no limit that men could set on their capacity. What white men could learn or had learned, they, or some of them, could learn." (Autobiography, 1907)

REFERENCE: William S. McFeely, *Yankee Stepfather: General O. O. Howard and the Freedmen* (1968).

Hiram Revels (1822–1901)

Revels, a clergyman, became one of the two black senators from Mississippi during Reconstruction.

Born a free man in Kentucky, Revels was of black and Indian ancestry. He first worked as a barber but then attended Knox College in Illinois and became a minister of the African Methodist Church.

He organized two black regiments in Maryland during the Civil War and then traveled widely in the South promoting religion and education for blacks. He was first elected an alderman in Natchez, Mississippi, despite his concern about mixing religion and politics. Many whites as well as blacks liked him, and he was elected to take Jefferson Davis's seat in the Senate. During his brief term he supported the moderate Republicans and not the radicals.

He later came under white Democratic influence and joined in the overthrow of Republican Reconstruction in 1875. Quiet and mild-mannered, he disliked political conflict.

Quote: "The colored members, after consulting together on the subject, agreed to give their influence and votes for one of their own race, as it would in their judgment be a weakening blow against color line prejudice, and they unanimously elected me for their nominee....Some of the Democracy favored it because they thought it would seriously damage the Republican party." (1884)

REFERENCE: Julius Thompson, *Hiram R. Revels, 1827–1901: A Biography* (1973).

Thaddeus Stevens (1792–1868)

Stevens was the Republican congressman who led radical Reconstruction and engineered the impeachment of Andrew Johnson.

Often sickly as a child, Stevens was partially physically disabled as an adult. He hated slavery from an early age and occasionally purchased fugitive slaves in order to give them their freedom.

In Congress Stevens constantly attacked Southerners in scurrilous language, and some of his speeches nearly provoked riots on the floor of the House. As soon as the Civil War broke out, he advocated arming the slaves and encouraging a slave insurrection. His hatred of the South was increased when Confederate soldiers destroyed his ironworks during Lee's invasion of Pennsylvania.

Stevens was well read and eloquent but relied heavily on vituperation and sarcasm and seemed in a constant state of barely suppressed rage. He died shortly after the Johnson trial, but only his nephew and his black housekeeper attended his funeral. He chose to be buried in a black cemetery.

Quote: "I repose in this quiet and secluded spot, not from any natural preference for solitude, but, finding other cemeteries limited by charter rules as to race, I have chosen this, that I might illustrate in my death the principle which I have advocated through a long life—Equality of Man before his Creator." (Inscription on Stevens's tombstone, written by himself, 1868)

REFERENCE: Hans Trefousse, *Thaddeus Stevens: Nineteenth-Century Egalitarian* (1997).

QUESTIONS FOR CLASS DISCUSSION

1. Could presidential Reconstruction have succeeded if politically skilled Abraham Lincoln instead of politically inept Andrew Johnson had been president?

2. How truly "radical" was "radical Reconstruction"?

3. How did both Southern and Northern racial attitudes shape Reconstruction, and what effect did Reconstruction have on race relations and the conditions of blacks? Did Reconstruction really address the problems of race?

4. Was Reconstruction a noble experiment that failed, a vengeful Northern punishment of the South, a weak effort that did not go far enough, or the best that could have been expected under the circumstances? What has been the historical legacy of Reconstruction? (Consider particularly the Fourteenth and Fifteenth Amendments.)

EXPANDING THE "VARYING VIEWPOINTS"

- William A. Dunning, *Reconstruction: Political and Economic* (1907).

    A view of Reconstruction as a national disgrace:

    "Few episodes of recorded history more urgently invited thorough analysis than the struggle through which the southern whites, subjugated by adversaries of their own race, thwarted the scheme which threatened permanent subjection to another race....The most rasping feature of the new situation to the old white element of the South was the large predominance of northerners and negroes in positions of political power....The most cunning and malignant enemy of the United States could not have timed differently this period of national ill-repute; for it came with the centennial of American independence...."

- Kenneth Stampp, *The Era of Reconstruction* (1965).

A favorable view of Reconstruction:

"Finally, we come to the idealistic aim of the radicals to make southern society more democratic, especially to make the emancipation of Negroes something more than an empty gesture. In the short run this was their greatest failure....Still, no one could quite forget that the Fourteenth and Fifteenth Amendments were now part of the federal Constitution....Thus Negroes were no longer denied equality by the plain language of law, as they had been before radical reconstruction, but only by coercion, by subterfuge, by deceit, and by spurious legalisms....The blunders of that era, tragic though they were, dwindle into insignificance. For if it was worth four years of civil war to save the Union, it was worth a few years of radical reconstruction to give the American Negro the ultimate promise of equal civil and political rights."

QUESTIONS ABOUT THE "VARYING VIEWPOINTS"

1. What does each of these historians see as the fundamental goals of Reconstruction? How well does each think it achieved those goals?

2. According to each of these viewpoints, what were the roles of Northern whites, Southern whites, and blacks in Reconstruction?

3. How would each of these historians interpret the overturning of Reconstruction and its continuing meaning for American society?

23

Political Paralysis in the Gilded Age, 1869–1896

CHAPTER THEME

Theme: Even as post–Civil War America expanded and industrialized, political life in the Gilded Age was marked by ineptitude, stalemate, and corruption. Despite their similarity at the national level, the two parties competed fiercely for offices and spoils, while doling out "pork-barrel" benefits to veterans and other special interest groups.

Theme: The serious issues of monetary and agrarian reform, labor, race, and economic fairness were largely swept under the rug by the political system, until revolting farmers and a major economic depression beginning in 1893 created a growing sense of crisis and demands for radical change.

CHAPTER SUMMARY

After the soaring ideals and tremendous sacrifices of the Civil War, the post–Civil War era was generally one of disillusionment. Politicians from the White House to the courthouse were often surrounded by corruption and scandal, while the actual problems afflicting industrializing America festered beneath the surface.

The popular war hero Grant was a poor politician and his administration was rife with corruption. Despite occasional futile reform efforts, politics in the Gilded Age was monopolized by the two patronage-fattened parties, which competed vigorously for spoils while essentially agreeing on most national policies. Cultural differences, different constituencies, and deeply felt local issues fueled intense party competition and unprecedented voter participation. Periodic complaints by "Mugwump" reformers and "soft-money" advocates failed to make much of a dent on politics.

The deadlocked contested 1876 election led to the sectional Compromise of 1877, which put an end to Reconstruction. An oppressive system of tenant farming and racial supremacy and segregation was thereafter fastened on the South, enforced by sometimes lethal violence. Racial prejudice against Chinese immigrants was also linked with labor unrest in the 1870s and 1880s.

Garfield's assassination by a disappointed office seeker spurred the beginnings of civil-service reform, which made politics more dependent on big business. Cleveland, the first Democratic president since the Civil War, made a lower tariff the first real issue in national politics for some time. But his mild reform efforts were eclipsed by a major economic depression that began in 1893, a crisis that deepened the growing outcry from suffering farmers and workers against a government and economic system that seemed biased toward big business and the wealthy.

DEVELOPING THE CHAPTER: SUGGESTED LECTURE OR DISCUSSION TOPICS

- Analyze the corruption of the Gilded Age in relation to the increasingly low moral and political standards of the time. Contrast the quality of politicians with those of the previous age—Clay, Jackson, Webster, and Lincoln.
  REFERENCE: Mark Summers, *The Era of Good Stealings* (1993).

- Examine the impact of the new political alignments in the South. Consider the role of "redeemers," poor whites, and blacks in the post-Reconstruction era.

    REFERENCE: Otto Olsen, *Reconstruction and Redemption in the South* (1980); Michael Perman, *The Road to Redemption* (1984).

- Consider the link between racial and labor conflict, especially in places like California, where the "racially different" Chinese were seen as threats to the advances of white (often Irish or other immigrant) working people.

    REFERENCE: Alexander Saxton, *The Indispensable Enemy: Labor and the Anti-Chinese Movement in California* (1975).

- Examine the depression of the 1890s as the immediate context for the growing sense of class crisis in America. Consider the different but related grievances of western and southern farmers and (largely) northern and eastern industrial works.

    REFERENCES: Charles Hoffman, *The Depression of the Nineties* (1970); Paul Krause, *The Battle for Homestead, 1880–1892* (1992); Robert McMath, *American Populism* (1993).

FOR FURTHER INTEREST: ADDITIONAL CLASS TOPICS

- Focus on the Tweed scandal as both event and symbol of the generally corrupt atmosphere of the times. The Nast cartoons make a good starting point.

- Discuss Grant's failures as president in contrast with his success as a general. Contrast his performance with that of other general-presidents like Washington or Jackson who were successful politicians.

- Consider the Compromise of 1877 in relation to race and sectional conflict. Ask whether a Republican unwillingness to compromise by ending Reconstruction might have led to renewed sectional violence.

- Examine the "corrupt" J.P. Morgan gold deal of 1895 as a symbol of what many Americans saw as the capture of the federal government by big business. Consider Morgan himself as an important political as well as economic figure, and ask whether he deserved the villainous treatment he received from critics and protestors.

CHARACTER SKETCHES

William Marcy Tweed (1823–1878)

Tweed was the New York political boss whose grand-scale corruption symbolized the low political standards of the Gilded Age.

He got his start in politics with volunteer fire companies, which were closely tied to Tammany Hall, and he soon learned tricky devices like running "dummy" candidates to divide the opposition. The City Council during his service was known as the "Forty Thieves."

Tweed offered $5 million to *The New York Times* if it would not print the information on his corruption and $500,000 to Nast if he would stop his anti-Tweed cartoons. Tweed was treated luxuriously in prison, even being allowed to take carriage rides. He escaped and fled to Cuba and Spain disguised as a sailor but was recognized and returned to harsher jail treatment.

Always genial and friendly, Tweed held no personal grudges against Thomas Nast and others who brought him down. He said he was only surprised that they wouldn't take his bribes.

Quote: (When asked how his ring had managed to keep the scandals hidden for so long): "Well, we used money wherever we could." (1869)

REFERENCE: Alexander Callow, *The Tweed Ring* (1966).

Horace Greeley (1811–1872)

Greeley was the most famous newspaper editor of the nineteenth century, whose eccentric involvements in reform and politics made him an object of humor and anger.

He started on a Vermont newspaper at age fourteen and in 1841 launched the *New York Tribune* in close association with Whig politicians Thurlow Weed and William Seward.

At various times he supported Fourierism, ending capital punishment, prohibition, cooperative labor unions, women's rights (though not suffrage), and homesteading. He once spent a few months in an unsuccessful farming venture and then published a book called *What I Know of Farming*.

He had a high, squeaky voice and whiskers and always wore a broad-brimmed hat and white socks. He tried numerous times for political office, but except for a few months in Congress, he always failed. He had often been satirized but took personally the attacks on him in the 1872 campaign: one cartoon depicted him shaking hands with Booth over Lincoln's body. He already showed signs of mental instability before the election and died shortly thereafter.

Quote: "We are henceforth to be one American people. Let us forget that we fought. Let us remember only that we have made peace." (1872)

REFERENCE: Lurton D. Ingersoll, *The Life of Horace Greeley* (1974).

James G. Blaine (1830–1893)

Blaine was the colorful Republican politician, presidential candidate, and secretary of state during the Gilded Age.

Blaine married his wife secretly because she was a schoolteacher who was supposed to remain single. She came from a well-off Maine family, and they helped him get his start in politics there.

Although he had the grand platform manner of earlier politicians, Blaine excelled at personal contact and humorous banter. He could easily remember thousands of names and connect each of them with an anecdote about the person.

By dramatically producing and reading the "Mulligan letters," which supposedly proved his involvement in railroad corruption, he convinced many people of his innocence. Although never charged with crime, he became wealthy by trading favors with the owners of railroads and other interests.

Quote: "This letter requires no answer. After reading it file it away in your most secret drawer or give it to the flames....Do not say a word...no matter who may ask you." (Letter to Sherman, 1884)

REFERENCE: R. Hal Williams, *Years of Decision* (1978).

QUESTIONS FOR CLASS DISCUSSION

1. Why did politics in the Gilded Age seemingly sink to such a low level? Did the Gilded Age party system have any strengths to compensate for its weaknesses?

2. Was the Compromise of 1877 another cynical political deal of the era or a wise adjustment to avoid a renewal of serious sectional conflict?

3. What were the short-term and long-term results of the "Jim Crow" system in the South? Why was the sharecropping system so hard to overcome?

4. Why was the political system so slow to respond to the economic grievances of farmers and workers, especially during the hard economic times of the 1890s? Were the Populists and others more effectively addressing the real problems that America faced, or was their approach fatally crippled by their nostalgia for a simpler, rural America?

MAKERS OF AMERICA: THE CHINESE

Questions for Class Discussion

1. How was the Chinese immigrant experience similar to that of such European groups as the Irish (Chapter 14), and how was it different? What effect did the racial distinctiveness of the Chinese have on their experience in America?

2. What were the greatest problems the Chinese-Americans experienced? How did they attempt to overcome them?

Suggested Student Exercises

- Consider various prejudicial stereotypes of Chinese-American immigrants from the movies or elsewhere (e.g., Charlie Chan). Compare these images with the actual experiences of Chinese-Americans.

- Consider how the history of California and the West Coast was significantly affected by the presence of even the relatively small number of Chinese immigrants. Examine whether that history has a new significance today, when modern China has again become a great power and new generations of Asian-American immigrants have arrived.

EXPANDING THE "VARYING VIEWPOINTS"

- Richard Hofstadter, *The Age of Reform* (1955).

  A view of the Populists as backward-looking and irrational reactionaries:

  "In the attempts of the Populists . . . to hold on to some of the values of agrarian life, to save personal entrepreneurship and individual opportunity and the character type they engendered, and to maintain a homogeneous Yankee civilization, I have found much that was retrograde and delusive, a little that was vicious, and a good deal that was comic. . . . Such tendencies in American life as isolationism and the extreme nationalism that often goes with it, hatred of Europe and

Europeans, racial, religious, and nationalist phobias, resentment of big business, trade-unionism, intellectuals, the Eastern seaboard and its culture—all these have been found not only in opposition to reform but also at times oddly combined with it."

- Lawrence Goodwyn, *Democratic Promise: The Populist Moment in America* (1976).

A view of the Populists as forward-looking and rational:

"For the triumph of Populism—its only enduring triumph—was the belief in possibility it injected into American political consciousness....Tactical errors aside, it was the élan of the agrarian crusade, too earnest ever to be decisively ridiculed, too creative to be permanently ignored, that lingers as the Populist residue....The creed centered on concepts of political organization and uses of democratic government that—even though in a formative stage—were already too advanced to be accepted by the centralizing, complacent nation of the Gilded Age....The issues of Populism were large. They dominate our world."

QUESTIONS ABOUT THE "VARYING VIEWPOINTS"

1. What does each of these historians see as the essential character of populism?

2. How does the holder of each of these viewpoints see the relationship between populism and the new corporate industrial order of the late nineteenth century?

3. How would each of these historians likely interpret the fact that populism disappeared as a political force but has remained a strong undercurrent in American political thinking?

24

Industry Comes of Age, 1865–1900

CHAPTER THEMES

Theme: America accomplished heavy industrialization in the post–Civil War era. Spurred by the transcontinental rail network, business grew and consolidated into giant corporate trusts, as epitomized by the oil and steel industries.

Theme: Industrialization radically transformed the practices of labor and the condition of American working people. But despite frequent industrial strife and the efforts of various reformers and unions, workers failed to develop effective labor organizations to match the corporate forms of business.

CHAPTER SUMMARY

Aided by government subsidies and loans, the first transcontinental rail line was completed in 1869, soon followed by others. This rail network opened vast new markets and prompted industrial growth. The power and corruption of the railroads led to public demands for regulation, which was only minimally begun.

New technology and forms of business organization led to the growth of huge corporate trusts. Andrew Carnegie and John D. Rockefeller led the way in the steel and oil industries. Initially, the oil industry supplied kerosene for lamps; it eventually expanded by providing gasoline to fuel automobiles. Cheap steel transformed industries from construction to rail building, and the powerful railroads dominated the economy and reshaped American society.

The benefits of industrialization were unevenly distributed. The South remained in underdeveloped dependence, while the industrial working class struggled at the bottom of the growing class divisions of American society. Increasingly transformed from independent producers and farmers to dependent wage earners, America's workers became vulnerable to illness, industrial accidents, and unemployment.

Workers' attempts at labor organization were generally ineffective. The Knights of Labor disappeared after the Haymarket bombing. Gompers founded the AF of L to organize skilled craft laborers but ignored most industrial workers, women, and blacks.

DEVELOPING THE CHAPTER: SUGGESTED LECTURE OR DISCUSSION TOPICS

- Explain the central role the railroads played in late-nineteenth-century America. Show how they not only moved goods and people but dominated politics, employed workers, promoted farms and cities, and created the models for American big business. Perhaps use the building of the transcontinental railroad as a key symbolic event of the age.

    REFERENCE: David Bain, *Empire Express: Building the First Transcontinental Railroad* (1999).

- Examine the dramatic impact of "big business" and the new industrial corporations on the American economy and American life generally. Use Andrew Carnegie and John D. Rockefeller as examples of how the new corporate industrial organizers became widely celebrated heroes as well. Consider their effects not only on the economy but also on American culture.

    REFERENCE: Alan Trachtenberg, *The Incorporation of America: Culture and Society in the Gilded Age* (1982).

- Consider the impact of industrialization on the nature of work and the lives of workers. Point out how most workers went from being self-employed or working in small enterprises to being employed in large, impersonal corporate enterprises.

    REFERENCE: Herbert Gutman, *Power and Culture: Essays on the American Working Class* (1987).

- Analyze the growing place of wage-earning women in the late-nineteenth-century industrial economy. Compare and contrast men's and women's attitudes toward work, family, and labor unions.

    REFERENCE: Alice Kessler-Harris, *Out to Work: A History of Wage-Earning Women in the United States* (1982).

FOR FURTHER INTEREST: ADDITIONAL CLASS TOPICS

- Discuss the railroads as both romantic enterprise (for example, the golden spike, the luxurious Pullman cars) and as controversial "exploitative" business (for example, the corruption of legislatures, price-fixing).

- Examine the benefits and drawbacks of industrialization for various groups (business, labor, women, minorities, immigrants).

- Using Edison as a symbol of the emerging technological and industrial age, show how his inventions were quickly taken up and incorporated into huge new industries.

- Use the Haymarket affair to illustrate the growing class conflicts in industrial America and to highlight the debates over how American workers should respond to the new industrial conditions.

CHARACTER SKETCHES

Thomas Edison (1847–1931)

Edison was the inventive genius of American industrialization who symbolized the modern fusion of science, technology, and industry.

Edison was regarded as a very slow student, and consequently his formal education lasted only three months. Still a boy, he turned to selling newspapers on the streets of Port Huron, Michigan, handing over some of the money to his family but spending the rest on books and chemicals. At age fifteen he went to work for the telegraph. His first inventions were electrical stock tickers and vote recorders.

He took out over a thousand patents in his life. Among his lesser-known inventions were synthetic chemicals, waxed paper, portland cement, the mimeograph machine, and light sockets and fixtures.

Although celebrated as a solitary genius, Edison actually developed the new forms of team research and systematic technological innovation. His laboratory at Menlo Park, New Jersey, was set up in 1880 and employed teams of researchers financed by industry.

Quote: "The first step is an intuition—and comes with a burst, then difficulties arise.... 'Bugs,' as such little faults and difficulties are called—show themselves, and months of anxious watching, study, and labor are requisite....I have the right principle and am on the right track, but time, hard work, and some good luck are necessary, too...." (Letter, 1878)

REFERENCE: Paul Israel, *Edison: A Life of Invention* (1998).

Andrew Carnegie (1835–1919)

Carnegie was a Scottish immigrant who became the leading industrialist of the American steel industry and a prominent philanthropist.

His parents, Scottish hand-loom weavers, were well informed and very interested in education. The family came to the United States when Carnegie's father was thrown out of work by the new textile mills. Carnegie's boyhood dream was to dress his mother in silks, and she lived long enough for him to shower her with expensive gifts.

Carnegie decided early in his career that he should eventually give away most of his money. He spent much of his time associating with literary people and writing magazine articles and books. Eventually, he gave away an estimated $350 million, including $60 million to American libraries.

Charming, smooth, and polished, Carnegie was generally popular with the public.

Quote: "Thirty-three, and an income of $50,000 per annum....Beyond this never earn—make no effort to increase fortune, but spend the surplus each year for benevolent purposes...." (Memo to himself, 1868)

REFERENCE: Joseph Frazier Wall, *Andrew Carnegie* (1970).

John D. Rockefeller (1839–1937)

Rockefeller was the industrialist who organized the Standard Oil Company and became the leading symbol of American capitalism.

His mother was harsh, austere, and religious, and Rockefeller inherited these qualities from her. He was generally frugal and humorless. As a young man, he taught Sunday school and always remained a committed member of the Baptist church.

Rockefeller avoided serving in the Civil War to devote himself to business. He began his career by working with a Cleveland merchant and bought his first refinery for $72,000.

He retired from active control of Standard Oil in 1897. By the 1920s his net worth was probably a billion dollars.

Quote: "In speaking of the real beginnings of the Standard Oil Company, it should be remembered that it was not so much the consolidation of the firms in which we had a personal interest, but the coming together of the men who had the combined brainpower to do the work....It is not merely capital and plans and the strictly material things that make up a business, but the character of the men behind these things...." (1909)

REFERENCE: Ron Chernow, *Titan: The Life of John D. Rockefeller, Sr.* (1998).

Samuel Gompers (1850–1924)

Gompers was the American labor leader who organized the American Federation of Labor and promoted the strategy of conservative craft organization.

Almost entirely self-educated, Gompers gained much of his knowledge by reading and attending lectures in New York City. He was very well acquainted with European socialist thinkers and even learned German so he could read Karl Marx in the original. But he always believed the Marxists and socialists were wrong and worked to develop arguments against them.

Gompers loved drama and pageantry but kept the "secret brotherhood" approach out of the AF of L unions. He disliked reformers and intellectuals, calling them "industrially impossible." Although strongly patriotic, after World War I Gompers and the AF of L were often accused of being "un-American" for promoting labor organization and strikes.

Quote: "The trusts are our employers, and the employer who is fair to us, whether an individual or a collection of individuals in the form of a corporation or a trust, matters little to us as long as we obtain fair wages." (1912)

REFERENCES: Harold Livesay, *Samuel Gompers and Organized Labor in America* (1987); David Montgomery, *The Fall of the House of Labor* (1987).

QUESTIONS FOR CLASS DISCUSSION

1. What were the costs and benefits of the industrial transformation of the post–Civil War era?

2. Should industrialists like Vanderbilt, Carnegie, and Rockefeller be viewed as "robber barons" or "captains of industry"?

3. Was the growing class division of the time a threat to American democracy? Why or why not?

4. Why did American workers have such trouble responding to the new industrial conditions of labor? Why were business and the middle-class public generally hostile to allowing workers to organize as industry did? Why did the AF of L survive while the Knights of Labor failed?

MAKERS OF AMERICA: THE KNIGHTS OF LABOR

Questions for Class Discussion

1. What was admirable and "progressive" in the Knights' outlook? What was largely nostalgic and doomed to failure?

2. What was the appeal of the Knights' emphasis on secrecy, ritual, and "brotherhood"? What elements of the Knights' emphasis on social solidarity remained part of the labor movement, and what disappeared?

Suggested Student Exercises

- Examine the Knights' role in the great industrial strikes of 1886. Explain why they experienced a boom in membership, especially with the advocacy of the eight-hour day, and then suddenly collapsed and soon disappeared.

- Examine the biographies of the Knights' two most prominent leaders, Terence Powderly and "Mother" Jones. Perhaps compare their "utopian" and "producer"-oriented outlook with that of more pragmatic unionists like Samuel Gompers and socialists like Eugene V. Debs.

EXPANDING THE "VARYING VIEWPOINTS"

- Matthew Josephson, *The Robber Barons: The Great American Capitalists, 1861–1901* (1934).

    A view of industrialization focused on business:

    "The members of this new ruling class were generally, and quite aptly, called 'barons,' 'kings,' 'empire-builders,' and even 'emperors.' They were aggressive men, as were the first feudal barons; sometimes they were lawless; in important crises, nearly all of them tended to act without those established moral principles which fixed more or less the conduct of the common people of the community. At the same time . . . many of them showed volcanic energy and qualities of courage which, under another economic clime, might have fitted them for immensely useful social constructions, and rendered them glorious rather than hateful to their people."

- Herbert Gutman, *Work, Culture, and Society in Industrializing America* (1976).

    A view of industrialization focused on labor and society:

    "In the half-century after 1843 industrial development radically transformed the earlier American social structure, and during this Middle Period…a profound tension existed between the older American preindustrial social structure and the modernizing institutions that accompanied the development of industrial capitalism.…In each of these distinctive stages of American society, a recurrent tension also existed between native and immigrant men and women fresh to the factory and the demands imposed upon them by the regularities and disciplines of factory labor."

QUESTIONS ABOUT THE "VARYING VIEWPOINTS"

1. What does each of these historians see as the most crucial feature of the new industrialization?

2. How does each of them see the relationship between industrial capitalism and the moral and cultural values of society?

3. How would each of them likely interpret the labor conflicts and strikes of the period—for example, the Haymarket affair and the decline of the Knights of Labor?

25

America Moves to the City, 1865–1900

CHAPTER THEME

Theme: In the late nineteenth century, American society was increasingly dominated by large urban centers. Explosive urban growth was accompanied by often disturbing changes, including the New Immigration, crowded slums, new religious outlooks, and conflicts over culture and values. While many Americans were disturbed by the new urban problems, cities also offered opportunities to women and expanded cultural horizons.

CHAPTER SUMMARY

The United States moved from the country to the city in the post–Civil War decades. Mushrooming urban development was exciting but also created severe social problems, including overcrowding and slums.

After the 1880s the cities were flooded with the New Immigrants from southern and eastern Europe. With their strange customs and non-Protestant religions, the newcomers sometimes met with nativist hostility and discrimination.

Religion had to adjust to social and cultural changes. Roman Catholicism and Judaism gained strength, while conflicts over evolution and biblical interpretation divided Protestant churches.

American education expanded rapidly, especially at the secondary and graduate levels. Blacks and immigrants tried, with limited success, to use education as a path to upward mobility.

Significant conflicts over moral values, especially relating to sexuality and the role of women, began to appear. The new urban environment provided expanded opportunities for women but also created difficulties for the family. Families grew more isolated from society, the divorce rate rose, and average family size shrank.

American literature and art reflected a new realism, while popular amusement became a big business.

DEVELOPING THE CHAPTER: SUGGESTED LECTURE OR DISCUSSION TOPICS

- Explain the strong connection among the new forces of industrialization, urbanization, and immigration. Show how each one tended to reinforce the others, creating a significantly new kind of urban environment.

  REFERENCE: Eric Monkkonen, *America Becomes Urban* (1988).

- Describe the experience of the New Immigrants and explain why they were often regarded with suspicion or hostility. The emphasis might be on the factors that made them different from most earlier immigrants—particularly their "strange" cultures, religions, poverty, and the fact that they crowded into urban slums.

  REFERENCE: John Bodnar, *The Transplanted: A History of Immigrants in Urban America* (1985).

- Relate the cultural conflicts over religion and values to the new social and cultural environment of the city. Show how urban life tended to undermine traditional standards of belief and behavior (for example, about drinking or divorce) while creating new institutions and values, including popular culture.

    REFERENCE: Gunther Barth, *City People: The Rise of Modern City Culture in Nineteenth-Century America* (1980).

- Consider the complicated effects of urbanization on women's roles and family—new opportunities arose but they imposed new strains on marriage and child-rearing.

    REFERENCES: Elaine May, *Great Expectations: Marriage and Divorce in Post-Victorian America* (1983); Steven Mintz, *A Prison of Expectations: The Family in Victorian Culture* (1985).

FOR FURTHER INTEREST: ADDITIONAL CLASS TOPICS

- Use Jane Addams's experiences to demonstrate how some Americans encountered the problems of new industrial metropolises like Chicago.

- Examine the myths and the realities of immigration. A good starting point might be Emma Lazarus's Statue of Liberty poem, which says, "Give me your tired, your poor, your huddled masses yearning to breathe free," but also called the immigrants "wretched refuse."

- Analyze the impact of urban life, immigration, Darwinism, and biblical higher criticism (literary scholarship) on religion, including the "immigrant religions" like Roman Catholicism, Eastern Orthodoxy, and Judaism.

- Consider the impact and meaning of new "popular amusements" like the circus, baseball, vaudeville, and so on.

CHARACTER SKETCHES

Jane Addams (1860–1935)

Addams, the founder of Hull House and the profession of social work, was the leading female reformer of the progressive era.

Her father was a prominent Illinois businessman and politician who had served in the state legislature with Lincoln. Her mother died when she was two, and she remained deeply devoted to her father until he suddenly died when she was twenty-one.

For the next eight years, she underwent a prolonged personal crisis, marked by physical ailments and deep depression. Her decision to open Hull House with her friend Ellen Gates Starr came partly out of her growing awareness of urban problems, but it also ended her personal struggles and gave meaning to her life.

Addams first used her own money for Hull House but later became a highly skilled fund-raiser. Her opposition to World War I lost her considerable popularity in the 1920s. Addams was benevolent, thoughtful, and modest but somewhat cool, aloof, and formal in personal relations.

Quote: "I found myself…with high expectations and a certain belief that whatever perplexities and discouragement concerning the life of the poor were in store for me, I should at least know something at firsthand and have the solace of daily activity….I had at last finished with the ever-lasting 'preparation for life,' however ill-prepared I might be."

REFERENCE: Allen F. Davis, *American Heroine: The Life and Legend of Jane Addams* (1973).

Dwight L. Moody (1837–1899)

Moody was the most prominent evangelical revivalist of the post–Civil War era and the founder of Moody Bible Institute and other schools.

After growing up in rural New England, in 1856 he moved to Chicago and became a successful shoe salesman. He began taking slum dwellers to church with him and in 1858 organized a Sunday school for Chicago street kids.

He traveled to Britain to study evangelical methods and conducted spectacularly well received revivals there. His musician and choir leader, Ira D. Sankey, contributed greatly to Moody's success with his popular, sentimental hymns.

Never officially ordained, Moody spoke the plain language of the ordinary person. His organization was large and sophisticated but developed techniques like the "conference room" to give each convert a sense of personal concern.

Quote: "Water runs down hill, and the highest hills are the great cities. If we can stir them, we can stir the whole nation….There is misery in the great city, but what is the cause of it? Why, the sufferers have become lost from the Shepherd's care." (1876)

REFERENCE: Lyle Dorsett, *A Passion for Souls: The Life of D.L. Moody* (1997).

Booker T. Washington (1856–1915)

A former slave who became the dominant American black leader in the period from 1890 to 1910, Washington was popular with whites but extremely controversial among blacks.

He was born in Virginia; his father was a white man from a neighboring plantation. As a boy Washington lived in a one-room, floorless cabin and slept on the ground.

After emancipation he and his mother walked over a hundred miles to Charleston, West Virginia, so that he could go to school. He was taken under the wing of whites at Hampton Institute and eventually was sent to organize Tuskegee Institute.

His 1895 speech at the Atlanta Exposition accepting segregation made him a national figure, but many blacks disagreed strongly. He eventually built up a large "machine" in the black community and controlled newspapers, jobs, and substantial patronage. His famous autobiography, *Up from Slavery,* was ghostwritten by a journalist and excluded many harsh facts of his life, especially in relation to his treatment by whites.

Quote: "The wisest among my race understand that the agitation of questions of social equality is the extremist folly….The opportunity to earn a dollar in a factory just now is worth infinitely more than the opportunity to spend a dollar in an opera house." (1895)

REFERENCE: Louis R. Harlan, *Booker T. Washington: The Making of a Black Leader* (1975); *Booker T. Washington: The Wizard of Tuskegee, 1901–1915* (1986).

Charlotte Perkins Gilman (1860–1935)

Gilman was the feminist theorist and writer whose work on economics influenced the early women's movement, and whose ideas and writings have attracted renewed attention since the revival of American feminism in the 1960s.

Gilman was a descendant of the famous Beecher family of American clergymen and writers. Her father abandoned the family, and her mother struggled to raise the family alone. Charlotte's unhappy marriage to Charles Stetson, an artist, led to a "nervous collapse" and depression. This experience was eventually described in her short story, "The Yellow Wall-Paper," published after her divorce from Stetson.

Gilman's major work, *Women and Economics,* differed from most progressive feminism in emphasizing the need for new communal social systems of child-rearing, cooking, and home maintenance, if women were ever to attain full economic and social equality. Her belief that women were morally superior to men was presented in her utopian novel *Herland,* in which she presented a perfect all-female society.

Quote: "In the school [the child] learns something of social values, in the church something, in the street something…but in the home he learns…every day and hour, that life, this deep, new, thrilling mystery of life consists mainly of eating and sleeping, of the making and wearing of clothes." (*The Home,* 1903)

REFERENCE: Mary A. Hill, *Charlotte Perkins Gilman: The Making of a Radical Feminist* (1980).

QUESTIONS FOR CLASS DISCUSSION

1. Did the development of American cities justify Jefferson's claim that "when we get piled up in great cities we will become as corrupt as Europe"?

2. Compare the "heroic" story of immigration, as illustrated in the Statue of Liberty, with the historical reality. What explains the ambivalence toward the New Immigrants reflected in Lazarus's poem?

3. Did urban life cause a decline in American religion or just an adjustment to new forms?

4. Why did urban life alter the condition of women and bring changes like birth control and rising divorce rates to the family?

MAKERS OF AMERICA: THE ITALIANS

Questions for Class Discussion

1. In what ways was the Italian experience typical of that of other New Immigrant groups, such as the Polish, Greeks, Jews, and others? (See Chapter 26 text.)

2. Why did so many Italian-Americans initially intend to return to Italy after a time? How does that fact fit with the common understanding of immigration to America?

Suggested Student Exercises

- Compare the ethnic "Little Italy" enclaves in various American cities with the "Chinatowns" established by the Chinese-Americans (Chapter 24). Consider what functions these communities served for the new immigrants, and how they affected other Americans' perceptions of the immigrants.

- Examine biographies of some recently prominent Italian-Americans (e.g., Congresswoman Geraldine Ferraro, New York Governor Mario Cuomo, Supreme Court Justice Antonin Scalia, actor Al Pacino, historian Eugene Genovese). Explore how their parents' and grandparents' experience fits into the general history of Italian immigration to America.

26

The Great West and the Agricultural Revolution, 1865–1896

CHAPTER THEMES

Theme: After the Civil War, whites overcame the Plains Indians' fierce resistance and settled the Great West, bringing to a close the long frontier phase of American history.

Theme: The farmers who populated the West found themselves the victims of an economic revolution in agriculture. Trapped in a permanent debtor dependency, in the 1880s they finally turned to political action to protest their condition. Their efforts culminated in the Populist Party's attempt to create an interracial farmer/labor coalition in the 1890s, but William Jennings Bryan's defeat in the pivotal election of 1896 signaled the triumph of urbanism and the middle class.

CHAPTER SUMMARY

At the close of the Civil War, the Great Plains and Mountain West were still occupied by Indians who hunted buffalo on horseback and fiercely resisted white encroachment on their land and way of life. But the whites' railroads, mining, and livestock broke up Indian territory, while diseases undercut their strength and numbers. A cycle of environmental destruction and intertribal warfare eventually overcame Indian resistance and soon threatened Native Americans' very existence. The federal government combined a misconceived "treaty" program with intermittent warfare to force the Indians onto largely barren reservations.

Attempting to coerce Indians into adopting white ways, the government passed the Dawes Act, which eliminated tribal ownership of land, while often insensitive "humanitarians" created a network of Indian boarding schools that further assaulted traditional culture.

The mining and cattle frontiers created colorful chapters in western history. Farmers carried out the final phase of settlement, lured by free homesteads, railroads, and irrigation. The census declared the end of the frontier in 1890, concluding a formative phase of American history. The frontier was less of a "safety valve" than many believed, but the growth of cities actually made the West the most urbanized region of the United States by the 1890s.

Beginning in the 1870s, farmers began pushing into the treeless prairies beyond the 100th meridian, using techniques of dry farming that gradually contributed to soil loss. Irrigation projects, later financed by the federal government, allowed specialized farming in many areas of the arid West, including California. The "closing" of the frontier in 1890 signified the end of traditional westward expansion, but the Great West remained a unique social and environmental region.

As the farmers opened vast new lands, agriculture was becoming a mechanized business dependent on specialized production and international markets. Once declining prices and other woes doomed the farmers to permanent debt and dependency, they began to protest their lot, first through the Grange and then through the Farmers' Alliances, the prelude to the People's (Populist) party.

The major depression of the 1890s accelerated farmer and labor strikes and unrest, leading to a growing sense of class conflict. In 1896 pro-silverite William Jennings Bryan captured the Democratic party's nomination, and led a fervent campaign against the "goldbug" Republicans and their candidate William McKinley. McKinley's success in winning urban workers away from Bryan proved a turning point in American politics, signaling the triumph of the city, the middle class, and a new party system that turned away from monetary issues and put the Republicans in the political driver's seat for two generations.

DEVELOPING THE CHAPTER: SUGGESTED LECTURE OR DISCUSSION TOPICS

- Place the dramatic Indian wars in the context of both irresistible white encroachment and the postwarfare history of American Indians. The Sioux experience—from Little Big Horn to Wounded Knee and after—might provide a good focus.

    REFERENCE: Robert Utley, *The Indian Frontier of the American West, 1846–1890* (1984).

- Examine the successive phases of economic activity in the Great West: mining, cattle raising, agriculture. Show how in each case an early "little person" era was ended by the coming of big business and new technology, and how the entry of corporate and investment capital shaped later western development.

    REFERENCE: Patricia Nelson Limerick, *Legacy of Conquest: The Unbroken Past of the American West* (1987).

- Examine the unique roles of women in the West, including the more "typical" pioneer farming women of the Great Plains, as well as the more unusual women who made their way in the mining towns and later cities of the Far West. Consider how their experience was similar to that of males in the West, and how it was different.

    REFERENCE: Glenda Riley, *The Female Frontier: A Comparative View of Women on the Prairie and Plains* (1988).

- Focus on the bitter labor conflicts of the decade, including the Homestead strike and the Pullman strike. Explain why the use of federal troops in the Pullman strike and the use of Pinkerton's antilabor agents in the Homestead strike embittered many workers against both industry and the government's executive and judicial authority.

    REFERENCE: Paul Krause, *The Battle for Homestead, 1880–1892* (1992).

- Examine the 1896 election as a "crucial election" in American history. Show how Mark Hanna and McKinley effectively organized the forces of the new urban industrialism against Bryan's agrarian-based crusade.

    REFERENCE: Stanley L. Jones, *The Presidential Election of 1896* (1964).

FOR FURTHER INTEREST: ADDITIONAL CLASS TOPICS

- Focus on one of the notable Indian chiefs (for example, Sitting Bull, Chief Joseph, or Geronimo). Examine their roles as leaders of their people both in resistance to white conquest and under the forced circumstances of reservation life. Consider their subsequent role as continuing symbols in later American history and culture.

- Discuss the validity of the frontier thesis first advanced by Frederick Jackson Turner in 1893. (See *Expanding the "Varying Viewpoints"* for an excerpt from Turner's famous essay.) Consider how his use of the word *frontier* contrasts with common understanding, in which the term refers almost entirely to the post–Civil War frontier of the Great West.

- Examine the life of the typical homesteader on the Great Plains, perhaps drawing on literary works like those of Ole Rolvaag or Willa Cather. Consider why such a person might be led to join the Farmers' Alliances. Perhaps compare the condition of pioneer farmers with those in the South, white and black.

- Consider the rapid rise and fall of the Populists in both the West and the South. Consider the attempt by Populists like Tom Watson to overcome racial division, and explain the reasons he and other disillusioned reformers later turned to a vicious racism.

- Examine Hanna's free-spending policies in the 1896 election. Assess what role campaign spending (and other political tactics) may have had in defeating Bryan, compared to the deeper social and political forces that kept most of the urban working class from supporting the pro-silver campaign.

- Analyze the long-term significance of the Republican victory in 1896. Consider McKinley as a symbol of triumphant urban industrial capitalism and the harbinger of an age of Republican political domination

CHARACTER SKETCHES

Sitting Bull (1834–1890)

Sitting Bull was the Sioux chief and shaman (medicine man) who organized the Indian coalition that defeated Custer at the Battle of Little Big Horn.

His Indian name was Ta-tan-ka I-yo-ta-ke, which translates literally as "Sitting Bull." As a young warrior he had led the Sioux against their traditional enemies, the Crow. He was friendly for a time with Father Pierre-Jean DeSmet, a Catholic priest who tried unsuccessfully to convert him to give up warfare.

Sitting Bull brought together over four thousand Sioux, Cheyenne, Arapahoe, and others in a single encampment before Little Big Horn. He did not fight in the battle himself because his job as shaman was to create the "good medicine" that would bring Indian victory.

After his return from Canada and surrender, he remained extremely hostile to whites. He participated in the "Ghost Dance" revival and agitation on a Sioux reservation and was shot by Indian police sent to arrest him.

Quote: "I don't want a white man over me. I don't want an agent....I want to do right by my people, and cannot trust anyone else to trade with them or talk with them." (1882)

REFERENCE: Robert Utley, *The Lance and the Shield: The Life and Times of Sitting Bull* (1993).

Chief Joseph (1840–1904)

Chief Joseph was the Nez Percé leader whose campaign against the U.S. Army in 1877 is considered a military classic.

Joseph's Indian name was Hinmaton-Yalaktit, meaning "Thunder-Coming-Across-the-Water-onto-Land." He had maintained peaceful relations with whites for years, but when some white civilians killed some Nez Percé, a group of young braves retaliated by killing whites, and the army under Gen. O. O. Howard (former head of the Freedmen's Bureau) was sent after Chief Joseph.

His maneuvers in defeating and eluding the army for over fifteen hundred miles were carried out with women and children in tow. He compelled his warriors to fight only against soldiers and not to kill or steal from white civilians. General Howard and other military personnel who met him after his surrender were all impressed by his intelligence and humanity.

His tribe was first moved to Oklahoma, where many of its members died, and then to the Colville reservation in Washington.

Quote: "I am tired of fighting. Our chiefs are killed....It is cold and we have no blankets. The little children are freezing to death....From where the sun now stands, I will fight no more forever." (Statement of surrender, 1877)

REFERENCE: Merrill D. Beal, *"I Will Fight No More Forever": Chief Joseph and the Nez Percé War* (1963).

Helen Hunt Jackson (1830–1885)

Jackson was the writer and advocate of Indian rights whose book *A Century of Dishonor* was one of the first to advocate more humane policies toward Native Americans.

A vivacious, intelligent, charming New Englander, Jackson turned to writing after her first husband was killed and her two young sons died. She became a very popular poet and novelist. Her novel *Mercy Philbrick's Choice* was based partly on the life of her schoolmate and friend Emily Dickinson.

She became interested in Indians after moving to Colorado with her second husband. Although Jackson did a good deal of research for *A Century of Dishonor,* she really understood little of Indian culture. Her subsequent novel about California Indians, *Ramona,* was a greater popular success. She also carried on a public controversy over Indian policy with Secretary of the Interior Carl Schurz.

Quote: "[This Congress] could cover itself with the lustre of glory as the first to cut short our nation's record of cruelties and perjuries—the first to attempt to redeem the United States from the shame of a century of dishonor!" (*A Century of Dishonor,* 1881)

REFERENCE: Siobhan Senier, *Voices of Indian Assimilation and Resistance: Helen Hunt Jackson, Sarah Winnemucca, and Victoria Howard* (2001).

Mark Hanna (1837–1904)

Hanna was the Cleveland businessman who engineered McKinley's election in 1896 and later became a prominent Republican senator.

He came from a strong antislavery Quaker background, which jeopardized his marriage to his first wife because she was an equally strong Democrat. Hanna made his fortune in coal and iron but focused much of his energy on forging an alliance between business and politics.

McKinley's political fortunes had declined for a time, until Hanna became interested in his ideas and began to promote McKinley for Ohio governor. He also got other business leaders to substantially aid

McKinley's personal finances. Hanna was later elected senator by a very narrow margin amid charges of bribery of state legislators.

Hanna was genial and popular with both businesspeople and politicians, whom he liked to bring together. Although a staunch conservative on most issues, he favored labor unions and was so generous to workers that his own companies never had a strike.

Quote: "I am glad that there is one member of the Convention who has the intelligence to ascertain how this nomination was made. By the people. What feeble efforts I have contributed to the result, I am here to lay at the feet of my party...." (Statement after McKinley's nomination, 1896)

REFERENCE: Wayne Morgan, *William McKinley and His America* (1963).

Eugene V. Debs (1855–1926)

Debs was a railway union leader who became the top socialist in the United States and the frequent presidential candidate of the Socialist party.

Debs's parents were French immigrants who settled in Indiana. During one period he worked three full-time jobs—as a grocery clerk, as a city clerk, and as secretary-treasurer of the Brotherhood of Locomotive Firemen.

When Debs was released from jail after the Pullman strike, there was a huge celebration in Chicago. He was always much-loved in his home town of Terre Haute, even by most people who disliked his socialism. A heavy drinker, Debs often had to be pulled away from his liquor by fellow socialists.

He was passionate, warmhearted, eloquent, and simple. Workers everywhere loved him and thronged to watch him jab his bony finger in the air and denounce capitalism, even if they did not vote for him.

Quote: "While there is a lower class I am in it....While there is a soul in prison I am not free."

REFERENCE: Nick Salvatore, *Eugene V. Debs: Citizen and Socialist* (1982).

William Jennings Bryan (1860–1925)

Bryan was the eloquent three-time-losing presidential candidate who later became Wilson's secretary of state and the prosecuting attorney in the Scopes evolution trial.

He began his career as a small-town Nebraska lawyer and journalist and retained a small-town outlook throughout his career. When not campaigning for president, he traveled widely as a Chautauqua lecturer. Two of his most popular lectures on religion were "The Prince of Peace" and "The Value of an Ideal." His voice was a remarkable instrument, which could carry with perfect clarity to the back of a crowd of thousands.

Although he became secretary of state, Bryan knew almost nothing about foreign policy or the world beyond the United States. On a visit to Turkey, he once asked the foreign-service officers, "Where are the Balkans?"

Bryan had long been an active crusader in Fundamentalist causes before becoming involved in the Scopes trial. He was deeply humiliated by Darrow in the trial and died shortly afterward.

Quote: "The poor man who takes property by force is called a thief but the creditor who can by legislation make the debtor pay a dollar twice as large as he borrowed it is lauded as the friend of sound currency. The man who wants the people to destroy the government is an anarchist but the man who wants government to destroy the people is a patriot." (Congressional speech, 1893)

REFERENCE: Paolo Coletta, *William Jennings Bryan* (3 Vols., 1964–1969).

John Peter Altgeld (1847–1902)

Altgeld was the Illinois governor whose pardon of the Haymarket anarchists and support for organized labor made him a hero to reformers and a hated figure among conservatives and businessmen.

Altgeld was born in Germany, and spent most of his youth as a poverty-stricken farm laborer in Ohio and elsewhere in the Midwest. He essentially educated himself by reading, especially in the law, and began a career as a prosecuting attorney and judge in Missouri and Illinois.

In 1892 Altgeld was elected the first Democratic governor of Illinois since the Civil War. The case of the Haymarket anarchists came to him for review shortly afterward, and his thorough study of the trial and the evidence convinced him that justice had not been done. The political furor set off by his pardon of three of the convicted men escalated when he protested President Cleveland's use of federal troops in the 1894 Pullman strike as unnecessary and unconstitutional. Aroused Republicans mounted a strong campaign against him in 1896, and his political career was ended by his defeat.

Quote: "There is no situation in Illinois which warrants the sending of federal troops. It is not soldiers that the railroads need so much as it is men to operate trains." (Statement, 1894)

REFERENCE: Harry Barnard, *Eagle Forgotten: The Life of John Peter Altgeld* (1938); Paul Avrich, *The Haymarket Tragedy* (1984).

GREAT DEBATES IN AMERICAN HISTORY

GREAT DEBATE (1890–1896): Government, finance, and the farmer: Should the government adopt monetary and other measures to aid American farmers and laborers?

Yes: Reformers: Populists led by Ignatius Donnelly, Jerry Simpson, and others; writers like Henry George and Henry Demarest Lloyd; free-silver Democrats like William Jennings Bryan and Richard Bland.

No: Conservatives: most Republican businesspeople and politicians like William McKinley and Mark Hanna; "gold Democrats" like Cleveland; most eastern newspapers and economists.

ISSUE #1: Free silver. Should the United States adopt free coinage of silver and thereby inflate the currency to aid farmers?

Yes: Reform Democrat William Jennings Bryan: "To recapitulate, there is not enough of either metal to form the basis for the world's metallic money; both metals must therefore be used as full legal tender primary money....If metallic money is sound money, then we who insist upon a base broad enough to support a currency redeemable in coin on demand are the real friends of sound money....If all the currency is built upon the small basis of gold those who hold the gold will be the masters of the situation."

No: Conservative Republican William McKinley: "Now they tell you that free silver is the panacea for all our ills....As free wool degraded your industry so free silver will degrade your money....We do not propose now to inaugurate a currency system that will cheat labor of its pay. The laboring men of this country whenever they give one day's work to their employers want to be paid in full dollars good everywhere in the world. We want in this country good work, good wages, and good money."

ISSUE #2: The tariff. Should the government maintain high protective tariffs against foreign imports?

No: Reform Populist Congressman "Sockless Jerry" Simpson of Kansas: "The enormous amount collected for this extraordinary privilege . . . fell heavily upon the agricultural classes. They are the consumers of sugar and window glass and of all those things that the four hundred and fifty trusts that have been formed under your protective system produce, and that is what has brought the agricultural interests of this country to poverty and bankruptcy today."

Yes: Conservative Republican William McKinley: "[The protective system] has dignified and elevated labor; it has made all things possible to the man who works for a living and cares for what he earns; it has opened to him every gateway to opportunity. We observe its triumphs on every hand: we see the mechanic become the manufacturer, the workman the proprietor, the employee the employer. Is this not worth something? Is it not worth everything? The Republican Protectionist would give the first chances to our people, and would so levy duties upon the products of other nations as to discriminate in favor of our own."

ISSUE #3: Trusts. Should the federal government act more forcefully to control trusts?

Yes: Reform Democrat William Jennings Bryan: "Every trust rests upon a corporation, and every corporation is a creature of law. The corporation is a man-made man....My contention is that the government that created must retain control, and that the man-made man must be admonished, 'Remember now thy creator.'...What government gives, the government can take away. What the government creates it can control....In my judgment a government of the people, by the people, and for the people will be impossible when a few men control all the source of production and dole out daily bread to all the rest on such terms as the few may prescribe....It will be a government of the syndicates, by the syndicates, and for the syndicates."

No: Conservative Democrat W. Bourke Cockran: "For the same reason I would suppress the monopoly built on favor I would protect the monopoly created by excellence. There is no way to suppress a monopoly arising from conspicuous merit except by the suppression of merit. If the producer of the best commodity may not dominate the market for that particular article, neither should the possessor of particular ability in any other department of human endeavor....Mr. Bryan's position is that monopoly in private hands is always oppressive. Instead of distinguishing between corporations which dominate the market by excellence and those dominating it by favor, he appears to distinguish between those which are successful and those which are not."

ISSUE #4: Government aid to farmers. Should the federal government adopt measures such as the subtreasury plan to provide economic aid to indebted farmers?

Yes: Texas Populist Harry Tracy: "Now if the government can loan these bankers money at one percent on collaterals, why can't the government loan it to the people on their collaterals? If the government can bridge the bankers over a close money market and keep them from having to sacrifice their collateral, why can't the government do the same by the people? What a burlesque on democratic government for 4000 men, because they are rich, to enjoy privileges that are denied 65,000,000 people."

No: Conservative Democrat Secretary of Agriculture J. Sterling Morton: "The free and independent farmers of this country…are not mendicants; they are not wards of the Government to be treated to annuities, like Indians upon a reservation.…Legislation can neither plow nor plant. The intelligent, practical, and successful farmer needs no aid from the Government. The ignorant, impractical, and indolent farmer deserves none."

REFERENCE: Paul Glad, *McKinley, Bryan, and the People* (1964).

QUESTIONS FOR CLASS DISCUSSION

1. Why has the Plains Indians' resistance to white encroachment played such a large part in the popular American view of the West? How is that mythical past related to the Indians' actual history?

2. What was "romantic" about the final phases of frontier settlement, and what was not?

3. Why was the "passing of the frontier" in 1890 a disturbing development for many Americans? Was the frontier more important as a particular place or as an idea?

4. Was the federal government biased against farmers and workers in the late nineteenth century? Why or why not?

5. Was McKinley's election really a "conservative" one, or was it Bryan and the Populists who represented the agrarian past resisting a progressive urban American future?

MAKERS OF AMERICA: THE PLAINS INDIANS

Questions for Class Discussion

1. Compare the Plains Indians' history and culture, especially before the coming of the whites, to that of the Iroquois (Chapter 2). How does this comparison prove the assertion that the cultures of various Indian peoples differed greatly?
2. In what ways did the Plains Indians benefit by the transformation of their way of life brought about by the horse? In what ways were they harmed?

Suggested Student Exercises

- Examine some photographs or artistic representations of Plains Indians from the late nineteenth century. Discuss what features of their culture are portrayed.

- Use the map of Indian reservations in the text (p. 594) to consider where the Plains Indians were particularly concentrated after the era of warfare ended. Consider what areas of the United States still have substantial populations of such plains peoples as the Sioux, Cheyenne, Kiowa, Crow, and Comanche. (Remember that the Oklahoma Indian territory included many originally eastern Indian peoples like the Cherokee and the Choctaw.)

EXPANDING THE "VARYING VIEWPOINTS"

- Frederick Jackson Turner, "The Significance of the Frontier in American History" (1893).

    A view of the West as a place permanently shaping the formerly "European" American character:

    "The existence of an area of free land, its continuous recession, and the advance of American settlement westward explain American development....This perennial rebirth, this fluidity of American life, this expansion westward with its new opportunities, its continuous touch with the simplicity of primitive society, furnish the forces dominating American character....In this advance, the frontier is the outer edge of the wave—the meeting point between savagery and civilization...."

- Richard White, *The Middle Ground* (1991).

    A view of the West as the product of the interaction of whites and Indians:

    "[The West] is not a traditional world either seeking to maintain itself unchanged or eroding under the pressure of whites. It is a joint Indian-white creation....The real crisis came...when Indians ceased to have power to force whites onto the middle ground. Then the desire of whites to dictate the terms of the accommodation could be given its head....Americans invented Indians and forced Indians to live with the consequences."

QUESTIONS ABOUT THE "VARYING VIEWPOINTS"

1. What does each of these historians understand to be the essential characteristics of the West?

2. How does White's assessment differ from Turner's view of the frontier as a "meeting point between savagery and civilization"?

3. How would each of these historians interpret the Plains Indian wars and the confinement of Indians on reservations?

27

The Path of Empire, 1890–1899

CHAPTER THEME

Theme: In the 1890s a number of economic and political forces sparked a spectacular burst of imperialistic expansionism for the United States that culminated in the Spanish-American War—a war that began over freeing Cuba and ended with the highly controversial acquisition of the Philippines and other territories.

CHAPTER SUMMARY

Various developments provoked the previously isolated United States to turn its attention overseas in the 1890s. Among the stimuli for the new imperialism were the desire for new economic markets, the sensationalistic appeals of the "yellow press," missionary fervor, Darwinist ideology, great-power rivalry, and naval competition.

Strong American intervention in the Venezuelan boundary dispute of 1895–1896 demonstrated an aggressive new assertion of the Monroe Doctrine and led to a new British willingness to accept American domination in the Western Hemisphere. Longtime American involvement in Hawaii climaxed in 1893 in a revolution against native rule by white American planters. President Cleveland temporarily refused to annex the islands, but the question of incorporating Hawaii into the United States triggered the first full-fledged imperialistic debate in American history.

The "splendid little" Spanish-American War began in 1898 over American outrage about Spanish oppression of Cuba. American support for the Cuban rebellion had been whipped up into intense popular fervor by the "yellow press." After the mysterious *Maine* explosion in February 1898, this public passion pushed a reluctant President McKinley into war, even though Spain was ready to concede on the major issues.

An astounding first development of the war was Admiral Dewey's naval victory in May 1898 in the rich Spanish islands of the Philippines in East Asia. Then in August, American troops, assisted by Filipino rebels, captured the Philippine city of Manila in another dramatic victory. Despite mass confusion, American forces also easily and quickly overwhelmed the Spanish in Cuba and Puerto Rico.

After a long and bitter national debate over the wisdom and justice of American imperialism, which ended in a narrow proimperialist victory in the Senate, the United States took over the Philippines and Puerto Rico as colonial possessions. Regardless of serious doubts about imperialism, the United States had strongly asserted itself as a proud new international power.

DEVELOPING THE CHAPTER: SUGGESTED LECTURE OR DISCUSSION TOPICS

- Explain more fully the different views of the causes of imperialism, including the idea of expansion as a way to create new economic markets. Show how these factors affected the Spanish-American War and the decision to take the Philippines.

    REFERENCE: Walter LaFeber, *The New Empire* (1963).

- Analyze the complicated mix of "idealism" and "realism" in the Spanish-American War, and explain why some Americans were deeply concerned about the oppressed Cubans while others were more interested in the war as an occasion to demonstrate and spread America's new national power abroad.

    REFERENCE: Ernest May, *Imperial Democracy* (1961).

- Demonstrate how the political impact of the war was much greater than the impact of the actual chaotic fighting. The focus might be on the ways in which the war raised up new heroes (Theodore Roosevelt and George Dewey) and created a new sense of the United States as a great world power.

    REFERENCE: David Trask, *The War with Spain in 1898* (1981).

- Consider why the question of whether to hold on to the Philippines was so controversial and why the proimperialist forces were able to win by a narrow margin. The discussion might center on both the short-term and long-term consequences of the Philippine acquisition.

    REFERENCE: H. W. Brands, *Bound to Empire: The United States and the Philippines* (1992).

FOR FURTHER INTEREST: ADDITIONAL CLASS TOPICS

- Examine Teddy Roosevelt as a central character in the events of the chapter: TR as imperialist advocate, assistant secretary of the navy, Rough Rider, legendary war hero, governor of New York, vice president, and then president.

- Analyze the "yellow press": what "yellow journalism" is, why it had such great appeal and popular impact in the late nineteenth century, how it sensationalized and distorted issues, how important it was (or was not) in really influencing President McKinley and others.

- Focus on Cuba and America: why, from the pre–Civil War era forward, Americans were concerned with Cuba; how they viewed the Cuban rebels; what issues dominated American debates about Cuban readiness for independence (for example, the Teller and Platt amendments); and what links developed to the subsequent history of American-Cuban relations.

- Consider the Philippines: where they are (point out that most Americans, even government officials, did not know their location in 1898), who the Filipino people were and are, why the islands have been viewed as strategically and commercially important (especially in relation to China). Discuss the nature of the Filipino rebellion against Spain, which became a rebellion against America. Perhaps tie in the subsequent history of American-Philippine relations.

CHARACTER SKETCHES

Queen Liliuokalani (1838–1917)

The refusal by Liliuokalani, the native ruler of Hawaii, to accept the white planters' revolt of 1893, and her eloquent pleas to President Cleveland, helped delay American annexation of Hawaii until 1898. Her devotion to her people and her resistance to white assimilation have made Liliuokalani a romantic symbol of traditional Hawaiian culture down to the present.

She became queen of Hawaii in 1891, at age fifty-two, after the death of her brother, King Kalakaua. She was a conscientious Christian with strong charitable interests, but she also had a disdain for "Protestant moralism." Despite her tireless efforts to preserve the power of the monarchy, she was deposed following the 1893 uprising, in which American troops openly aided the rebellious white minority.

A contemporary newspaper described Liliuokalani's face as "strong and resolute." She spoke a pure and graceful English, and her voice was musical and well modulated. Throughout her life she composed beautiful Hawaiian songs, including the famous "Aloha Oe" ("Farewell to Thee").

Quote: "Some of my subjects, aided by aliens, have renounced their loyalty and revolted against the constitution and government of my kingdom. . . . Upon receiving incontestable proof that His Excellency the Minister of the United States aided and abetted their unlawful movements, and caused United States troops to be landed for that purpose, I submitted to force." (To President Grover Cleveland, 1893)

REFERENCE: Helena Allen, *The Betrayal of Liliuokalani: Last Queen of Hawaii, 1838–1917* (1982).

William Randolph Hearst (1863–1951)

Hearst's sensationalistic "yellow journalism" and bombastic warmongering in 1897–1898 have long provoked the debatable charge that he was personally responsible for the Spanish-American War—a view to which Hearst himself was willing to subscribe. "You furnish the pictures and I'll furnish the war," Hearst allegedly responded to the assertion of artist-correspondent Frederic Remington (who covered Cuba during the war) that Remington had witnessed little evidence of Spanish cruelty. (Although the statement was reported by another correspondent, there is no proof that Hearst ever actually said it.)

A native San Franciscan, Hearst had been raised primarily by his mother and given an elite education, but he was expelled from Harvard (where he worked on the humor magazine *Lampoon*) for a stunt that involved sending chamber pots to professors. In 1887 he used family wealth to take control of the *San Francisco Examiner,* which he turned into a commercially successful paper. In 1895 he acquired the *New York Journal* and entered a fierce circulation war with Pulitzer's *New York World*. In June 1898 Hearst personally sailed to Cuba, where he helped round up Spanish prisoners while writing headline-grabbing stories.

Ever an extremely flamboyant and controversial figure, Hearst was active in politics and remained a dynamic force in journalism for many decades.

Quote: "The journalism that talked was a great advance from no journalism at all. But the future belongs to the journalism that acts." (1898)

REFERENCES: David Nasaw, *The Chief: The Life of William Randolph Hearst* (2000).

Theodore Roosevelt (1858–1919)

Although Roosevelt was a great president, a skilled international diplomat, and a gifted writer, it was his brief actions during the Spanish-American War that created the enduring Roosevelt legend the public always loved best: Teddy the Rough Rider charging up San Juan Hill. Roosevelt himself never regretted that these exploits overshadowed his more substantive achievements, because he too loved the image of the rugged hero.

After graduation from Harvard in 1880, Roosevelt began his public life by writing lively works of naval and western history. An assistant secretary of the navy under William McKinley, he pushed for a big navy and expansionism. His famous order to Commodore George Dewey, issued when Secretary of the Navy Long was away for a weekend, led to the American victory at Manila Bay and the conquest of the Philippines, which Roosevelt and his friends strongly desired. Although lacking military experience, Roosevelt used his political connections to obtain his army commission for service in Cuba and, along with writer Richard Harding Davis, effectively promoted the legend of the Rough Riders that made him "the most famous man in America."

Quote: "There comes a time in the life of a nation, as in the life of an individual, when it must face great responsibilities, whether it will or no. We have now reached that time....The guns of our warships in the tropic seas of the West and the remote East have awakened us to the knowledge of new duties."

REFERENCES: Edmund Morris, *The Rise of Theodore Roosevelt* (1979); John M. Cooper, Jr., *The Warrior and the Priest* (1983).

GREAT DEBATES IN AMERICAN HISTORY

GREAT DEBATE (1899): American imperialism. Should the United States become an imperialist power by keeping the Philippine Islands?

For: The "proimperialists"—led by expansionists like Theodore Roosevelt, Henry Cabot Lodge, and Albert Beveridge; some business publications like the *Review of Reviews* and business spokespersons like Mark Hanna; and some religious leaders like the Rev. J. H. Barrows and the Rev. Josiah Strong.

Against: The "anti-imperialists"—led by writers like William James and Mark Twain; some business spokespersons like Andrew Carnegie; some labor leaders like Samuel Gompers; and some clergymen like the Rev. Charles Ames and the Rev. Henry Van Dyke.

ISSUE #1: Manifest Destiny. Is overseas expansion, and therefore control of the Philippines, part of the inevitable manifest destiny of the United States?

For: Proimperialist Theodore Roosevelt: "Our whole national history has been one of expansion. Under Washington and Adams we expanded westward to the Mississippi. Under Jefferson we expanded across the continent to the mouth of the Columbia....The same will be true of the Philippines. Nations that expand and nations that do not expand may ultimately go down, but the one leaves heirs and a glorious memory, and the other leaves neither."

Against: Anti-imperialist Carl Schurz: "Whenever there is a project on foot to annex a foreign territory to this republic the cry of 'manifest destiny' is raised to produce the impression that all opposition to such a project is a struggle against fate. The fate of the American people is in their own wisdom and will. If they devote their energies to the development of what they possess within their present limits...their 'manifest destiny' will be the preservation of the exceptional and invaluable advantages they now enjoy...."

ISSUE #2: Democracy. Would ruling another nation be compatible with basic American ideals of democracy and self-government?

For: Proimperialist *New York Tribune:* "Cannibals govern themselves. The half-ape creatures of the Australian bush govern themselves. The Eskimo governs himself, and so do the wildest tribes of darkest Africa. But what kind of a government is it?"

Against: Anti-imperialist Rev. Henry Van Dyke: "How can we pass by the solemn and majestic claim of our Declaration of Independence, that 'government derives its powers from the consent of the governed'? How can we face the world as a union of free states holding vassal states in subjection, a mighty mongrel nation in which a republic is tied to an empire, and democracy bears children not to be distinguished from the offspring of absolutism?"

ISSUE #3: Economic benefit. Is acquiring the Philippines essential for America's economic health and future trade with Asia?

For: Proimperialist *American Wool and Cotton Exporter:* "Annexation is important because the contingencies of our China trade bid fair to be such as to make the Philippines exceedingly valuable to us as a basis for operations in the continent of China."

Against: Anti-imperialist Carl Schurz: "I agree that we cannot have too many foreign markets. But can such markets be opened only by annexing to the United States the countries in which they are situated?"

ISSUE #4: Race. Should the dark-skinned Filipinos be brought under the rule of white-skinned Americans?

For: Proimperialist *The Textile Record:* "Supremacy in the world appears to be the destiny of the race to which we belong, the most competent governor of inferior races....The clear path of duty for us appears to be to bring to the people of the Spanish islands in the Pacific and the Atlantic an opportunity to rise from misery and hopelessness to a promise of just government and commercial success."

Against: Anti-imperialist Henry Labouchère: [A parody of Rudyard Kipling's "The White Man's Burden." See text]
"Pile on the brown man's burden
    Nor do not deem it hard
If you should earn the rancor
    Of those ye yearn to guard.
The screaming of your eagle
    Will drown the victim's sob
Go on through fire and slaughter
    There's dollars on the job.
Pile on the brown man's burden
    And through the world proclaim
That ye are freedom's agent—
    There's no more paying game!
And should your own past history
    Straight in your teeth be thrown
Retort that Independence
    Is good for whites alone."

REFERENCES: E. Berkeley Tompkins, *Anti-Imperialism in the United States: The Great Debate, 1890–1920* (1970); Richard Welch, ed., *Imperialists vs. Anti-Imperialists* (1972).

QUESTIONS FOR CLASS DISCUSSION

1. What were the causes and consequences of the Spanish-American War? Did the results of the war (particularly the acquisition of the Philippines) flow from the nature of the war, or were they unexpected?

2. How was American expansionism overseas similar to previous continental expansion westward, and how was it different?

3. Was the taking of Hawaii, Puerto Rico, and the Philippines really a violation of fundamental American ideals of self-government and democracy?

4. What were the elements of "idealism" and "realism" in American expansionism in the 1890s? How have Americans incorporated both of these seemingly contradictory philosophies in their foreign policy?

MAKERS OF AMERICA: THE PUERTO RICANS

Questions for Class Discussion

1. How has Puerto Rico's special relationship to the United States made Puerto Ricans unique among all immigrant groups?

2. Compare the experience of Puerto Ricans with that of other Latino immigrants, especially the Mexicans (see Chapter 42).

Suggested Student Exercises

- Examine the continuing debate over Puerto Rico's relationship with the United States. Consider how Puerto Rican statehood or independence would affect Puerto Ricans in the mainland United States.

- Consider the particularly important role that Puerto Ricans have played in the life of New York City in the twentieth century, and the transformations their community has undergone there. Daniel Patrick Moynihan and Nathan Glazer, *Beyond the Melting Pot* (1963) is an older sociological work that examines Puerto Ricans in New York; Virginia Sanchez Korral, *From Colonia to Community: The History of Puerto Ricans in New York City* (1983) is a good study of the evolution of the Puerto Rican community.

28

America on the World Stage, 1899–1909

CHAPTER THEME

Theme: In the wake of the Spanish-American War, President Theodore Roosevelt pursued a bold and sometimes controversial new policy of asserting America's influence abroad, particularly in East Asia and Latin America.

CHAPTER SUMMARY

America's decision to take the Philippines aroused violent resistance from the Filipinos, who had expected independence. The brutal war that ensued was longer and costlier than the Spanish-American conflict.

Imperialistic competition in China deepened American involvement in Asia. Hay's Open Door policy helped prevent the great powers from dismembering China. The United States joined the international expedition to suppress the Boxer Rebellion.

Theodore Roosevelt brought a new energy and assertiveness to American foreign policy. When his plans to build a canal in Panama were frustrated by the Colombian Senate, he helped promote a Panamanian independence movement that enabled the canal to be built. He also altered the Monroe Doctrine by adding a "Roosevelt Corollary" that declared an American right to intervene in South America.

Roosevelt negotiated an end to the Russo-Japanese War but angered both parties in the process. Several incidents showed that the United States and Japan were now competitors in East Asia.

DEVELOPING THE CHAPTER: SUGGESTED LECTURE OR DISCUSSION TOPICS

- Show how the United States after the Spanish-American War was increasingly acting like a "great power" in world affairs, especially in Asia, and how Roosevelt energetically promoted this involvement despite the traditional belief in American "isolationism."

    REFERENCES: Marilyn Young, *The Rhetoric of Empire: America's China Policy, 1895–1901* (1968); Charles E. Neu, *Troubled Encounter: The United States and Japan* (1975).

- Explain why the Philippine-American War was the most serious consequence of the Spanish-American War. Consider the disturbing questions it raised about America's new international involvements, especially imperial control of a distant, hostile people.

    REFERENCE: Richard E. Welsh, *Response to Imperialism: The United States and the Philippine-American War, 1899–1902* (1975).

- Examine Roosevelt's aggressive determination to build the Panama Canal in relation to America's growing international assertiveness, particularly in Latin America. Show how American involvement in the Panama coup and the Roosevelt Corollary to the Monroe Doctrine aroused sharp Latin American opposition.

    REFERENCE: Richard H. Collin, *Theodore Roosevelt's Caribbean: The Panama Canal, the Monroe Doctrine, and the Latin American Context* (1990).

- Discuss the role of Asian immigration and the fear of the "yellow peril" in shaping America's relations with East Asia in the early twentieth century.

    REFERENCE: Alexander DeConde, *Ethnicity, Race, and American Foreign Policy* (1992).

FOR FURTHER INTEREST: ADDITIONAL CLASS TOPICS

- Discuss the Philippine-American War in relation to the debate over imperialism considered in Chapter 27.

- Examine Roosevelt's theory and practice of the "big stick" in foreign policy, especially in his relations with Latin America.

- Examine the role of American missionaries in shaping U.S. foreign policy in this period, especially in China.

- Take up the question of gender in relation to American foreign policy and American imperialism, particularly the idea that aggressive overseas action was one way for men (including Theodore Roosevelt) to assert their masculinity in an era of growing feminine influence in society and culture.

CHARACTER SKETCHES

John Hay (1838–1905)

Hay was Abraham Lincoln's private secretary, secretary of state under McKinley and Roosevelt, and a noted poet and historian.

Hay's uncle's law office in Springfield, Illinois, was next to Lincoln's, and Hay's childhood friend John Nicolay arranged for Hay to become Lincoln's private secretary, even though Hay was only twenty-three. He performed many personal chores for the Lincolns at the White House and was sometimes awakened by a sleepless Lincoln, who would tell him jokes. Hay and Nicolay later wrote a ten-volume biography of Lincoln that presents the president in a highly favorable light but reflects serious scholarship rather than mythologizing the national hero.

In the 1870s Hay became a celebrated literary figure. His poetry, such as *Pike County Ballads and Other Pieces,* was quite popular, but his novels were mostly attacks on labor unions. Hay was the closest friend of historian Henry Adams, and the two built adjoining houses across the street from the White House. Hay appreciated Adams's philosophical distance from politics but could not accept his friend's dark pessimism about public affairs.

Quote: "I need not tell you the lunatic difficulties under which we labor....All the powers treat us as a central Hello Office, and we strive to please the public. If I looked at things as you do, in the light of reason, history, and mathematics, I should go off after lunch and die." (Letter to Henry Adams about Open Door policy, 1900)

REFERENCE: Tyler Dennett, *John Hay: From Poetry to Politics* (1933).

Philippe Bunau-Varilla (1859–1940)

Bunau-Varilla was the French engineer who energetically promoted the Panama Canal and the Panamanian revolution, and negotiated the Hay–Bunau-Varilla Treaty with the United States.

As a young engineering student, Bunau-Varilla had come under the spell of Suez Canal builder Ferdinand Lesseps, and Bunau-Varilla became convinced that his mission in life was to complete Lesseps's work by building the canal across Panama. Besides distributing stamps showing Nicaraguan volcanoes, he bombarded senators with favorable information about Panama, while carefully concealing the overwhelming problems the French builders had experienced there in nearly twenty years of effort.

He played a key role in fomenting the "revolution" in Panama, having obtained assurances that the United States would intervene as soon as independence was declared. He wrote the constitution and designed the flag of the new republic, and he gave both to one of the plotters.

Quote: "I have been exposed to calumny in my long fight against ignorance and falsehood....I have served the Republic of Panama, and her interests are coincident with those of the canal. Once the treaty is ratified, I will have fulfilled the pledge I made to myself twenty-three years ago."

REFERENCE: G. A. Anguizola, *Philippe Bunau-Varilla: The Man Behind the Panama Canal* (1980).

George Goethals (1858–1928)

Goethals was the American engineer who built the Panama Canal.

Although a career military officer in the Army Corps of Engineers, Goethals never fired a weapon except in basic training. After the first two engineers assigned to the canal job resigned, Goethals was given near-absolute power over the Canal Zone in order to speed up the job.

Besides planning and supervising the construction, he managed over thirty thousand employees and their families, and created social institutions like jails, courts, hospitals, and so on. He set aside every Sunday morning to hear individual complaints from the workers.

Goethals was a tough, unsmiling, chain-smoking martinet. Someone once asked a family member how Goethals amused himself, and the reply was, "He does not amuse himself."

Quote: "The real builder of the Panama Canal was Theodore Roosevelt. It could not have been more Roosevelt's triumph if he had personally lifted every shovelful of earth in its construction." (1919)

REFERENCE: David McCulloch, *The Path Between the Seas* (1977).

QUESTIONS FOR CLASS DISCUSSION

1. Why was the Philippine-American War such a brutal affair, and why is it not as well remembered as the less costly Spanish-American War?

2. Did Roosevelt more often "speak softly" or use the "big stick"? Was his approach to foreign policy aggressive or simply energetic?

3. How did the Roosevelt Corollary distort the Monroe Doctrine? What were the consequences of the Roosevelt Corollary for American relations with Latin America?

4. Was the United States essentially acting as a "white, Western imperialist" power, or did American democratic ideals substantially restrain the imperialist impulse?

MAKERS OF AMERICA: THE FILIPINOS

Questions for Class Discussion

1. Compare the Philippine immigration to America with that of the Chinese (Chapter 23). How did American imperial ownership of the Philippines make the Filipinos' experience different from that of other Asians?

2. Even though more immigrants have come from the Philippines than from China or Japan, it seems that most Americans do not regard Filipinos as they view other Asian immigrants. Why might that be so? Is the awareness of the Filipino presence greater in Hawaii and the West Coast than in other parts of the country?

Suggested Student Exercises

- Analyze the political history of American-Philippine relations as described in this chapter of the text. Consider its relation to the history of Filipino immigration described here.

- Compare the "old" Filipino immigration described here with the "new" post–World War II immigration from the Philippines.

EXPANDING THE "VARYING VIEWPOINTS"

- Julius Pratt, *Expansionists of 1898* (1951).

  A "traditional" view of imperialism:

  "The Manifest Destiny of the 1840s had been largely a matter of emotion. Much of it had been simply one expression of a half-blind faith in the superior virility of the American race and the superior beneficence of American political institutions. In the intervening years, much had been done to provide this emotional concept with a philosophic backing....Far-fetched and fallacious as their reasoning may appear to us, it nevertheless carried conviction....The observation must be made that the rise of an expansionist philosophy in the United States owed little to economic influences....The need of American business for colonial markets and fields for investment was discovered not by businessmen but by historians and other intellectuals, by journalists and politicians."

- William Appleman Williams, *The Tragedy of American Diplomacy* (1959).

  A "revisionist" view of imperialism as a product of economic expansionism:

  "Men like McKinley and other national leaders thought about America's problems and welfare in an inclusive, systematized way that emphasized economics. Wanting democracy and social peace, they argued that economic depression threatened those objectives, and concluded that overseas economic expansion provided a primary means of ending that danger. They did not want war per se, let alone war in order to increase their own personal fortunes. But their conception of the world ultimately led them into war in order to solve the problems in the way that they considered necessary and best."

QUESTIONS ABOUT THE "VARYING VIEWPOINTS"

1. Which of these two interpretations better explains (a) the war with Spain, (b) the decision to keep the Philippines, and (c) the U.S. involvement as a "great power" in world affairs?

2. Which historian would see American imperialism more as "inevitable," and which would see it more as a matter of choice?

3. Which of the two would judge American imperialism more harshly as a violation of moral principles and a threat to American democracy?

29

Progressivism and the Republican Roosevelt, 1901–1912

CHAPTER THEMES

Theme: The strong progressive movement successfully demanded that the powers of government be applied to solving the economic and social problems of industrialization. Progressivism first gained strength at the city and state level, and then achieved national influence in the moderately progressive administrations of Theodore Roosevelt.

Theme: Roosevelt's hand-picked successor, William H. Taft, aligned himself with the Republican Old Guard, causing Roosevelt to break away and lead a progressive third-party crusade.

CHAPTER SUMMARY

The progressive movement of the early twentieth century became the greatest reform crusade since abolitionism. Inaugurated by Populists, socialists, social gospelers, female reformers, and muckraking journalists, progressivism attempted to use governmental power to correct the many social and economic problems associated with industrialization.

Progressivism began at the city and state level, and first focused on political reforms before turning to correct a host of social and economic evils. Women played a particularly important role in galvanizing progressive social concern. Seeing involvement in such issues as reforming child labor, poor tenement housing, and consumer causes as a wider extension of their traditional roles as wives and mothers, female activists brought significant changes in both law and public attitudes in these areas.

At the national level, Roosevelt's Square Deal used the federal government as an agent of the public interest in the conflicts between labor and the corporate trusts. Rooseveltian progressivism also acted on behalf of consumer and environmental concerns. Conservatism became an important public crusade under Roosevelt, although sharp disagreements divided "preservationists" from those who favored the "multiple use" of nature. The federal emphasis on "rational use" of public resources generally worked to benefit large enterprises, and to inhibit action by the smaller users.

Roosevelt personally selected Taft as his political successor, expecting him to carry out "my policies." But Taft proved to be a poor politician who was captured by the conservative Republican Old Guard and rapidly lost public support. The conflict between Taft and pro-Roosevelt progressives finally split the Republican party, with Roosevelt leading a third-party crusade in the 1912 election.

DEVELOPING THE CHAPTER: SUGGESTED LECTURE OR DISCUSSION TOPICS

- Analyze the roots of progressivism and the various elements that made up the progressive coalition. Show particularly the role of muckraking journalists and female reformers in arousing public opinion in favor of reform.

    REFERENCE: William L. O'Neill, *The Progressive Years: America Comes of Age* (1975).

- Examine the critical role of women in progressive reform, and show how their efforts were largely—although not entirely—focused and successful in areas that seemed consistent with their social roles as protectors and nurturers of the family.

    REFERENCE: Robyn Muncy, *Creating a Female Dominion in American Reform* (1991).

- Discuss consumer protection and environmental conservation as examples of "middle-class" concerns that progressivism and progressive political leaders like Roosevelt promoted.

    REFERENCES: Elmo Richardson, *The Politics of Conservation* (1968); James Harvey Young, *Pure Food: Securing the Federal Food and Drug Act of 1906* (1989).

- Discuss the contrast between Roosevelt's regulatory New Nationalism and Wilson's more libertarian New Freedom in the campaign of 1912.

    REFERENCE: Morton Keller, *Regulating a New Economy: Public Policy and Economic Change in America, 1900–1933* (1990).

FOR FURTHER INTEREST: ADDITIONAL CLASS TOPICS

- Consider one city or state as a case study in the actual conflicts and achievements of progressivism. Cincinnati or Cleveland are good urban examples, and Wisconsin is the best state example.

- Use excerpts from the work of some muckrakers to show how journalists aroused public concern and promoted involvement in progressive reform. Steffens, Tarbell, or especially Sinclair's *The Jungle* are all valuable for this purpose.

- Discuss Roosevelt as both personality and progressive political leader.

- Examine the rise of conservationism as a national concern to (a) Roosevelt's concern to preserve "rugged" American values and (b) the increasing needs of an urban populace for escape and revival in nature.

CHARACTER SKETCHES

Lincoln Steffens (1866–1936)

Steffens was the muckraking journalist who helped stir the nation to progressive reform and in the 1930s wrote an influential autobiography claiming to show the limits of progressivism.

After growing up in a moderately affluent San Francisco family, Steffens spent some years randomly studying and traveling in Europe. He had difficulty finding a career, but a young German student whom he had met in Europe died and left Steffens his substantial estate, enabling Steffens to live independently and pursue unconventional journalism.

Steffens's *The Shame of the Cities* was so shocking because he used massive documentation to supposedly demonstrate that practically everyone was not merely corrupt but abusing power for his or her private interests. After a disillusioning fling with "Christian reform," Steffens turned toward "tougher" movements and wrote favorably about revolutionary Mexico, Mussolini's Italy, and Lenin's Russia. When he returned from Russia in 1919, he said, "I have seen the future, and it works."

Quote: "I was not the original muckraker—the prophets of the Old Testament were ahead of me....I did not intend to be a muckraker; I did not know that I was one till President Roosevelt picked the name out of Bunyan's *Pilgrim's Progress* and pinned it on us." (Autobiography, 1931)

REFERENCE: Justin Kaplan, *Lincoln Steffens: A Biography* (1974).

Ida Tarbell (1857–1944)

Tarbell was the muckraking journalist and reformer whose critical articles on Standard Oil helped bring about the breakup of Rockefeller's giant petroleum trust.

Tarbell's father made wooden kegs for the infant Pennsylvania oil industry. When she was researching the Standard Oil articles, she learned that one of her father's business partners had committed suicide after being squeezed out by Rockefeller oil interests.

Originally an ardent feminist who traveled to France to write about the role of women in the French Revolution, Tarbell later turned against feminism and suffragism, perhaps because she felt that feminism had deprived her of marriage and motherhood.

She was a very popular biographer and lecturer, and wrote best-selling books about Lincoln, Napoleon, and Madame Roland. Despite her sharp criticism of Rockefeller, she admired much of American business and looked favorably on Henry Ford and "scientific management."

Quote: "[Rockefeller] has never lowered [the price of oil] a point if it could be avoided, and in times of public stress he has taken advantage of the very misery of the poor to demand higher prices....Does it pay the public to trust the control of a great necessity of life to such a man?" (1904)

REFERENCE: Kathleen Brady, *Ida Tarbell: Portrait of a Muckraker* (1984).

Upton Sinclair (1878–1968)

Sinclair was the reform-minded journalist and novelist whose works helped inspire consumer protection and other progressive movements.

Raised in an "aristocratic" southern family impoverished by the Civil War, Sinclair moved to the Lower East Side of New York and worked his way through the City College of New York by writing "hack" journalism.

He was an enthusiast who got carried away by almost any cause with which he came in contact. Sinclair spent months in the stockyards researching *The Jungle* and donated the proceeds to a utopian commune. He founded the Intercollegiate Socialist Society with Jack London and wrote many more muckraking novels attacking financiers (*The Moneychangers*), coal mines (*King Coal*), the petroleum industry (*Oil!*), and so on. By age eighty-four he had written seventy-nine books.

In 1934 he ran for governor of California on a tax and pension program called EPIC (End Poverty In California). The campaign was unsuccessful but attracted much national attention.

Quote: "And as for the other men who work in tank rooms full of steam, where there were open vats near the level of the floor, their peculiar trouble was that they fell into the vats; and when they were fished out, there was never enough of them left to be worth exhibiting—sometimes they would be overlooked for a day, till all but the bones of them had gone out to the world as Durham's Pure Beef Lard." (*The Jungle*, 1906)

REFERENCE: Leon Harris, *Upton Sinclair: American Rebel* (1975).

Copyright © Houghton Mifflin Company. All rights reserved.

MAKERS OF AMERICA: THE ENVIRONMENTALISTS

Questions for Class Discussion

1. What really caused the sudden upsurge in concern for preserving America's environment at the beginning of the twentieth century? To what extent was this concern motivated by nostalgia for an older America, and to what extent by a desire to preserve nature and natural resources for future generations?

2. What were the underlying issues in the debate between "rational use" environmentalists and the more thoroughgoing "preservationists"? How did the rise of modern ecological science tilt that debate?

Suggested Student Exercises

1. Examine a comprehensive map of all of American's national parks, wildlife preserves, and national forests, along with the dates they were established. See what patterns can be discovered regarding the relationship between areas set aside for preservation and recreation and changing American society (e.g., where and when were preserved areas established near to major urban populations, and where and when were very remote lands set aside?)

2. Examine the ideas and actions of some of the major national figures who shaped American environmental awareness, e.g., Henry David Thoreau, John Muir, Gifford Pinchot, Ansel Adams, Rachel Carson, or others. Compare and contrast their different approaches to nature and preservation, and consider what tensions as well as shared outlooks have shaped the environmental movement.

QUESTIONS FOR CLASS DISCUSSION

1. Why did the progressives believe that strong government action was the only way to tackle the social and economic problems of industrialization? How did this approach differ from traditional American emphasis on voluntary solutions to social problems?

2. Why were women so critical to the successes of the progressive movement? Were there any weaknesses in their ideas and approaches to social reform?

3. Why was Roosevelt such a popular progressive leader? In what ways did he sound like a more ardent reformer than he really was?

4. To what extent was progressivism really a "middle class" reform effort that did not really reflect the interests or concerns of the poor and working classes it claimed to benefit? How did some of the progressive concern for conservation and environment reflect the perspectives of more affluent Americans?

30

Wilsonian Progressivism at Home and Abroad, 1912–1916

CHAPTER THEMES

Theme: After winning a three-way election focused on different theories of progressivism, Woodrow Wilson successfully pushed through a sweeping program of domestic economic and social reform in his first term.

Theme: Wilson's attempt to promote an idealistic progressive foreign policy failed, as dangerous military involvements threatened in both Latin America and the North Atlantic.

CHAPTER SUMMARY

Wilson and his New Freedom defeated Roosevelt and his New Nationalism in a contest over alternative forms of progressivism. Eloquent, idealistic former professor Wilson successfully carried out a broad progressive economic reform of the tariff, finances, and the trusts. He also achieved some social reforms that benefited the working classes, but not blacks.

Wilson's attempt to implement progressive moral goals in foreign policy was less successful, as he stumbled into military involvements in the Caribbean and revolutionary Mexico. The outbreak of World War I in Europe also brought the threat of American involvement, especially from German submarine warfare.

Wilson temporarily avoided war by extracting the precarious *Sussex* pledge from Germany. His antiwar campaign of 1916 narrowly won him reelection over the still-quarreling Republicans.

DEVELOPING THE CHAPTER: SUGGESTED LECTURE OR DISCUSSION TOPICS

- Examine Wilson's complex personality and explain how it influenced both his great successes and his failures in politics.

  REFERENCE: August Mecksher, *Woodrow Wilson* (1991).

- Examine Wilson's idealistic approach to both domestic and foreign policy. Show how he used his eloquence and moral appeals to arouse the public and achieve his goals at home, and explain why this approach was not as successful abroad.

  REFERENCE: John Morton Blum, *Woodrow Wilson and the Politics of Morality* (1956).

- Consider how Wilson's attempt to promote American-style democracy in Mexico led him into military intervention and near-war. The focus might be on the difficulties even well-intentioned policies encountered in the face of a revolutionary upheaval such as Mexico was experiencing.

REFERENCE: P. Edward Haley, *Revolution and Intervention: The Diplomacy of Taft and Wilson with Mexico, 1910–1917* (1970).

- Analyze why Wilson found himself headed to the brink of war with Germany over the submarine. Show how America's traditions, geography, and interests tended to create sympathy for the Allies, while the "barbarous" new weapon struck directly at Wilson's moral approach to foreign policy.

REFERENCE: John M. Cooper, Jr., *The Vanity of Power: American Isolation and the First World War, 1914–1917* (1969).

FOR FURTHER INTEREST: ADDITIONAL CLASS TOPICS

- Examine the events in Europe before and after the outbreak of World War I, and discuss how both Germany and the Allies tried to influence the United States.

- Compare and contrast Wilson's and Roosevelt's policies in Latin America. Consider how each policy might have looked from a Latin American standpoint.

- Examine the role of both British and German propaganda in the United States in the years before American entry into World War I. Consider the extent to which these attempts to shape American public opinion affected both official and popular views of the two sides (including among different ethnic groups).

- Consider women's issues in relation to Roosevelt's and Wilson's progressivism, especially prominent figures like Jane Addams and Lillian Wald.

CHARACTER SKETCHES

Louis Brandeis (1856–1941)

Brandeis was the progressive lawyer who became the first Jewish justice of the Supreme Court.

His parents came to the United States as refugees from the failed liberal revolution in Hungary in 1848. The family strongly emphasized culture and education, and Louis returned to Europe several times to travel and study at leading institutions.

Although he was a star student at Harvard Law School and a successful private attorney, the Homestead Steel strike turned Brandeis toward involvement in labor and progressive causes, to which he donated his legal services. His "Brandeis brief" on behalf of women workers in *Muller* v. *Oregon* made him nationally famous. His efforts on behalf of eastern European Jewish garment workers led him to a rediscovery of his own Jewish heritage and a growing involvement in Zionism.

He was frequently a Supreme Court dissenter in the 1920s, but later many of his views became accepted as law. He endorsed New Deal legislation in the 1930s but opposed Roosevelt's Court-packing plan.

Quote: "Refuse to accept as inevitable any evil in business (e.g., irregularity of employment). Refuse to tolerate any immoral practice (e.g., espionage)....[Democracy] demands continuous sacrifice by the individual and more exigent obedience to the moral law than any other form of government." (1922)

REFERENCE: Philippa Strum, *Louis D. Brandeis: Justice for the People* (1984).

Woodrow Wilson (1856–1924)

Wilson was an influential academic scholar and administrator before he became president. He held public office for only two years before his election to the White House.

Brought up under the close guidance of his Presbyterian pastor father, Wilson seldom played with his childhood peers. He failed as a lawyer before pursuing graduate studies in political science at Johns Hopkins. His book *Congressional Government* (1885) was a classic study of the American legislative process.

As president of Princeton after 1902, he battled against the snobbish "eating clubs" and tried to establish a more democratic system on campus but was defeated.

Wilson first fell seriously ill during the Paris Conference in April 1919. There is now substantial medical evidence that he suffered a series of minor strokes over several years before the massive stroke that nearly killed him on his western tour. After his collapse, his second wife kept him in virtual isolation from all advisers, including his most intimate friend, Colonel House.

Quote: "Those senators do not understand what the people are thinking. They are far from the people, the great mass of the people." (1919)

REFERENCE: Kendrick Clements, *The Presidency of Woodrow Wilson* (1992).

Francisco ("Pancho") Villa (1878–1923)

Villa was the so-called Robin Hood of the Mexican Revolution, whose raids into the United States provoked Wilson to intervene in Mexico.

Born to a poor peasant family, Villa became a thief and cattle rustler who was accused of several murders. He eventually headed up a large gang of desperadoes, but in 1910 he announced that he was joining the Mexican Revolution's fight for social justice against oppressive landlords and foreign interests.

He did sometimes redistribute land and goods to the peasants, but he also became wealthy himself through questionable means. Among his enterprises were meat-packing plants and gambling casinos. Villa was at first friendly with Americans and was even rumored to have received funds from powerful Americans like Hearst. Because of his thorough knowledge of northern Mexico, he successfully eluded Pershing, but he finally laid down his arms in 1920. Three years later he was gunned down in his home village by unknown assassins.

Quote: "It is unfair for some to have a lot when others have nothing. The poor who work but earn too little have a claim on the wealth of the rich." (1915)

REFERENCES: Manuel Machado, *Centaur of the North: Francisco Villa, the Mexican Revolution, and Northern Mexico* (1988); Clarence C. Clendenen, *The United States and Pancho Villa* (1961).

QUESTIONS FOR CLASS DISCUSSION

1. Were Wilson's progressive legislative achievements in his first term consistent with his New Freedom campaign? Why or why not?

2. How was Wilson's progressive presidency similar to Theodore Roosevelt's, and how was it different? Were the differences ones of personality or policy?

Copyright © Houghton Mifflin Company. All rights reserved.

3. Why did Wilson fail in his attempt to develop a more "moral," less imperialistic policy in Latin America? Were his involvements really an attempt to create a new mutual relationship between the United States and the neighboring republics, or was it just an alternative form of American domination?

4. Was the United States genuinely neutral during the first years of World War I, or was it biased in favor of the Allies and against Germany?

EXPANDING THE "VARYING VIEWPOINTS"

- Richard Hofstadter, *The Age of Reform* (1955).

    A view of progressives as backward-looking individualists:

    "Progressivism, at its heart, was an effort to realize familiar and traditional ideals under novel circumstances....At the core of their conception of politics was a figure quite as old-fashioned as the figure of the little competitive entrepreneur who represented the most commonly accepted economic ideal. This old-fashioned character was the Man of Good Will, the same innocent, bewildered, bespectacled, and mustached figure we see in the cartoons today labeled John Q. Public—a white collar or small business voter-taxpayer with perhaps a modest home in the suburbs."

- Gabriel Kolko, *The Triumph of Conservatism* (1963).

    A view of progressivism as a victory for business conservatism:

    "The New Freedom, in its concrete legislative aspects, was little more than the major demands of politically oriented big businessmen. They had defined the issues, and it was they who managed to provide the direction for change....In its larger outlines it was they who gave progressivism its essential character. By the end of 1914 they had triumphed, and to the extent that the new laws were vague and subject to administrative definitions by boards and commissions, they were to totally dominate the extensive reign of political capitalism that had been created in the United States by 1915."

- Robert Wiebe, *The Search for Order, 1877–1920* (1967).

    A view of progressives as forward-looking bureaucrats:

    "Experts in administration supported by a variety of professionals sought solutions to the city's problems through proper procedures and continuous enforcement....A blend of many ideas, the new political theory borrowed its most revolutionary qualities from bureaucratic thought....Trained, professional servants would staff a government broadly and continuously involved in society's operations....This revolutionary approach to government, incomplete as it was, eventually dominated the politics of the early twentieth century."

QUESTIONS ABOUT THE "VARYING VIEWPOINTS"

1. According to each of these historians, who were the progressives, and what were their central values?

2. How would each of these historians relate the progressive constituency to the basic progressive approach to government?

3. How would each interpret the progressive attack on political bosses and the establishment of independent regulatory commissions to monitor businesses like the railroads, meat packing, and banking?

31

The War to End War, 1917–1918

CHAPTER THEMES

Theme: Entering World War I in response to Germany's unrestricted submarine warfare, Wilson turned America's participation into a fervent ideological crusade for democracy that successfully stirred the public to a great voluntary war effort, but at some cost to traditional civil liberties.

Theme: After America's limited but important contribution to the Allied victory, a triumphant Wilson attempted to construct a peace based on his idealistic Fourteen Points. But European and senatorial opposition, and especially his own political errors, doomed American ratification of the Versailles Treaty and participation in the League of Nations.

CHAPTER SUMMARY

Germany's declaration of unlimited submarine warfare, supplemented by the Zimmerman note proposing an alliance with Mexico, finally caused the United States to declare war. Wilson aroused the country to patriotic heights by making the war an idealistic crusade for democracy and permanent peace based on his Fourteen Points.

Wartime propaganda stirred voluntary commitment to the war effort, but at the cost of suppressing dissent. Voluntary efforts also worked wonders in organizing industry, producing food, and financing the war. Labor, including women, made substantial wartime gains. The beginnings of black migration to northern cities led to racial tensions and riots.

America's soldiers took nearly a year to arrive in Europe, and they fought in only two major battles at the end of the war. America's main contribution to the Allied victory was to provide supplies, personnel, and improved morale. Wilson's immense prestige created high expectations for an idealistic peace, but his own political blunders and the stubborn opposition of European statesmen forced him to compromise his lofty aims.

As Lodge stalled the treaty, Wilson tried to rouse the country on behalf of his cherished League, but his own physical collapse and refusal to compromise killed the treaty and the League. Republican isolationists effectively turned Harding's victory in 1920 into a death sentence for the League.

DEVELOPING THE CHAPTER: SUGGESTED LECTURE OR DISCUSSION TOPICS

- Explain the importance of Wilson's definition of war aims. Show why his sweeping declaration of the Fourteen Points stirred tremendous enthusiasm in both America and Europe, where seemingly meaningless slaughter had dragged on for years.

    REFERENCE: Thomas Knock, *To End All Wars: Woodrow Wilson and the Quest for a New World Order* (1992).

- Analyze America's "voluntary" method of organizing for war (as opposed to the governmental coercion of European wartime regimes). Show how the feverish propaganda necessary for this approach caused war opponents to be treated as traitors.

    REFERENCE: David M. Kennedy, *Over Here: The First World War and American Society* (1980).

- Examine Wilson's negotiations at Paris. Point out how his own high idealism forced him onto the defensive, since every practical compromise appeared to be a betrayal, and how he came to focus all his hopes on the League.

    REFERENCE: Arthur Link, *Woodrow Wilson: War, Revolution, and Peace* (1979).

- Explain the defeat of the League and the treaty. Consider the way Lodge effectively exploited Wilson's weaknesses, especially his unwillingness to compromise what he saw as absolute principles.

    REFERENCES: Thomas Bailey, *Woodrow Wilson and the Lost Peace* (1944); Robert H. Ferrell, *Woodrow Wilson and World War I* (1985).

FOR FURTHER INTEREST: ADDITIONAL CLASS TOPICS

- Use samples of wartime propaganda to show how the war was presented to the public and how patriotic commitment was aroused.

- Analyze the treatment of war opponents, especially socialists and German-Americans. Discuss whether stifling them was necessary for the war effort or whether it corrupted the war to "make the world safe for democracy."

- Analyze the impact of the war on women and African-Americans. Consider the significance of passing the Nineteenth Amendment.

- Emphasize the Wilson-Lodge feud. Consider how their great political controversies were deepened by personal hatred and pride.

CHARACTER SKETCHES

George Creel (1876–1953)

Creel was the progressive journalist who became the energetic head of the American propaganda effort in World War I.

Creel quit high school after one year to become an ardent progressive journalist. He founded a newspaper, the *Kansas City Independent,* that crusaded against the Pendergast machine, prostitution, and child labor. Creel was a flamboyant figure who married a vaudeville actress and liked to associate with boxers and other athletes.

Besides war propaganda, Creel organized a massive effort to spread a "wholesome" view of the American way of life throughout the world via films, magazines, and books. Creel remained a liberal California journalist through the New Deal, but during and after World War II, he became an extreme right-winger who called for harsh vengeance against Germany and Japan.

Quote: "[I decided that] the desired results could be obtained without paying the price that formal law would have demanded....Better to have the desired compulsions proceed from within than to apply them from without." (1920)

REFERENCE: Stephen L. Vaughn, *Holding Fast the Inner Line: Democracy, Nationalism, and the Committee on Public Information* (1980).

John J. Pershing (1860–1948)

Pershing was the commander of the "Pershing expedition" into Mexico and of the American Expeditionary Force in World War I.

He attended a "normal school" before winning a competition to enter the U.S. Military Academy. His first service was among the Indians, and for a time he led a company of Sioux scouts. His nickname, "Black Jack," came from his having commanded a black cavalry unit but was also a reference to his tough drillmaster methods.

In the Mexican campaign he applied new devices like radios, airplanes, and machine guns to military uses. His ability to stay within the strict political guidelines given him in Mexico won him Wilson's favor and command of forces in World War I. Pershing was a model soldier—square-jawed, of rigid bearing, calm, forceful, discreet. Many of his junior officers later became the great American commanders in World War II.

Quote: "The most important question that confronted us in the preparation of our forces of citizen soldiery for efficient service was training....Few people can realize what a stupendous undertaking it was to teach these vast numbers their various duties when most of them were ignorant of practically everything pertaining to the business of the soldier in war." (Memoirs, 1931)

REFERENCE: Gene Smith, *Until the Last Trumpet Sounds: The Life of General of the Armies John J. Pershing* (1998).

Henry Cabot Lodge (1850–1924)

Lodge was the aristocratic New England scholar and senator who successfully battled against Wilson's League of Nations.

A descendant of the ancient Lodge and Cabot lines of Massachusetts, Lodge married his cousin Ann Cabot Davis. He studied history under Henry Adams and wrote scholarly but strongly pro-Federalist biographies of Washington, Hamilton, Webster, and his grandfather George Cabot.

He was a close friend of Theodore Roosevelt and was also a friend of Wilson's antagonist at Princeton, Dean West.

Although highly intelligent, Lodge was narrow in outlook and comfortable only with those of his own background and class. He was rigid and opinionated and, like Wilson, tended to turn political disagreements into personal animosities.

Quote: "We have twice succeeded in creating a situation where Wilson either had to take the Treaty with strong reservations...or else was obliged to defeat it. He has twice taken the latter alternative. His personal selfishness goes beyond what I have seen in any human being. It is so extreme that it is entirely unenlightened and stupid...." (Letter, 1920)

REFERENCE: William C. Widenor, *Henry Cabot Lodge and the Search for an American Foreign Policy* (1980).

GREAT DEBATES IN AMERICAN HISTORY

GREAT DEBATE (1919–1920): Versailles Treaty and League of Nations. Should the United States ratify the Versailles Treaty and join the League of Nations?

Yes: Pro-League forces, led by President Wilson and his administration; most Democrats, led by Senators Pittman and Williams; many eastern business interests and international law advocates, led by former President Taft.

No: Anti-League forces: including strong reservationists, led by Lodge, Elihu Root, and Senator Cummins; irreconcilables, led by Senators Borah and Johnson; many midwesterners, Irish-Americans, and other ethnic groups.

ISSUE #1: The treaty. Would the Versailles Treaty ensure a just and workable peace?

Yes: Pro-League President Wilson: "The Treaty is a readjustment of all those great injustices that underlie the whole structure of European and Asian society….The heart of the Treaty is that it undoes the injustice that Germany did…[and] organizes the world to see that such injustice will in the future be impossible….[I]t has very, very few compromises in it, and is, most of it, laid down in straight lines according to American specifications."

No: Anti-League British economist John Maynard Keynes: "In the first place, this treaty ignores the economic solidarity of Europe, and by aiming at the destruction of the economic life of Germany it threatens the health and prosperity of the Allies themselves. In the second place, by making demands the execution of which is in the literal sense impossible, it stultifies itself and leaves Europe more unsettled than it found it. The treaty, by overstepping the limits of the possible, has in practice settled nothing."

ISSUE #2: Warmaking power. Would joining the League of Nations amount to a surrender of the sovereign power of the United States to decide matters of war and peace?

No: Pro-League President Wilson: "Article Ten has no operative force unless we vote that it shall operate. The member of the Council representing the United States has to vote 'aye' before the United States or any other country can be advised to go to war under that agreement….There is no compulsion upon us…except the compulsion of our good conscience and judgment. So it is perfectly evident that if, in the judgment of the people of the United States the Council adjudged wrong and that this is not a case of the use of force, there would be no necessity on the part of the Congress of the United States to vote the use of force."

Yes: Anti-League Sen. Charles Townshend: "We are to be linked up in a league of more than thirty nations….If trouble occurs in Europe, which under the League and the Treaty the United States is bound to enter, our government must settle the trouble and pay the bills, even though a majority of its men are sacrificed and its whole treasure is exhausted, for morally we cannot turn our back or surrender when we enter the contract. In a partnership each partner is responsible for all the obligations of the firm….American boys from American homes will have to serve in both Europe and Asia for many years."

ISSUE #3: Monroe Doctrine. Would the League permit international interference with American privileges under the Monroe Doctrine?

No: Pro-League President Wilson: "I spoke to the conference in Paris, and they at once inserted the provision which is now there that nothing in that Covenant shall be construed as affecting the validity of the Monroe Doctrine.

...At last, in the Covenant of the League of Nations, the Monroe Doctrine has become the doctrine of the world."

No: Anti-League Senator Henry Cabot Lodge: "In the first draft of the treaty that was presented to us the Monroe Doctrine was left somewhere among the voices heard in the air and the visions that are seen by capable visionaries, and we were told that the doctrine was safe because it had been extended to the whole world....Now, however, there comes back a second draft with a direct statement in regard to the Monroe Doctrine putting it in a far worse position, in my judgment, than it was under the first draft, and that was bad enough."

ISSUE #4: Would the League violate America's long tradition of "no entangling alliances"?

No: Pro-League President Wilson: "When men tell you that we are, by going into the League of Nations, reversing the policy of the United States, they have not thought the thing out. The statement is not true....The point is that the United States is the only nation in the world that has sufficient moral force with the rest of the world....What Washington had in mind was exactly what these gentlemen want to lead us back to. The day we have left behind us was a day of alliances....This project of the League of Nations is a great policy of disentanglement."

Yes: Anti-League Senator William Borah: "If I have had a conviction throughout my life, it has been the conviction that we should stay out of European and Asiatic affairs. I do not think we can have here a great, powerful, independent, self-governing Republic and do anything else; I do not think it is possible for us to continue to be the leading intellectual and moral power in the world and do anything else....Let the people of this country who are opposed to entering into an alliance with Europe, who are opposed to surrendering the policy of Washington and the doctrine of Monroe, understand that reservations...are made to get votes...."

REFERENCES: Thomas A. Bailey, *Woodrow Wilson and the Lost Peace* (1944); Bailey, *Woodrow Wilson and the Great Betrayal* (1945); Ralph Stone, *The Irreconcilables: The Fight Against the League of Nations* (1970); William Widenor, *Henry Cabot Lodge and the Search for an American Foreign Policy* (1980).

QUESTIONS FOR CLASS DISCUSSION

1. What were the ideological results of Wilson's proclamation of World War I as a "war to end war" and "a war to make the world safe for democracy"?

2. Was it necessary to suppress dissent in order to win the war?

3. Was the Treaty of Versailles a violation of Wilson's high wartime ideals or the best that could have been achieved under the circumstances?

4. What was the fundamental reason America failed to join the League?

EXPANDING THE "VARYING VIEWPOINTS"

- George Kennan, *American Diplomacy* (1950).

A view of Wilson's diplomacy as naïve idealism:

"Under the protecting shadow of this theory [Wilsonian idealism], the guns continued their terrible work for a final year and a half after our entry. Under the shadow of this theory Wilson went to Versailles unprepared to face the sordid but all-important details of the day of reckoning. Under this theory he suffered his tragic and historic failure. Under this theory things advanced with a deadly logic and precision to a peace which was indeed 'forced upon the loser, a victor's terms imposed upon the vanquished, accepted in humiliation, in duress'—a peace that did indeed leave a sting, a resentment, a bitter memory, and upon which its own terms came later to rest 'as upon quicksand.' "

- Arthur Link, *Wilson the Diplomatist* (1957).

A view of Wilsonian diplomacy as a noble effort:

"For Woodrow Wilson the Paris Peace Conference was more a time of heroic striving and impressive achievement than of failure. By fighting against odds that would have caused weaker men to surrender, he was able to prevent the Carthaginian kind of peace that we have seen to our regret in our own time; and he was able to create the machinery for the gradual attainment of the kind of effort that he would have liked to impose at once. The Paris settlement, therefore, was not inevitably a 'lost peace.' It could have been, rather, the foundation of a viable and secure world order and therefore a lasting memorial to its chief architect, if only the victors had maintained the will to enforce what Wilson had signed."

32

American Life in the "Roaring Twenties," 1919–1929

CHAPTER THEMES

Theme: A disillusioned America turned away from idealism and reform after World War I and toward social conservatism and the pleasures of prosperity.

Theme: New technologies, mass-marketing techniques, and new forms of entertainment fostered rapid cultural change along with a focus on consumer goods. But the accompanying changes in moral values and uncertainty about the future produced cultural anxiety as well as sharp intellectual critiques of American life.

CHAPTER SUMMARY

After the crusading idealism of World War I, America turned inward and became hostile to anything foreign or different. Radicals were targeted in the red scare and the Sacco-Vanzetti case, while the resurgent Ku Klux Klan joined other forces in bringing about pronounced restrictions on further immigration. Sharp cultural conflicts occurred over the prohibition experiment and evolution.

A new mass-consumption economy fueled the spectacular prosperity of the 1920s. The automobile industry, led by Henry Ford, transformed the economy and altered American lifestyles.

The pervasive media of radio and film altered popular culture and values. Birth control and Freudian psychology overturned traditional sexual standards, especially for women. Young literary rebels, many originally from the Midwest, scorned genteel New England and small-town culture and searched for new values as far away as Europe. The stock-market boom symbolized the free-wheeling spirit of the decade.

DEVELOPING THE CHAPTER: SUGGESTED LECTURE OR DISCUSSION TOPICS

- Analyze the social "turning inward" of the 1920s as a disillusioned reaction to World War I. Show how the rise of the Klan and immigration restriction especially reflected a desire to preserve America against "alien" influences.

    REFERENCE: Nancy MacLean, *Behind the Mask of Chivalry: The Making of the Second KKK* (1993).

- Discuss the Scopes trial as a focal point of the deep conflicts over religion and culture in the 1920s.

    REFERENCE: George Marsden, *Fundamentalism and American Culture* (1980).

- Examine the economic and cultural consequences of the new mass-consumption economy. Show how innovations such as credit buying, advertising, and automobile travel weakened the old Protestant ethic with a new emphasis on pleasure and excitement.

    REFERENCE: Ronald Marchand, *Advertising the American Dream: Making Way for Modernity* (1985).

- Consider the radical cultural transformations in moral and sexual values brought about by such developments as movies, birth control, Freudian psychology, jazz, and "advanced" literature, especially as they affected women. Examine the rise of the "consumer culture" and its impact on traditional moral and social values (e.g., the impact of credit buying on the "Puritan ethic").

    REFERENCE: Stanley Coben, *Rebellion Against Victorianism: The Impetus for Cultural Change in 1920s America* (1991).

FOR FURTHER INTEREST: ADDITIONAL CLASS TOPICS

- Explore the ideology and actions of the 1920s Klan. Consider similarities and differences in relation to the Klan of Reconstruction.

- Discuss the role of prohibition during the 1920s and its close relation to the rise of organized crime.

- Explore the complex and sometimes contradictory cultural values of the decade as symbolically represented by Charles Lindbergh's flight. Discuss how he symbolized technological innovation but also individual heroism in an increasingly "mass" society.

- Consider the role of both black and white artists in changing American culture in the 1920s. Consider where writers like Fitzgerald and Hughes were reflecting similar concerns, and where their outlook was different.

CHARACTER SKETCHES

Henry Ford (1863–1947)

Ford was the automobile genius and industrialist who epitomized the new age of mass consumer production.

Although he hated farm work as a boy, Ford was always nostalgic about rural life and later re-created an idealized version of it in his Greenfield Village.

He was widely praised for paying his workers $5 a day—although not all of them earned that. In 1915, Ford paid for a "Peace Ship" full of American antiwar activists who sailed to Norway in a futile effort to end World War I. In the 1920s he published a viciously anti-Semitic paper, *The Dearborn Independent,* which was distributed through Ford dealerships.

Ford enjoyed his own reputation as the voice of the uneducated common person and often sounded off on subjects about which he knew nothing. For example, he asserted that earlier civilizations had had airplanes and cars, that cows should be eliminated and milk produced artificially, and that all the art in the world was not worth five cents.

Quote: "I don't like to read books. They mess up my mind." (1919)

REFERENCE: David L. Lewis, *The Public Image of Henry Ford* (1976).

Alphonse Capone (1899–1947)

Capone was the brutal gangster who dominated Chicago organized crime in the late 1920s and early 1930s.

Capone's parents were Italian immigrants from Sicily who came to New York in 1893. Capone quit school after the fourth grade and soon linked up with other gang members, including Johnny Torrio. In one early gang fight Capone was slashed across the face with a knife, giving him his nickname of "Scarface."

When Torrio moved from New York to Chicago, Capone followed him to help run the giant prostitution operation and other rackets in the city. In 1925 Torrio retired, and Capone seized control of all of Chicago's prohibition-era organized crime by gunning down his rivals. Capone's worth was estimated at over $100 million and for a time in the late 1920s he had extensive power within Chicago's political, journalistic, and law-enforcement communities.

After his conviction for income-tax evasion and imprisonment on Alcatraz Island, he was discovered to be suffering from syphilis. He was released on parole in 1939.

Quote: "What's your racket?" (1927)

REFERENCE: John Kobler, *The Life and World of Al Capone* (1992); Laurence Bergreen, *Capone: The Man and the Era* (1994).

Charles A. Lindbergh (1902–1974)

Lindbergh was the pilot whose solo flight made him the greatest hero of the 1920s and who later became a leading isolationist spokesman before World War II.

A group of St. Louis businessmen put up the money for Lindbergh's plane, which had never been fully tested before he headed across the Atlantic. He dozed off several times during the flight but was awakened each time by the erratic movements of the plane. Vast crowds greeted him in Paris, although he landed in the dark.

Lindbergh was stunned by the unrelenting publicity and tried unsuccessfully to withdraw from the public eye. He married the daughter of diplomat Dwight Morrow. Anne Morrow Lindbergh later became a popular author. The kidnapping and murder of their two-year-old son in 1932 horrified America and caused the Lindberghs to move to Europe. Lindbergh's association with Nazism and isolationism in the 1930s cost him some popularity, but he sometimes advised the government on aviation matters even into the 1950s and 1960s.

Quote: "These wars in Europe are not wars in which our civilization is defending itself against some Asiatic intruder….This is not a question of banding together to defend our white race against foreign invasions. This is simply one more of those age-old quarrels among our family of nations." (Radio address, 1939)

REFERENCE: Scott Berg, *Lindbergh* (1998).

Marcus Garvey (1887–1940)

Garvey was the black nationalist leader whose "Back to Africa" movement had a major influence on African-American culture in the 1920s.

Garvey was born in Jamaica and worked as a printer and union organizer. During travels to South America and Britain, he learned a great deal about the history and culture of African peoples, which led him to emphasize black racial pride and to formulate his plans for a return of all blacks to Africa.

His Universal Negro Improvement Association attracted tremendous support from American blacks in the early 1920s, but the government of Liberia (where Garvey hoped to migrate) thought him a revolutionary plotter and withdrew support from his Black Star steamship lines. His conviction for fraud and his deportation to Jamaica effectively ended his political career, but he remained a hero among many blacks for his emphasis on African culture and self-determination.

Quote: "Never allow anyone to convince you of your inferiority as a man. Rise in your dignity to justify all that is noble in your race.

> My race is mine and I belong to it.
> It climbs with me and I climb with it.
> My pride is mine and I shall honor it.
> It is the height on which I daily sit."
> (*The Negro World*, 1923)

REFERENCE: J. Stein, *The World of Marcus Garvey* (1986).

F. Scott Fitzgerald (1896–1940)

Fitzgerald was the novelist whose literature and life symbolized and promoted the values of the "jazz age" in the 1920s.

His father was from an old aristocratic Maryland family whose ancestors included the author of "The Star-Spangled Banner." His mother was from a poor Irish background, and Fitzgerald claimed his dual ancestry gave him a unique view of American life.

At Princeton Fitzgerald worked harder for social than academic success and was distressed when academic probation forced him to give up his campus literary activities. Fitzgerald's glamorous postwar life in Europe fell victim to lavish spending, alcoholism, and the mental illness of his wife Zelda.

In the 1930s he returned to America and wrote *Tender Is the Night* (1934) and a brilliant story, "The Crack-Up," about his own mental distress and feared loss of talent. When he was sober, Fitzgerald was charming, elegant, and a fine conversationalist.

Quote: "America was going on the greatest, gaudiest spree in history.... The whole golden boom was in the air—its splendid generosities, its outrageous corruptions, and the death struggle of the old America in prohibition." (1935)

REFERENCE: William A. Fahey, *F. Scott Fitzgerald and the American Dream* (1973).

MAKERS OF AMERICA: THE POLES

Questions for Class Discussion

1. How did both economic and religious factors contribute to Polish immigration?

2. How was the Polish influence in America similar to that of other "New Immigrants" such as the Italians (see Chapter 25)? How was it different?

Suggested Student Exercises

- The text lists five cities that were centers of Polish immigration to America: Chicago, Buffalo, Pittsburgh, Detroit, and Milwaukee. Examine the impact of Polish-Americans in one of these cities over several generations.

- Critically analyze negative cultural stereotypes of Polish immigrants in the press and elsewhere in the 1920s and after. Consider what biases may underlie these stereotypes, and how some of the social and cultural changes in recent decades, in both the United States and Poland (e.g., the Polish Pope John Paul II and the fall of communism), may work to undercut such stereotyping.

QUESTIONS FOR CLASS DISCUSSION

1. Why did the United States, which had welcomed so many millions of immigrants for nearly a century, suddenly become so fearful of immigration in the 1920s that it virtually ended mass immigration for two decades?

2. To what extent was the Scopes Trial only about competing theories of human origins, and to what extent was it simply a focal point for deeper concerns regarding the role of religion and traditional moral authorities in American life and the new cultural power of science?

3. Was the new "mass culture" as reflected in Hollywood films and radio a source of moral and social change, or did it really reinforce the essentially conservative business and social values of the time? (Consider the role of commercial advertising in particular.)

4. Were the intellectual critics of the 1920s really disillusioned with the fundamental character of American life, or were they actually loyal to a vision of a better America, and only hiding their idealism behind a veneer of disillusionment and irony?

33

The Politics of Boom and Bust, 1920–1932

CHAPTER THEMES

Theme: The Republican administrations of the prosperous 1920s pursued conservative, probusiness policies at home and economic unilateralism abroad.

Theme: The great crash of 1929 led to a severe, prolonged depression that devastated the American economy and spirit, and resisted Hoover's limited efforts to correct it.

CHAPTER SUMMARY

The Republican governments of the 1920s carried out active, probusiness policies while undermining much of the progressive legacy by neglect. The Washington Naval Conference indicated America's desire to withdraw from international involvements. Sky-high tariffs protected America's booming industry but caused severe economic troubles elsewhere in the world.

As the Harding scandals broke, the puritanical Calvin Coolidge replaced his morally easygoing predecessor. Feuding Democrats and La Follette progressives fell easy victims to Republican prosperity.

American demands for strict repayment of war debts created international economic difficulties. The Dawes plan provided temporary relief, but the Hawley-Smoot Tariff proved devastating to international trade.

The stock-market crash of 1929 brought a sudden end to prosperity and plunged America into a horrible depression. Herbert Hoover's reputation collapsed as he failed to relieve national suffering, although he did make unprecedented but limited efforts to revive the economy through federal assistance.

DEVELOPING THE CHAPTER: SUGGESTED LECTURE OR DISCUSSION TOPICS

- Explain the central features of Republican economic and political conservatism in the 1920s: probusiness government, hostility to progressive social and economic regulation, and high tariffs to isolate the American economy from the troubled world economy.

  REFERENCE: Burl Noggle, *Into the Twenties* (1974).

- Contrast Warren Harding and his corrupt cronies with the upright Coolidge and Hoover. Perhaps show how each of the three presidents represented a different emphasis within the general political consensus of the probusiness 1920s.

  REFERENCES: John D. Hicks, *Republican Ascendancy, 1921–1933* (1960); Joan Hoff Wilson, *Herbert Hoover, Forgotten Progressive* (1975).

- Describe the stock-market crash and the depression. Examine various causes of the depression and indicate its paralyzing effect on ordinary citizens as well as on the business and political leadership.

    REFERENCE: Robert McElvaine, *The Great Depression* (1984).

- Consider the changing role of American workers in both the probusiness 1920s and during the early years of the Great Depression.

    REFERENCE: Robert Zieger, *American Workers, American Unions, 1920–1985* (1986).

FOR FURTHER INTEREST: ADDITIONAL CLASS TOPICS

- Focus on Harding's cronies and the Teapot Dome scandals.

- Discuss the futile Democratic and progressive efforts of the 1920s. The focus might be on the deep cultural divisions within the Democratic party between urban immigrants and the rural South, epitomized in the 103-ballot Democratic convention of 1924.

- Examine Hoover's career, from humane administrator to business organizer to hapless president. Discuss why someone so successful proved so helpless in the face of the depression.

- Analyze the human consequences of the depression for both the unemployed and the many others who feared unemployment and found their living standard severely reduced.

CHARACTER SKETCHES

Warren G. Harding (1865–1923)

This simple, genial president was deeply mourned when he died in 1923, just before the news broke of the thoroughgoing corruption in his administration.

Rumors throughout Harding's career that he was part black were based only on hometown gossip and the fact that one of his great-grandparents had lived in a black neighborhood. There is no historical evidence that he had any black ancestors.

Harding was happy as a small-town editor and poker-playing U.S. senator, although his ambitious wife, "The Duchess," constantly pushed him to do greater things. Harding maintained several mistresses, and one of them—Nan Britton of Marion, Ohio—bore a child by him in 1919. As president, he would frequently sneak away to play poker with the "Ohio gang" at "the little green house on K street."

Harding was deeply distressed as he learned of his cronies' corrupt dealings. He seemed near collapse during his presidential trip to Alaska, on which he died, and frequently asked Secretary of Commerce Herbert Hoover what a president should do if there was dishonesty around him.

Quote: "My God, this is a hell of a job. I have no troubles with my enemies…but my God-damn friends!…" (1923)

REFERENCE: Robert K. Murray, *The Harding Era* (1969); Eugene P. Trani, *The Presidency of Warren G. Harding* (1977).

Calvin Coolidge (1872–1933)

Coolidge's rectitude and old-fashioned virtues provided welcome relief from the Harding scandals, while also offering the public a reassuring counterpoint to the wild cultural changes of the 1920s.

At Amherst College, Coolidge astounded classmates by constantly seeking ways to live more cheaply. He was personally kind and generous, but he was frequently moody and had few close friends. Even after he became a successful attorney, he used a party-line phone and refused to buy a car because it was too expensive.

Coolidge was generally ignorant of history and political theory, but he loved classical languages and sometimes translated Latin literary works into English. He had a malicious sense of humor and loved to play practical jokes like ringing for White House servants and then hiding from them. His poker-faced silence was the subject of much commentary and humor. When writer Dorothy Parker was told that Coolidge had died, she said, "How could they tell?"

Quote: "There are two ways to be self-respecting: to spend less than you make, and to make more than you spend." (1925)

REFERENCE: Hendrik Booraem, *The Provincial: Calvin Coolidge and His World* (1994); Robert Ferrell, *The Presidency of Calvin Coolidge* (1998).

Herbert Hoover (1874–1964)

Hoover was an international hero as food relief administrator during World War I and a popular secretary of commerce, but his single term as president made him a permanent symbol of economic and political disaster.

Hoover was the product of a strong Iowa Quaker background. His parents died before he was ten, and he was then raised by an uncle in Oregon. After graduating from Stanford, he lived outside the United States for nearly twenty years while working as an engineer and businessman. One of his interests was the history of mining, and he collected and had translated Renaissance classics on the subject.

As a public official, Hoover developed a large staff of deferential subordinates who called him "The Chief" and generated favorable publicity on his behalf. He was stiff, formal, humorless, and unyielding in his opinions once he had taken a stand. Those who worked intimately with him always liked him, but he was comfortable only in the company of people who he knew were on his side.

Quote: "We in America today are nearer to the final triumph over poverty than ever before in the history of any land....We have not yet reached the goal, but given a chance to go forward with the policies of the last eight years, we shall soon with the help of God be in sight of the day when poverty will be banished from this nation." (Convention acceptance speech, 1928)

REFERENCE: Joan Hoff Wilson, *Herbert Hoover: Forgotten Progressive* (1975).

QUESTIONS FOR CLASS DISCUSSION

1. In what ways were the 1920s a reaction against the progressive era?

2. Was the American isolationism of the 1920s linked to the rise of movements like the Ku Klux Klan? In what ways did movements like fundamentalism reflect similar "antimodern" outlooks, and in what ways did they reflect more basic religious disagreements?

3. To what extent did the policies of the booming 1920s contribute to the depression?

4. How did the depression challenge the traditional belief of Hoover and other Americans in "rugged individualism"?

34

The Great Depression and the New Deal, 1933–1938

CHAPTER THEME

Theme: Roosevelt's New Deal tackled the Great Depression with massive federal programs designed to bring about relief, recovery, and reform.

CHAPTER SUMMARY

Confident, aristocratic Roosevelt swept into office with an urgent mandate to cope with the depression emergency. His bank holiday and frantic Hundred Days lifted spirits and created a host of new agencies to provide for relief to the unemployed, economic recovery, and permanent reform of the system.

Roosevelt's programs put millions of the unemployed back on the job through federal action. As popular demagogues like Huey Long and Father Charles Coughlin increased their appeal to the suffering population, Roosevelt developed sweeping programs to reorganize and reform American history, labor, and agriculture. The TVA, Social Security, and the Wagner Act brought far-reaching changes that especially benefited the economically disadvantaged.

Conservatives furiously denounced the New Deal, but Roosevelt formed a powerful coalition of urbanites, labor, "new immigrants," blacks, and the South that swept him to victory in 1936.

Roosevelt's Court-packing plan failed, but the Court finally began approving New Deal legislation. The later New Deal encountered mounting conservative opposition and the stubborn persistence of unemployment. Although the New Deal was highly controversial, it saved America from extreme right-wing or left-wing dictatorship.

DEVELOPING THE CHAPTER: SUGGESTED LECTURE OR DISCUSSION TOPICS

- Describe the impact of Roosevelt and the New Deal on deeply depressed ordinary Americans, perhaps focusing on how Roosevelt revived spirits and restored faith in the system, even for those who did not agree with all his programs. Include the experiences of ordinary men and women in the 1930s.

    REFERENCES: Studs Terkel, *Hard Times* (1970); Ann Banks, *First Person America.*

- Examine the goals and activities of the major New Deal programs. The "relief-recovery-reform" distinction (pp. 781 and 784) is useful for sorting out the alphabet agencies, as is the distinction between the early NRA-AAA approach and the later TVA–Social Security–Wagner Act reforms. A unifying theme for the whole New Deal is the search to provide greater "security" against the storms and uncertainties of unregulated capitalism.

    REFERENCE: David M. Kennedy, *Freedom from Fear* (1999).

- Explain the various challenges to Roosevelt from both the popular demagogues and the conservatives. Show how he skillfully "stole the thunder" from the former and used the latter as political whipping boys.

    REFERENCE: Alan Brinkley, *Voices of Protest: Huey Long, Father Coughlin, and the Great Depression* (1982).

- Consider the experience of women in the Depression and in the making of the New Deal. Look at both ordinary women in urban and rural areas, as well as more prominent reformers and government figures.

    REFERENCES: Lois Scharf, *To Work and to Wed: Female Employment, Feminism, and the Great Depression* (1980); Susan Ware, *Beyond Suffrage: Women in the New Deal* (1981).

FOR FURTHER INTEREST: ADDITIONAL CLASS TOPICS

- Compare and contrast the images and activities of FDR and Eleanor Roosevelt. Show how he pursued realistic political goals, while she took up the cause of the most disadvantaged citizens.

- Discuss the particular impact of the depression on women, families, and children.

- Use Steinbeck's *The Grapes of Wrath* (and perhaps the film) to discuss the plight of Dust Bowl farmers in the depression. Point out that, for most, the problem was not dust but impossibly low prices.

- Discuss the long-term, continuing impact of the New Deal today. Consider the controversies in the 1980s and after over the legacy of "big government" programs started by the New Deal.

CHARACTER SKETCHES

Franklin Roosevelt (1882–1945)

Roosevelt came from a wealthy patrician family, and his advocacy on behalf of the common person in the depression led him to be called a "traitor to his class."

Thoroughly indulged as an only child, Roosevelt was taught primarily by private tutors. His mother, Sara Delano, was a strong-willed woman who exercised a dominant influence on him even during his adult life.

Roosevelt had been very athletic before being struck with polio in 1921. It took him several years of constant effort to regain his strength; after he discovered the therapeutic waters at Warm Springs, Georgia, he again participated in swimming, fishing, and sailing. Roosevelt was almost never photographed in a wheelchair, so many Americans did not know that the wheelchair was his normal means of getting around.

Roosevelt enjoyed political maneuvering and often pitted his advisers against one another. He once told two officials with contradictory proposals to "go in a room and weave them together."

Quote: "In every dark hour of our national life a leadership of frankness and vigor has met with that support and understanding of the people themselves which is essential to victory.…The money changers have fled from their high seats in the temple of our civilization.…This nation asks for action, and action now." (Inaugural address, 1933)

REFERENCE: Frank Freidel, *Franklin D. Roosevelt: Rendezvous with Destiny* (1990).

Eleanor Roosevelt (1884–1962)

Besides her role as Franklin Roosevelt's wife and adviser, Eleanor Roosevelt became an influential reformer and political leader in her own right, both before and after FDR's death.

Eleanor Roosevelt did not change names when she married her distant cousin. Her father, Elliott Roosevelt, was Theodore Roosevelt's younger brother and a troubled alcoholic who separated from his family when Eleanor was young. Her mother died when Eleanor was eight, and she was raised by a grandmother who made her feel unattractive and unwanted.

Her discovery of her husband's unfaithfulness led to a crisis in their marriage and her determination to create a political identity and career on her own. Her newspaper column, "My Day," became a highly popular feature in the 1930s and 1940s. She grew to be a skilled political operator and helped to engineer the nomination of Adlai Stevenson for president in 1952 and 1956.

Quote: "As time went by, I found that people no longer considered me a mouthpiece for my husband but realized that I had a point of view of my own with which he might not at all agree. Then I felt freer to state my views." (Autobiography, 1949)

REFERENCE: Blanche Wiesen Cook, *Eleanor Roosevelt: A Life* (1992).

Huey Long (1893–1935)

Long was the colorful "Kingfish" whose populist politics dominated Louisiana and who eventually challenged Roosevelt's leadership during the depression.

Originally from rural north Louisiana, Long always had a strong following among poor farmers. He was elected state railroad commissioner at age twenty-five, and used the office flamboyantly to attack monopolistic utilities. As governor and senator he ruled Louisiana with near-absolute control; every police officer, firefighter, and teacher in the state owed his or her job directly to Long.

Long spent lavishly for public works, roads, and schools, especially for the "redneck" areas. He also built up Louisiana State University, with particular emphasis on the football team and the band, and was known for leading the band on the sidelines during games.

Long would often hold court in hotel rooms in his pajamas, with reporters and advisers and citizens listening to his clever, humorous, obscene monologues. Long's plan was to run as an independent presidential candidate in 1936, building a base of support so he could win the White House in 1940.

Quote: "Why weep or slumber, America,
Land of brave and true?
With castles, and clothing, and food for all
All belongs to you.
Every Man a King! Every Man a King!" (Radio address, 1935)

REFERENCE: William Hair, *The Kingfish and His Realm: The Life and Times of Huey P. Long* (1991).

QUESTIONS FOR CLASS DISCUSSION

1. Which of Roosevelt's measures were most effective in fighting the depression? Why?

2. How did Roosevelt alter the role of the federal government in American life?

3. How did ordinary workers and farmers effect social change in the 1930s?

4. What were the positive and negative effects of the New Deal's use of the federal government as an agency of social reform?

MAKERS OF AMERICA: THE DUST BOWL MIGRANTS

Questions for Class Discussion

1. In what ways was the migration of the "Okies" and "Arkies" to California similar to European or Asian immigration to the United States, and in what ways was it different?

2. How does the actual historical experience of the Dust Bowl migrants compare with the fictional portrayal of one such family in John Steinbeck's *The Grapes of Wrath*? Is the knowledge that most Americans have of this migration primarily shaped by that novel?

Suggested Student Exercises

- Use a map to trace the Dust Bowl migrants' route from Arkansas, Oklahoma, and Texas to the San Joaquin Valley.

- Read some of the descriptive passages from Steinbeck's novel. Consider why he found in these migrants' experience a suitable subject for a socially conscious work about the Great Depression.

EXPANDING THE "VARYING VIEWPOINTS"

- Arthur M. Schlesinger, Jr., *The Age of Roosevelt: The Coming of the New Deal* (1959).

    A view of the New Deal as a radical transformation:

    "By bringing to Washington a government determined to govern, Roosevelt unlocked new energies in a people who had lost faith, not just in government's ability to meet the economic crisis, but almost in the ability of anyone to do anything. The feeling of movement was irresistible....A despairing land had a vision of America as it might some day be.... 'It's more than a New Deal,' said Harold Ickes. ' It's a new world. People feel free again. They can breathe naturally. It's like quitting a morgue for the open woods.' 'We have had our revolution,' said Collier's, 'and we like it.' "

- William E. Leuchtenberg, *Franklin D. Roosevelt and the New Deal* (1963).

    A view of the New Deal as a "halfway revolution":

    "The New Deal achieved a more just society by recognizing groups which had been largely unrepresented—staple farmers, industrial workers, particular ethnic groups, and the new intellectual-administrative class. Yet this was still a halfway revolution. It swelled the ranks of the bourgeoisie but left many Americans—sharecroppers, slum dwellers, most Negroes—outside the new equilibrium....The New Dealers perceived that they had done more in those years than had been done in any comparable period of American history, but they also saw that there was much still to be done, much, too, that continued to baffle them."

QUESTIONS ABOUT THE "VARYING VIEWPOINTS"

1. What does each of these historians regard as the fundamental achievement of the New Deal?

2. What weaknesses does Leuchtenberg see in the New Deal?

3. How might each of these historians interpret such programs as the AAA, Social Security, and the Wagner Act?

35

Franklin D. Roosevelt and the Shadow of War, 1933–1941

CHAPTER THEME

Theme: In the early and mid-1930s, the United States attempted to isolate itself from foreign involvements and wars. But by the end of the decade, the spread of totalitarianism and war in Europe forced Roosevelt to provide more and more assistance to desperate Britain, despite strong isolationist opposition.

CHAPTER SUMMARY

Roosevelt's early foreign policies, such as wrecking the London economic conference and establishing the Good Neighbor policy in Latin America, were governed by concern for domestic recovery and reflected America's desire for a less active role in the world. America virtually withdrew from all European affairs, and promised independence to the Philippines as an attempt to avoid Asian commitments.

Depression-spawned chaos in Europe and Asia strengthened the isolationist impulse, as Congress passed a series of Neutrality Acts designed to prevent America from being drawn into foreign wars. The United States adhered to the policy for a time, despite the aggression of Italy, Germany, and Japan. But after the outbreak of World War II in Europe, Roosevelt began to provide some aid to the Allies.

After the fall of France, Roosevelt gave greater assistance to desperate Britain in the destroyers-for-bases deal and in lend-lease. Still-powerful isolationists protested these measures, but Wendall Willkie refrained from attacking Roosevelt's foreign policy in the 1940 campaign.

Roosevelt and Winston Churchill issued the Atlantic Charter, and by the summer of 1941, the United States was fighting an undeclared naval war with Germany in the North Atlantic. After negotiations with Japan failed, the surprise attack on Pearl Harbor plunged the United States into World War II.

DEVELOPING THE CHAPTER: SUGGESTED LECTURE OR DISCUSSION TOPICS

- Explain the causes of American isolationism in the 1930s: domestic depression, disillusion with World War I, hostility to arms dealers and other "merchants of death."

  REFERENCE: Manfred Jonas, *Isolationism in America, 1935–1941* (1966).

- Examine the erosion of isolationism in response to the aggressions of Benito Mussolini, Adolf Hitler, and the Japanese warlords. Show the transition in American thinking from indifference to fear for democracy, as appeasement only fed the dictators' appetites.

  REFERENCE: David M. Kennedy, *Freedom from Fear* (1999).

- Describe the fierce debates between internationalists and isolationists, especially from 1939 to 1941. The emphasis might be on Roosevelt's carefully calibrated strategy of increasing aid at each stage, but never so rapidly as to hand the isolationists a political victory.

    REFERENCE: Kenneth S. Davis, *Franklin D. Roosevelt: Into the Storm, 1937–1941* (1993).

- Discuss the Japanese-American negotiations and the conflicts that set the stage for Pearl Harbor.

    REFERENCE: Donald Cameron Watt, *How the War Came: The Immediate Origins of the Second World War, 1938–1939* (1989).

FOR FURTHER INTEREST: ADDITIONAL CLASS TOPICS

- Focus on the "merchants of death" Nye hearings. Discuss how 1930s isolationism was strongly aimed at the factors that had supposedly led the United States into World War I.

- Examine the rise of Mussolini, Hitler, and the Japanese militarists. Consider why Americans were appalled by their doctrines, even if they did not want to fight them.

- Analyze the isolationist-internationalist debate, especially over lend-lease. Point out the isolationists' argument that such aid would inevitably lead to war and the internationalists' argument that helping Britain was the way to stay out of war. Consider whether FDR acted wisely in moving the United States closer to involvement.

- Discuss the causes of the Pacific war from the Japanese point of view. Consider whether the war was "inevitable."

CHARACTER SKETCHES

Adolf Hitler (1889–1945)

Hitler was regarded as a vulgar laughingstock in Germany in the 1920s, but he eventually ruled more of Europe than anyone since Napoleon.

The son of a minor Austrian bureaucrat who was over fifty years old when Adolf was born, Hitler constantly envisioned himself as a great artist, but his grades and talent were so poor that he failed to get into a Vienna art school. He later painted pictures and baked them so he could sell them for high prices as valuable works by old masters.

Hitler was a total failure until he joined the German army during World War I and became completely caught up in the German cause. Through long years of speaking in beer halls, Hitler became adept at reading audiences. His emotional, ranting speeches had great hypnotic power. Except on matters of war and politics, Hitler was totally ignorant and had banal or vicious views that he nevertheless considered the thoughts of genius.

Quote: "Man has become great through struggle....Whatever goal man has reached is due to his originality plus his brutality....Through all the centuries force and power are the determining factors...." (*Mein Kampf,* 1924)

REFERENCE: Alan Bullock, *Hitler: A Study in Tyranny* (1962).

Copyright © Houghton Mifflin Company. All rights reserved.

Winston Churchill (1874–1965)

Churchill was a powerful British politician and statesman long before his heroic leadership against the Nazis in World War II.

Churchill's father was Lord Randolph Churchill, a descendant of the seventeenth-century duke of Marlborough. Churchill later wrote a biography of his distinguished ancestor, Marlborough. His mother was an American, and he always cherished his half-American ancestry.

The brash young Churchill dashed around the remote spots of the British Empire at its height in the 1890s, seeking adventure and glory. He found it during the Boer War, and wrote dramatic accounts of how he escaped from Boers by hiding under floorboards.

Churchill became the powerful first lord of the admiralty during World War I at age thirty-nine, but the daring Gallipoli campaign in Turkey that he organized proved a disaster. Churchill then lost influence and spent much of the 1920s and 1930s as a political outcast, until the rise of Nazism gave him a new opportunity. He was stubborn and self-willed, and almost childish in his vanity and outbursts of temper. Yet he was warm-hearted, generous, courageous, and capable of strong sympathy with others. During the London blitz, he insisted on sharing the hardships of the people and often wept when he saw bombed-out houses and churches.

Quote: "We shall fight on the beaches, we shall fight in the fields and streets, we shall fight in the hills, we shall never surrender." (Speech, 1940)

REFERENCE: William Manchester, *The Last Lion: Winston Spencer Churchill*, 2 vols. (1983, 1988).

Joseph Stalin (1879–1953)

Stalin's name and picture were everywhere in Russia during his brutal rule, but after "de-Stalinization" his name and image were completely erased from the Soviet Union.

Stalin's real name was Joseph Dzhugashvili. He later chose Stalin (steel) as his revolutionary name. Stalin's parents sent him to a seminary to become a priest, but he joined revolutionary movements and was expelled.

At the height of his tyranny in the 1930s, Stalin exiled or killed millions of people, including even his closest associates and one of his own family members. His second wife committed suicide in 1932, leaving a letter accusing him of numerous crimes. For many years, all Soviet artists, writers, musicians, scientists, and others had to sing Stalin's praises and have their work approved by him. He was suspicious, cruel, and paranoid but could exude great charm on occasion.

Quote: "It may be asked how could the Soviet government have consented to conclude a non-aggression pact with such perfidious…fiends as Hitler and Ribbentrop? Was this not an error on the part of the Soviet government? No.…We secured to our country peace for a year and a half and the opportunity of preparing our forces." (1941)

REFERENCE: Adam Ulam, *Stalin: The Man and His Era* (1973).

GREAT DEBATES IN AMERICAN HISTORY

GREAT DEBATE (1939–1941): Isolationism versus internationalism. Should the United States move away from isolationist neutrality and toward aiding the Allies in the fight against Hitler?

Yes: The internationalists, led by President Roosevelt and the administration; most big-business leaders and cosmopolitan city-dwellers; the Committee to Defend America by Aiding the Allies, led by William Allen White.

No: The isolationists, led by the America First Committee and Charles A. Lindbergh; some senators and representatives, led by William Borah, Robert Taft, and Hamilton Fish; some writers, like Charles Beard and Harry Elmer Barnes; some small-business and ethnic groups, especially in the Midwest; some leftists and socialists, led by Norman Thomas.

ISSUE #1: Isolation. Should the United States have any interest in events overseas?

Yes: Internationalist Roosevelt: "It becomes clearer and clearer that the world will be a shabby and dangerous place to live in—yes, even for Americans to live in—if it is ruled by force in the hands of a few....I hope that we shall have fewer American ostriches in our midst. It is not good for the ultimate health of ostriches to bury their heads in the sand."

No: Isolationist poet Oliver Allstrom:
"Over there," there's mud and shedding of blood
And tongues confusing and strange.
So why lend a hand to an alien band
Whose dreams we can never change?

"No, no," comes the cry from the U.S. sky,
"We'll never be Allied tools.
Nor again parade in a foreign brigade
Like saps in a squad of fools."

"And Europe may strut through its bloody rut
And scheme with her Babel-snares.
But we'll stay home, this side of the foam
And mind our own affairs!"

ISSUE #2: Democracy. Are the Allies fighting for the democratic principles America believes in?

Yes: Internationalist Congressman Jerry Voorhis: "I have an interest in the way of life wherein free men can freely struggle to better their conditions, freely worship and believe according to their own conscience....I know that this is not possible in a Nazi- or Communist-dominated nation. So...to aid Great Britain and the other nations attempting to resist the totalitarians has become part of American policy."

No: Isolationist Congressman Hamilton Fish: "The cause for which Hitler has thrown the German masses into war is damnably unholy. But the war of Chamberlain and Reynaud is not thereby rendered holy. The fact that Hitler is the opponent does not make the Allied war a fight for democracy....The Allied governments have no idealism in the conflict, no war aims worthy of the sacrifice...of their peoples...."

ISSUE #3: War. Will aiding the Allies inevitably lead the United States into war?

No: Internationalist Roosevelt: "There is a far less chance of the United States getting into war if we do all we can now to support the nations defending themselves against attack by the Axis than if we acquiesce in their defeat, submit tamely to an Axis victory, and wait our turn to be the object of attack in another war later on....There is no demand for sending an American Expeditionary Force outside our own borders. There is no intention by any member of your government to send such a force. You can, therefore, nail any talk about sending armies to Europe as deliberate untruth."

Yes: Isolationist Senator Arthur Vandenberg: "When H.R. 1776 [lend-lease] passed the Senate...we did vastly more than 'aid Britain.' We have thrown ourselves squarely into the power politics and the power wars of Europe, Asia, and Africa....We have said to Britain, 'We will see you through to victory.' And it would be unbelievably dishonorable for us to stop short of full participation in the war if that be necessary to a victory....But I fear this means we must actively engage in the war ourselves."

ISSUE #4: War and democracy. Would another war require dictatorial methods and destroy democracy within the United States?

No: Internationalist Roosevelt: "I reject the idea that only by abandoning our freedom, our ideals, our way of life, can we build our defenses adequately, can we match the strength of the aggressors....I do not share these fears."

Yes: Isolationist socialist Norman Thomas: "The method of modern totalitarian warfare is self-defeating in terms of ideal ends. War itself is the only victor. Each particular war begets its more deadly successors. Intolerance, dictatorship, brutality, are its inevitable accompaniments...."

REFERENCES: William Langer and S. Everett Gleason, *The Challenge to Isolation, 1937–1940* (1952); Kenneth Davis, *FDR: Into the Storm, 1937–1940* (1993); Wayne Cole, *Charles Lindbergh and the Battle Against American Intervention in World War II* (1974).

QUESTIONS FOR CLASS DISCUSSION

1. Why did the neutrality laws fail to prevent America's growing involvement with the military conflicts in Europe and Asia?

2. How did the process of American entry into World War II compare with the entry into World War I?

3. Would it have been more straightforward of Roosevelt to have openly called for a declaration of war against Hitler rather than increasing involvement gradually while claiming that he did not want war?

4. Would the United States have entered World War II even if the Japanese had not attacked Pearl Harbor?

MAKERS OF AMERICA: REFUGEES FROM THE HOLOCAUST

Questions for Class Discussion

1. In what ways were the refugees from Hitler's anti-Semitic persecutions similar to other immigrant groups, and in what ways were they different?

2. How did the earlier history of American Jewish immigration affect the experience of the Holocaust refugees in America?

3. Was American government policy toward the refugees, and toward the Holocaust generally, an adequate response to the crisis?

Suggested Student Exercises

- Use various aids (photographs, films, documents) to illustrate the Holocaust. Consider why many of the refugees felt grateful to America for providing a haven, but frustrated at their inability to do more for their fellow Jews.

- Use some examples of the work of Jewish refugee artists, composers, scientists, or writers (e.g., Marc Chagall, Kurt Weill, Albert Einstein, Hannah Arendt, and Erich Fromm) to illustrate the refugee immigrants' cultural contribution to America. Consider how such contributions may have differed from the second- and third-generation cultural achievements of some other immigrant groups.

36

America in World War II, 1941–1945

CHAPTER THEMES

Theme: Unified by Pearl Harbor, America effectively carried out a war mobilization effort that produced vast social and economic changes within American society.

Theme: Following its "get Hitler first" strategy, the United States and its Allies invaded and liberated conquered Europe from Fascist rule. The slower strategy of "island-hopping" against Japan also proceeded successfully until the atomic bomb brought a sudden end to World War II.

CHAPTER SUMMARY

America was wounded but roused to national unity by Pearl Harbor. Roosevelt settled on a fundamental strategy of dealing with Hitler first, while doing just enough in the Pacific to block the Japanese advance.

With the ugly exception of the Japanese-American concentration camps, World War II proceeded in the United States without the fanaticism and violations of civil liberties that occurred in World War I. The economy was effectively mobilized, using new sources of labor such as women and Mexican *braceros*. Numerous African-Americans and Indians also left their traditional rural homelands and migrated to war-industry jobs in the cities of the North and West. The war brought full employment and prosperity, as well as enduring social changes, as millions of Americans were uprooted and thrown together in the military and in new communities across the country. Unlike European and Asian nations, however, the United States experienced relatively little economic and social devastation from the war.

The tide of Japanese conquest was stemmed at the Battles of Midway and the Coral Sea, and American forces then began a slow strategy of "island hopping" toward Tokyo. Allied troops first invaded North Africa and Italy in 1942–1943, providing a small, compromise "second front" that attempted to appease the badly weakened Soviet Union as well as the anxious British. The real second front came in June 1944 with the D-Day invasion of France. The Allies moved rapidly across France, but faced a setback in the Battle of the Bulge in the Low Countries.

Meanwhile, American capture of the Marianas Islands established the basis for extensive bombing of the Japanese home islands. Roosevelt won a fourth term as Allied troops entered Germany and finally met the Russians, bringing an end to Hitler's rule in May 1945. After a last round of brutal warfare on Okinawa and Iwo Jima, the dropping of two atomic bombs ended the war against Japan in August 1945.

DEVELOPING THE CHAPTER: SUGGESTED LECTURE OR DISCUSSION TOPICS

- Explain the basic strategic military decisions of the war. The emphasis might be on the fact that there were, in a sense, two separate wars that had to be conducted simultaneously and that the European war required delicate political and military coordination with Britain and Russia.

  REFERENCE: H. P. Willmott, *The Great Crusade: A New Complete History of the Second World War* (1990).

- Describe the social and economic changes brought by the war. Particular attention could be given to war-spawned prosperity after the depression and to the beginnings of the Sunbelt migrations that continued in the postwar era, including the African-American exodus to the North and West.

    REFERENCE: John W. Jeffries, *Wartime America: The World War II Homefront* (1996).

- Examine the major military battles in Europe, Asia, and the Middle East, and their relation to the political tensions among the United States, Britain, and the Soviet Union.

    REFERENCE: Gerhard Weinberg, *A World at Arms* (1990); David M. Kennedy, *Freedom from Fear* (1999).

- Analyze the events of the war against Japan, including the development and use of the atomic bomb. The emphasis might be on the controversy over why the bomb was used.

    REFERENCES: Martin J. Sherwin, *A World Destroyed: The Atomic Bomb and the Grand Alliance* (1975); Ronald Spector, *Eagle Against the Sun: The American War with Japan* (1985).

FOR FURTHER INTEREST: ADDITIONAL CLASS TOPICS

- Examine the role of women during the war. Discuss the text's point (p. 837) that American women's lives were not altered as much as were the lives of women in other belligerent nations.

- Discuss the varieties of warfare conducted by American forces during the conflict, ranging from the savage island fighting in the Pacific to the strategic bombing of German and Japanese military and civilian targets.

- Focus on Roosevelt, Churchill, and Stalin as the "Big Three" wartime leaders. Perhaps use their major decision-making meetings—Casablanca, Teheran, Yalta—to define the stages of the war.

- Analyze the immediate and long-term consequences of the war. Show how the basic international structure of the postwar world was determined by World War II, including the rivalry between the United States and the Soviet Union.

CHARACTER SKETCHES

A. Philip Randolph (1889–1979)

Randolph was the longtime head of the Brotherhood of Sleeping Car Porters and an early black civil rights advocate.

A black minister's son, Randolph became converted to socialism. In 1917 he and Chandler Owen started a radical black magazine, *The Messenger,* which called World War I a "white man's war" and urged blacks to refuse to fight—in contrast to W. E. B. Du Bois's support for the war effort and black soldiers.

In the 1920s Randolph was considered a political spokesman for the racially conscious "new negro," who emerged especially in Harlem and other northern ghettos. In 1925 Pullman porters, who were the lowest-paid rail workers and were all patronizingly called "George," approached Randolph and asked him to head their union. In 1937 the brotherhood finally won a contract.

Copyright © Houghton Mifflin Company. All rights reserved.

Randolph's proposed March on Washington in 1941 never occurred, but the idea remained alive in the black community, and Randolph was one of the speakers at the 1963 March on Washington where Martin Luther King, Jr. delivered his "I Have a Dream" speech.

Quote: "This is an hour of crisis....To American Negroes, it is the denial of jobs in government defense projects. It is racial discrimination in government departments. It is widespread Jim-Crowism in the armed forces of the Nation....What a runaround! What a disgrace! What a blow below the belt!" (Call for March on Washington, 1941)

REFERENCE: Paula Pfeffer, *A. Philip Randolph: Pioneer of the Civil Rights Movement* (2001). William Harris, *Keeping the Faith: A. Philip Randolph, Milton Webster, and the Brotherhood of Sleeping Car Porters* (1977).

Douglas MacArthur (1880–1964)

MacArthur was the American army commander in the Pacific in World War II, the governor of occupied Japan, and the U.N. commander who was fired by President Truman during the Korean War.

His father, Arthur MacArthur, was a famous American officer in the Civil War, Spanish-American War, and Philippine War. Douglas MacArthur's strong-arm tactics in ousting the "Bonus Army" from Washington in 1932 made him a controversial figure, and he remained surrounded by controversy for much of his career.

Although he is best known for saying "I shall return" to the Philippines, MacArthur's greatest military accomplishment in World War II was actually his difficult battles in New Guinea and Los Negros.

MacArthur was virtually the absolute ruler of Japan from 1945 to 1947, and many Japanese looked on him as a kind of "white emperor." Republicans several times approached MacArthur about running for president, but he always refused. In public MacArthur was arrogant, egotistical, and self-promoting, but in private he was more genial and easygoing.

Quote: "When I joined the Army, even before the turn of the century, it was the fulfillment of all my boyish hopes and dreams....I still remember the refrain of one of the most popular barrack ballads of that day, which proclaimed, most proudly, that 'Old soldiers never die. They just fade away.' And like the old soldier of that ballad, I now close my military career and just fade away." (Speech to Congress, 1951)

REFERENCE: William Manchester, *American Caesar* (1978); Geoffrey Parrett. *Old Soldiers Never Die: The Life of Douglas MacArthur* (1996).

George Patton (1885–1945)

Patton was the American tank commander of World War II whose belligerent behavior and ideas made him a focus of controversy.

Descended from Revolutionary and Confederate officers, Patton grew up captivated by tales of his ancestors' heroic military exploits. He was raised on his wealthy grandfather's California estate and did not attend school until he was twelve years old.

Patton's tactical skill, especially in the conquest of Sicily, earned great praise, but he was nearly fired from his command when he slapped and browbeat two shell-shocked GIs in an army hospital. Eisenhower reprimanded Patton but permitted him to remain at his post, deciding that his military ability was necessary to the war.

After his spectacular tank breakthrough across France, he entered Germany but became embroiled in further controversy when he advocated that American forces continue on and fight the Russians and that they use Nazi officials and soldiers to do so. Patton was an extreme personality, known for his hysterical outbursts, his constant profanity, and his sentimentality.

Quote: "Americans love to fight, traditionally. All real Americans love the sting and clash of battle. America loves a winner. America will not tolerate a loser." (Speech to his troops before D-Day, 1944)

REFERENCE: Martin Bluminson, *Patton: The Man Behind the Legend, 1888–1945* (1985).

QUESTIONS FOR CLASS DISCUSSION

1. How did America's domestic response to World War II differ from its reaction to World War I?

2. What was the wisest strategic decision in World War II, and what was the most questionable?

3. How were the European and Pacific wars similar, and how were they different?

4. What was the significance of the dropping of the atomic bomb, then and now?

MAKERS OF AMERICA: THE JAPANESE

Questions for Class Discussion

1. How were the Japanese immigrants similar to other immigrants from East Asia, such as the Chinese and Filipinos? How were they different?

2. Should the World War II internment experience be seen as the most significant event in the Japanese-American experience? How did it affect those who lived through it and their descendants?

Suggested Student Exercises

- Use photographs or documents from early Japanese immigrants to glean their views of the United States.

- Consider the lives and careers of some prominent Japanese-Americans (such as Senator Daniel Inouye of Hawaii) in relation to the general Japanese-American experience.

MAKERS OF AMERICA: THE GREAT AFRICAN-AMERICAN MIGRATION

Questions for Class Discussion

1. Why did World War II finally provide the historic impetus to cause African-Americans to leave their ancient conditions of oppression in the rural South?

2. What benefits did African-Americans gain from their migration north and west, and what problems did they still have?

Copyright © Houghton Mifflin Company. All rights reserved.

Suggested Student Exercises

- Use photographs or other documents of the African-American migration to northern cities in the World War II era. Examine what evidence the photographs provide about the economic conditions of the migrants.

- Read passages from one of the novels of the era, for example, Richard Wright's *Native Son* or Ralph Ellison's *Invisible Man,* to illustrate the feelings and perceptions of African-Americans as they entered life in the large northern cities. Wright's autobiography, *Black Boy,* also explains the conditions and aspirations that led many young blacks to leave the rural South and move north.

EXPANDING THE "VARYING VIEWPOINTS"

- Gar Alperovitz, *Atomic Diplomacy* (rev. ed., 1985).

    A view of the atomic bomb as aimed at Russia rather than Japan:

    "The decision to use the weapon did not derive from overriding military considerations....*Before the atomic bomb was dropped each of the Joint Chiefs of Staff advised that it was highly likely that Japan could be forced to surrender 'unconditionally,' without use of the bomb and without an invasion.*...Unquestionably, political considerations related to Russia played a major role in the decision; from at least mid-May American policy makers hoped to end the hostilities before the Red Army entered Manchuria....A combat demonstration was needed to convince the Russians to accept the American plan for a stable peace."

- Martin Sherwin, *A World Destroyed* (1975).

    A view of the atomic bomb as primarily aimed at Japan:

    "Caught between the remnants of war and the uncertainties of peace, policymakers and scientists were trapped by their own unquestioned assumptions....The secret development of this terrible weapon, during a war fought for a total victory, created a logic of its own: a quest for a total solution of a set of related problems that appeared incapable of being resolved incrementally....As Szilard first suggested in January 1944, the bomb might provide its own solution....The decision to use the bomb to end the war could no longer be distinguished from the desire to use it to stabilize the peace."

QUESTIONS ABOUT THE "VARYING VIEWPOINTS"

1. What does each of these historians see as American officials' thinking about the relationship between the bomb and the ending of the war against Japan?

2. What does each regard as the primary reason for the use of the bomb?

3. What conclusions might be drawn from each of these views about the political and moral justifications for dropping the bomb?

37

The Cold War Begins, 1945–1952

CHAPTER THEMES

Theme: America emerged from World War II as the world's strongest economic power, and commenced a postwar economic boom that lasted for two decades. A bulging population migrated to the suburbs and Sunbelt, leaving the cities increasingly to minorities and the poor.

Theme: The end of World War II left the United States and the Soviet Union as the two dominant world powers, and they soon became locked in a Cold War confrontation. The Cold War spread from Europe to become a global ideological conflict between democracy and communism. Among its effects were a nasty hot war in Korea and a domestic crusade against "disloyalty."

CHAPTER SUMMARY

In the immediate postwar years there were widespread fears of a return to depression. But fueled by cheap energy, increased worker productivity, and government programs like the GI Bill of Rights, the economy began a spectacular expansion that lasted from 1950 to 1970. This burst of affluence transformed American industry and society, and particularly drew more women into the workforce.

Footloose Americans migrated to the Sunbelts of the South and West, and to the growing suburbs, leaving the northeastern cities with poorer populations. Families grew rapidly, as the "baby boom" created a population bulge that would last for decades.

The Yalta agreement near the end of World War II left major issues undecided and created controversy over postwar relations with the Soviet Union. With feisty Truman in the White House, the two new superpowers soon found themselves at odds over Eastern Europe, Germany, and the Middle East.

The Truman Doctrine announced military aid and an ideological crusade against international communism. The Marshall Plan provided economic assistance to starving and communist-threatened Europe, which soon joined the United States in the NATO military alliance.

The Cold War and revelations of spying aroused deep fears of communist subversion at home that culminated in McCarthy's witch-hunting. Fear of communist advances abroad and social change at home generated national and local assaults on many people perceived to be "different." Issues of the Cold War and civil rights fractured the Democratic Party three ways in 1948, but a gutsy Truman campaign overcame the divisions to win a triumphant underdog victory.

The Communist Chinese won a civil war against the Nationalists. North Korea invaded South Korea, and the Americans and Chinese joined in fighting the seesaw war to a bloody stalemate. MacArthur's insubordination and threats to expand the war to China led Truman to fire him.

DEVELOPING THE CHAPTER: SUGGESTED LECTURE OR DISCUSSION TOPICS

- Explain the changes in American economic development since World War II. The emphasis might be on America's uncontested postwar economic domination and on the eventual weakening of the heavy-industrial base and the turn to other economic activities.

    REFERENCE: John Patrick Diggins, *The Proud Decades: America in War and Peace, 1941–1960* (1988).

- Explain the complex causes of the Cold War. The emphasis might be on the vacuum of power created by the destruction of Europe and the decline of Britain, as well as on the specific ideological and political battles over Poland, Germany, and Greece.

    REFERENCES: Daniel Yergin, *Shattered Peace* (1977); Melvyn P. Leffler, *A Preponderance of Power: National Security, the Truman Administration, and the Cold War* (1992).

- Examine the rise of suburbs in relation to the changes in postwar economic, social, and racial life. Consider suburbia as an expression of both rising affluence and geographical mobility (especially in the South and West). Perhaps consider some of the critics and defenders of the suburbs in the 1950s.

    REFERENCE: Kenneth Jackson, *Crabgrass Frontier* (1986).

- Analyze the connection between the Cold War abroad and the hunt for subversion at home, perhaps focusing on the difference between the attacks on actual Soviet spies and the broader attack on all American Communists and the use of the "Communist" charge as a way to smear and suppress all sorts of people with unconventional views and lifestyles.

    REFERENCE: Richard Fried, *Nightmare in Red* (1990); Ellen Schrecker, *Many Are the Crimes* (1998).

FOR FURTHER INTEREST: ADDITIONAL CLASS TOPICS

- Contrast the economic, social, and cultural life of a "typical" family of the 1940s and 1950s and a similar family of the 1990s.

- Examine the significance of divided Germany and the "captive nations" of Eastern Europe in the Cold War.

- Analyze one or more of the key subversion cases—for example, the Hiss or Rosenberg cases. Consider how they became decades-long symbols of Cold War divisiveness.

- Discuss the frustrations of Korea as a "limited" and stalemated war. Special emphasis could be placed on the firing of MacArthur.

CHARACTER SKETCHES

Benjamin Spock (1903–)

Spock is the pediatrician whose child-rearing guide *Baby and Child Care* has been used by millions of American parents.

A 1929 graduate of Columbia Medical School, Spock became a well-known New York pediatrician for such people as Margaret Mead. He wrote *Baby and Child Care* while serving in the navy during World War II. The book has sold over 25 million copies—the best-selling original title ever published in the United States.

Although the book was criticized as "permissive," it was actually a moderate reaction against the rigid feeding schedules and strict discipline imposed by child-care experts of the 1920s and 1930s.

Spock became an active opponent of the Vietnam War in the 1960s. He was indicted and convicted for encouraging draft resistance, but the conviction was overturned on appeal in 1969. In 1972 he ran as the presidential candidate of the small People's party. Even in his radical political activities, his image was that of a kindly, grandfatherly gentleman.

Quote: "I may as well let the cat out of the bag as far as my opinion goes and say that strictness or permissiveness is not the real issue. Good-hearted parents who aren't afraid to be firm when necessary can get good results with either strictness or moderate permissiveness." (*Baby and Child Care,* 1946)

REFERENCE: Thomas Maier, *Dr. Spock: An American Life* (1998).

Harry S Truman (1884–1972)

Truman was the Missouri haberdasher and machine politician who came to be regarded as one of the great American presidents.

The *S* in the middle of Truman's name did not stand for anything. Both of his grandfathers had *S* names, so his parents just gave Harry the letter rather than choose either one.

Being very nearsighted, even as a boy, Truman spent much time playing the piano and reading history. His hero in American history was Andrew Jackson.

Truman worked on the family farm and at many odd jobs before becoming a popular artillery officer in World War I—an experience that remained one of the highlights of his life. The men's clothing store he started in 1919 failed two years later, and he then began his career in machine politics. Judge Truman controlled a large patronage army but was never involved in corruption.

His quick temper and blunt-spoken ways were legendary. He often wrote angry letters to critics but only occasionally mailed them.

Quote: "The Republicans work for the benefit of the few bloodsuckers who have offices in Wall Street. This is a crusade of the people against the special interests, a crusade to keep the country from going to the dogs. You back me up and we'll win that crusade." (Campaign speech, 1948)

REFERENCE: David McCulloch, *Truman* (1992).

George Kennan (1904–)

Kennan was the American diplomat and ambassador to Russia who is credited with formulating the containment policy but later became a critic of many American Cold War policies, including Vietnam.

There was a distantly related nineteenth-century George Kennan whose career eerily paralleled that of the twentieth-century Kennan. Both were born on the same day, and both became leading American Russia scholars and diplomats of their time.

Kennan served as a U.S. diplomat in Germany and Riga, Latvia, before World War II. He became a scholarly expert on Russia, and his telegrams to Washington, based partly on his close observations of Stalin and the Russians, set out the basic principles of containment even before he wrote his "X" article in *Foreign Affairs.*

Kennan's brief term as ambassador to the Soviet Union in 1952 was cut short when the Soviet government expelled him, supposedly for critical remarks he had made about the communist rulers. Kennan later objected to the "militarization" of American foreign policy and ironically became in the 1960s and 1970s probably the most influential critic of the American Cold War policies he is credited with initiating.

Quote: "There is nothing—I repeat nothing—in the history of the Soviet regime which could justify us in assuming that the men who are now in power in Russia, or even those who have chances of assuming power within the foreseeable future, would hesitate for a moment to apply this power against us if by so doing they thought it would materially improve their power position in the world." (Telegram to Washington, 1945)

REFERENCE: George F. Kennan, *Memoirs, 1925–1950* (1967); David Meyers, *George Kennan and the Dilemmas of U.S. Foreign Policy* (1998); A biography of Kennan by historian John Lewis Gaddis forthcoming.

Thomas Dewey (1902–1971)

Dewey was the losing Republican presidential candidate in 1944 and 1948.

Originally a student of music, Dewey tried for an opera-singing career in Chicago. In 1931 he became the youngest ever United States attorney and in 1935 became a special prosecutor for racketeering, going after such notorious gangsters as Dutch Schultz and Lucky Luciano. His career as a relentless prosecutor formed the basis for several Hollywood movies.

Dewey grew his mustache to please his wife, who liked it, but his advisers constantly urged him to shave it off, saying it made him look sinister. Although he was lively and pungent in private, Dewey was obsessed with maintaining a proper public image. He never allowed himself to be photographed except in a tie and vest.

He long remained a power in Republican politics and helped engineer the nominations of Dwight Eisenhower and Richard Nixon.

Quote: "I do not know about the accommodations at the White House for the family....There is of course no rush about it." (Letter, fall 1948)

REFERENCE: Richard Norton Smith, *Thomas E. Dewey and His Times* (1982).

QUESTIONS FOR CLASS DISCUSSION

1. Which development caused the greatest change in American society in the immediate postwar years: increased affluence, the migration to the suburbs, the entry of women into the workforce, or the "baby boom"?

2. Was the primary threat from the Soviet Union military or ideological—that is, was the danger that the Soviet army would invade Western Europe or that more and more people in Europe and elsewhere would be attracted to communist ideas?

3. Were there any legitimate concerns behind the "red-hunting" anticommunism of the late 1940s and early 1950s? How were McCarthy and others able to turn the search for spies and subversives into an assault on freethinkers, adulterers, homosexuals, and others deemed "different" in some way?

4. Was Truman right to fire MacArthur when and how he did? What would have happened if MacArthur had gotten his way and expanded the conflict with the Chinese?

MAKERS OF AMERICA: THE SUBURBANITES

Questions for Class Discussion

1. To what extent was the migration to suburbia a "flight from" the city and its problems, and to what extent was it a "flight to" a vision of a new "pastoral" way of life?

2. Were the new problems that accompanied the early growth of suburbia, e.g., traffic congestion, pollution, racial segregation, and the confinement of women to domestic roles a result of the suburban migration itself? Or would they have come to the fore even if most postwar Americans had continued to live in central cities?

Suggested Student Exercises

- Examine the maps of four or five major metropolitan areas of the United States to discover the geographical relations of central cities to suburbs. Looking at maps over the course of several decades (e.g., from 1950, 1965, 1980, and 1995), examine the growth of suburban settlement patterns, and consider their relation to patterns of railroads, highways, and mass transit in areas where it has a prominent role (e.g., Washington D.C., Chicago, Atlanta, San Francisco).

- Select a dozen or more major American corporations, and determine the location of their corporate headquarters in relation to central cities and suburbs. Consider the extent to which the traditional pattern of "live in the suburbs, work in the city" has been altered in some metropolitan areas, and to what extent it remains in place.

EXPANDING THE "VARYING VIEWPOINTS"

- Walter LaFeber, *America, Russia, and the Cold War, 1945–1984* (1985).

  A view of the United States as primarily responsible for the Cold War:

  "Having failed to budge the Russians in face-to-face negotiations, even when backed by atomic bombs, the State Department next tried to buckle Stalin's iron fence with economic pressures....More important, it made American officials ponder the awful possibility that Stalin's ambitions included not only strategic positions in Eastern Europe, but the imposition of Communist regimes upon Asia and the Middle East. Stating the Soviet dictator's alternatives in this way no doubt badly distorts his true policies....Stalin's thrusts after 1944 were rooted more in the Soviets' desire to secure certain specific strategic bases, raw materials, and above all, to break up what

Stalin considered to be the growing Western encirclement of Russia....However, American officials saw little reason to worry about such distinctions."

- John Lewis Gaddis, *The United States and the Origins of the Cold War* (1972).

A view of the Cold War as caused primarily by Soviet aggression:

"If one must assign responsibility for the Cold War, the most meaningful way to proceed is to ask which side had the greater opportunity to accommodate itself, at least in part, to the other's position, given the range of alternatives as they appeared at the time. Revisionists have argued that American policy-makers possessed greater freedom of action, but their view ignores the constraints imposed by domestic policies....The Russian dictator was immune from pressures of Congress, public opinion, or the press....This is not to say that Stalin wanted a Cold War....But his absolute powers did give him more chances to surmount the internal restraints on his policy than were available to his democratic counterparts in the West."

QUESTIONS ABOUT THE "VARYING VIEWPOINTS"

1. How does each of these historians see American and Soviet motives in the Cold War?

2. On what basis does each assign primary responsibility for initiating Cold War conflicts?

3. How would each of these historians likely interpret the confrontation over Greece and the Truman Doctrine?

38

The Eisenhower Era, 1952–1960

CHAPTER THEME

Theme: The Eisenhower years were characterized by prosperity and moderate conservatism at home and by the tensions of the Cold War abroad.

Theme: While Dwight Eisenhower and the majority of Americans held to a cautious, family-oriented perspective on domestic social questions, an emerging civil rights movement and the influence of television and popular music presented challenges to the spirit of national "consensus."

CHAPTER SUMMARY

Using the new medium of television to enhance his great popularity, grandfatherly "Ike" was ideally suited to soothe an America badly shaken by the Cold War and Korea. Eisenhower was slow to go after Joseph McCarthy, but the demagogue's bubble finally burst. Eisenhower also reacted cautiously to the beginnings of the civil rights movement but sent troops to Little Rock to enforce court orders. While his domestic policies were moderately conservative, they left most of the New Deal in place.

Despite John Dulles's tough talk, Eisenhower's foreign policies were also generally cautious. He avoided military involvement in Vietnam, although aiding Diem, and pressured Britain, France, and Israel to resolve the Suez crisis.

He also refused to intervene in the Hungarian revolt and sought negotiations to thaw the frigid Cold War. Dealing with Nikita Khrushchev proved difficult, as *Sputnik,* the Berlin Crisis, the U-2 incident, and Fidel Castro's Cuban revolution all kept Cold War tensions high. In a tight election, Senator John Kennedy defeated Eisenhower's vice president, Richard Nixon, by calling for the country to "get moving again" by more vigorously countering the Soviets.

American society grew ever more prosperous in the Eisenhower era, as science, technology, and the Cold War fueled burgeoning new industries like electronics and aviation. Women joined the movement into the increasingly white-collar workforce, and chafed at widespread restrictions they faced.

A new consumer culture, centered around television, fostered a new ethic of leisure and enjoyment, including more open expressions of sexuality in popular entertainment. Intellectuals and artists criticized the focus on private affluence rather than the public good. Jewish, African-American, and southern writers had a striking new impact on American culture.

DEVELOPING THE CHAPTER: SUGGESTED LECTURE OR DISCUSSION TOPICS

- Describe the general domestic atmosphere of the Eisenhower years: broad economic prosperity (with occasional recessions) and broad social consensus based on the New Deal and anticommunism. The emphasis might be on seeing this harmony as a reaction to the turbulent 1930s and 1940s and also noting some of the hidden anxieties of the time.

  REFERENCE: David Halberstam, *The Fifties* (1993).

- Explain the up-and-down atmosphere of the Cold War in the 1950s. Note the general improvement in relations from Stalin's day, but also the numerous conflicts and the arms race that constantly threatened nuclear annihilation.

    REFERENCE: Thomas J. McCormick, *America's Half Century: U.S. Foreign Policy in the Cold War* (1989).

- Examine the growing importance of civil rights issues in the 1950s, as illustrated by *Brown* v. *Board of Education* and King's Montgomery bus boycott. The slow pace of court-ordered desegregation might be contrasted with the increasing determination of blacks to attack the still-pervasive Jim Crow system.

    REFERENCE: Taylor Branch, *Parting the Waters: America in the King Years, 1954–1963* (1988).

- Consider the initial impact of television on all areas of American life in the 1950s, including politics, consumption (advertising), family life, religion, and popular culture.

    REFERENCE: Lynn Spiegel, *Make Room for TV: Television and the Family Ideal in Postwar America* (1992).

FOR FURTHER INTEREST: ADDITIONAL CLASS TOPICS

- Focus on the Army-McCarthy hearings and the decline at last of "low-blow Joe." Perhaps discuss Eisenhower's reluctance to take on McCarthy when he was popular.

- Consider America's relation to the French war in Vietnam or the installation of the Shah in Iran. Discuss how American policies, while avoiding immediate conflicts, sowed the seeds of later, more serious difficulties.

- Examine the Kennedy-Nixon campaign of 1960 for the specific light it shed on wider themes of the time, including anti-communism, the new importance of television, and tensions that accompanied the movement of previously marginal groups like Catholics into the center of American life.

- Consider the relation between economic transformations and the role of women in the 1950s. Show both the new emphasis on domesticity and childrearing, and the beginnings of rebellion by suburban women.

CHARACTER SKETCHES

Joseph McCarthy (1908–1957)

McCarthy was the demagogic Wisconsin senator whose name has entered the dictionary as a synonym for exaggerated and irresponsible attacks on others' reputations.

He began his career as a small-time Wisconsin judge before serving as an intelligence officer in World War II. McCarthy never saw military action and resigned before the war was over, but he later fabricated the story that, as "tail-gunner Joe," he had been wounded in air battles.

Before he launched his anticommunist crusade, McCarthy was primarily known in the Senate for his personal rudeness and for backing the soft-drink industry. McCarthy's speeches attacking alleged communists in government were nothing new, but his constant claim to have evidence (which somehow never appeared) kept him always on the offensive. McCarthy was loud, vulgar, boisterous, and self-promoting. He lied so constantly and grandly that no one knew when he was telling the truth, perhaps not even himself.

Quote: "[General Marshall] is part of a conspiracy so immense and in infamy so black as to dwarf any previous such venture in the history of man....[There is] a pattern which finds his decisions maintained with great stubbornness and skill, always and invariably serving the world policy of the Kremlin." (1951)

REFERENCES: Arthur Herman, *Joseph McCarthy* (1999); Richard Rovere, *Senator Joe McCarthy* (1959).

John Foster Dulles (1888–1959)

Dulles was Eisenhower's secretary of state and a leading architect of American strategy in the Cold War.

The son of a New York Presbyterian minister, Dulles grew up under strong religious influences, which stayed with him all his life. His maternal grandfather, John Watson Foster, had been secretary of state under Benjamin Harrison, and Dulles met men like William Taft, Andrew Carnegie, and Bernard Baruch when they visited his father.

Dulles served in the American delegation at Versailles but in the 1930s became the leading Republican expert on foreign policy. In 1936 he made a controversial speech that expressed sympathy for Germany and appeared to welcome Nazism. Dulles's brother Allen was a top American intelligence officer in World War II and later head of the CIA.

Always a controversial personality, Dulles expressed firm opinions and engaged in moral posturing that grated on many people, including Churchill and Eisenhower, but he often won them over by the force of his character and intelligence.

Quote: "Some say we were brought to the verge of war. Of course we were brought to the verge of war....If you try to run away from it, if you are scared to go to the brink, you are lost." (1956)

REFERENCE: Leonard Mosely, *Dulles* (1978).

Dwight David Eisenhower (1890–1969)

Eisenhower's rise from obscure colonel to supreme Allied commander in World War II was spectacular, but Marshall and others had long taken note of his talents and marked him for future advancement.

His parents were basically of middle-class background, but at the time of Eisenhower's birth, his father had been laid off, and the family had temporarily moved from Abilene, Kansas, to Denison, Texas, where "Ike" was born.

Eisenhower and George Patton were both reprimanded for urging the use of tanks in World War I. During his World War II years in Europe, "Ike" spent much time with his driver, Kay Summersby, leading to rumors that he and Mamie planned to divorce.

His excellent personal relations with Soviet Marshal Zhukov gave Eisenhower a different view of the Russians and led him to seek personal contacts with them.

Before the 1952 campaign he tried to teach Nixon how to fish and was disappointed when his running mate proved unwilling or unable to learn the sport.

Quote: "My first day at the President's desk. Plenty of worries and difficult problems. But such has been my portion for a long time. The result is that this seems (today) like a continuation of all I've been doing since July 1941—even before that." (Diary entry, January 1953)

REFERENCE: Stephen Ambrose, *Eisenhower* [2 vols.] (1983, 1984).

Rosa Parks (1913–   )

Parks is the black seamstress whose refusal to move to the back of a bus in Montgomery, Alabama, on December 5, 1955, set off a bus boycott and the beginning of the civil rights movement.

Even though she took her action on her own, Parks had previous acquaintance with black protest ideas and leaders. As a young woman, she had tried to organize an NAACP youth chapter in Montgomery, though without success. She had met A. Philip Randolph and Roy Wilkins and knew black leaders in Montgomery. She was also a leader in her local church, St. Paul AME church.

She had planned ahead that she was going to sit in the front of the bus that day and refuse to move. After her arrest, she went to E. D. Nixon, head of the local Brotherhood of Sleeping Car Porters, who circulated leaflets calling for the wider protest.

Parks worked with the civil rights movement for years. She moved to Detroit in 1967 and remained active in black causes.

Quote: "I just decided I was not going to be moved out of that seat." (Interview, 1978)

REFERENCE: Douglas Brinkley, *Rosa Parks* (2000).

Elvis Aron Presley (1935–1977)

Presley was the rock-and-roll star who helped transform American popular musical styles in the 1950s and after.

Presley grew up in Memphis, Tennessee, where he learned both gospel music and black blues music. His first recordings were done for Sam Phillips, a producer who had been looking for a white singer who sounded like a black man. After signing a contract with RCA Victor in 1955, his career came under the control of Colonel Tom Parker, who promoted him into a national phenomenon.

Presley's sexually suggestive style led to many protests from parents and conservative groups, as a result of which he was shown only from the waist up in his first television appearance in 1956. Presley's thirty-three movies were nearly as popular as his records, and his drafting into the army in 1960 was treated as a major event. After his death, his home in Memphis became a virtual pilgrimage shrine for his fans.

Quote: "Please, Mr. Sholes, don't make me stand still. If I can't move I can't sing." (To a record producer, 1954)

REFERENCE: Albert Harry Goldman, *Elvis* (1981).

QUESTIONS FOR CLASS DISCUSSION

1. How does Eisenhower's political leadership compare with that of other general-presidents: Washington, Jackson, Taylor, and Grant?

2. Was Eisenhower's seeming caution and inactivity a lack of vigorous leadership or a wise prudence in the exercise of power?

3. Was the 1950s a time of American triumph abroad and affluence at home, or was it a period that actually suppressed many problems of race, women's roles, and cultural conformity?

4. Which writers and artists best expressed the concerns of American culture in the 1950s? Was there a connection between the rise of pop-culture figures like Elvis Presley and Marilyn Monroe and the changes in art and writing (like the beats and the new southern writers)?

39

The Stormy Sixties, 1960–1968

CHAPTER THEMES

Theme: The Kennedy administration's "flexible response" doctrine to combat Third World communism bore ill fruit in Cuba and especially Vietnam. Johnson's massive escalation of the war failed to defeat the Communist Vietnamese forces, while growing domestic opposition finally forced him from power.

Theme: The Kennedy administration's domestic stalemate ended in the mid-1960s, as Johnson's Great Society and the black civil rights movement brought a tide of liberal social reform. But the diversion of resources and the social upheavals caused by the Vietnam War wrecked the Great Society.

CHAPTER SUMMARY

Kennedy's New Frontier initiatives bogged down in congressional stalemate. Cold War confrontations over Berlin and Russian missiles in Cuba created threats of war. Countering Third World communism through flexible response led the administration into dangerous involvement in Vietnam and elsewhere.

Johnson succeeded Kennedy and overwhelmingly defeated Goldwater. The black movement for integration and voting rights won great victories. Johnson used his huge congressional majorities to push through a mass of liberal Great Society legislation. Northern black ghettos erupted in violence amid calls for black power.

Johnson escalated military involvement in the Dominican Republic and Vietnam. As the number of troops and casualties grew without producing military success, dovish protests against the war gained strength. Political opposition forced Johnson not to seek reelection, and the deep Democratic divisions over the war allowed Nixon to win the White House.

DEVELOPING THE CHAPTER: SUGGESTED LECTURE OR DISCUSSION TOPICS

- Explain the Kennedy administration's vigorous activism in the Cold War, both against the Russians and against Third World communists. The emphasis might be on the contrast between relative success dealing with the Russians (for example, the Cuban missile crisis) versus frustration in the Third World (for example, the Bay of Pigs and Vietnam).

    REFERENCE: James N. Giglio, *The Presidency of John F. Kennedy* (1991).

- Examine the black movements of the sixties, from civil rights to black power, perhaps focusing on the fact that the nonviolent movement's great successes in integration and voting rights were not considered adequate by those trapped in northern black ghettos.

    REFERENCE: Harvard Sitkoff, *The Struggle for Black Equality, 1954–1980* (1981).

- Describe the escalation of the Vietnam War. Explain the political as well as the military side of the war (for example, the constant fear that the Saigon government would collapse if the United States did not provide greater support).

    REFERENCE: Stanley Karnow, *Vietnam: A History* (1983); Marilyn B. Young, *The Vietnam Wars, 1945–1990* (1991).

- Consider the domestic political and social turmoil of the sixties, brought on by social and cultural upheavals as well as Vietnam. Point out the deep polarization of American society, as evidenced by the turbulent events of 1968.

    REFERENCE: Allen Matusow, *The Unraveling of America* (1984); Maurice Isserman and Michael Kazin, *America Divided: The Civil War of the 1960s* (2000).

FOR FURTHER INTEREST: ADDITIONAL CLASS TOPICS

- Focus on the "Kennedy image." Compare the vision of "Camelot" with the historical realities of Kennedy's performance as president and controversies over his private behavior and character.

- Use Martin Luther King Jr.'s life and work to explain the principles of the nonviolent civil rights movement. Perhaps show how King came under assault from some whites and blacks during his lifetime for being either too militant or not militant enough.

- Discuss the causes and consequences of the Vietnam War. Consider why it so divided American society.

- Examine the cultural rebellions of the 1960s in relation to traditional American values like distrust of authority and individualism. Examine the "sexual revolution" and the changes in the family as they impacted broader issues of public authority and the role of institutions like the school and church.

CHARACTER SKETCHES

Lyndon Baines Johnson (1908–1973)

Johnson was a highly skilled Senate majority leader in the 1950s and was frustrated by his powerlessness as Kennedy's vice president.

The son of a flamboyant Texas state senator, Lyndon often joined him amid the colorful, corrupt atmosphere of Austin. Johnson's first venture into politics came at San Marcos Teachers' College, where he formed a student political group, the White Stars, to take control of campus activities and jobs from a rival group, the Black Stars.

Johnson briefly taught high school in Houston and organized successful student debate teams that traveled all over the state. He became a congressional assistant in Washington and learned to imitate the congressman's voice on the phone well enough to carry on extensive conversations with callers.

Roosevelt treated Johnson as a special young protégé and invited him to go sailing as a particular favor. Johnson lost his first senate race in 1941 but won his next try in 1948 by 87 votes—a result that earned him the nickname "Landslide Lyndon."

Quote: "I knew from the start that I was bound to be crucified either way I moved. If I left the woman I loved—the Great Society—in order to get involved with that bitch of a war on the other side of the world, then I would lose everything at home. All my programs, all my dreams. But if I left that war and let the communists take over South Vietnam, then I would be seen as a coward and my nation would be seen as an appeaser and we would find it impossible to accomplish anything for anyone anywhere on the entire globe." (Conversation, 1970)

REFERENCE: Robert Dallek, *Lone Star Rising: Lyndon Johnson and His Times, 1908–1960* (1991).

Martin Luther King, Jr. (1928–1968)

King was much criticized in his lifetime, but in 1986 his birthday began to be celebrated as a national holiday—the first such honor given to a black American.

He came from a long line of Baptist preachers. His father, Martin Luther King, Sr., was pastor at Ebenezer Baptist church in Atlanta, and Martin, Jr., was for a time copastor with him.

King and his wife, Coretta Scott, both came from the middle-class Atlanta black community. He experienced sharper discrimination when he went north to study theology. King earned his doctorate from Boston University with a dissertation on the doctrine of God and also studied the nonviolent teachings of Gandhi. Later he and his wife visited India to learn more about Gandhian techniques.

During King's civil rights campaign in Chicago in 1966, he lived in a ghetto slum on the West Side. His outspoken attacks on the Vietnam War caused considerable criticism that he was not sticking to civil rights issues. At the time of his assassination, he was conducting a campaign for black garbage workers in Memphis.

Quote: "When we let freedom ring, when we let it ring from every village and every hamlet, from every state and every city, we will be able to speed up that day when all of God's children, black men and white men, Jews and Gentiles, Protestants and Catholics, will be able to join hands and sing in the words of that old Negro spiritual, 'Free at last! Free at last! Thank God almighty, we are free at last!' " ("I Have a Dream" speech, 1963)

REFERENCE: David L. Garrow, *Bearing the Cross*: *Martin Luther King and the Southern Christian Leadership Conference* (1986).

John Fitzgerald Kennedy (1917–1963)

Kennedy achieved a narrow victory in 1960 and for most of his time in office had to battle for political support, but after his assassination he entered the pantheon of national heroes.

Through much of his youth, Kennedy struggled to compete with his more athletic and glamorous older brother, Joseph Kennedy, Jr. After Joe's combat death in World War II, John took his place as the focus of his father's ambitions for the presidency.

Kennedy's Harvard senior thesis was published as a book, *Why England Slept,* with the aid of his father. During his youth, Kennedy was often seriously ill with back troubles compounded by Addison's disease, which was thought to be life-threatening. In 1954 he underwent major back surgery and missed the Senate vote censuring Joseph McCarthy.

Kennedy was cool, skeptical, sardonic, and well read. He had a reputation as a playboy but was also a sober, well-disciplined, determined politician who used his abilities to the fullest.

Quote: "Let the word go forth from this time and place, to friend and foe alike, that the torch has been passed to a new generation of Americans, born in this century, tempered by war, disciplined by a hard and bitter peace, proud of our ancient heritage, and unwilling to witness or permit the slow undoing of those human rights to which this nation has always been committed, and to which we are committed today at home and throughout the world." (Inaugural address, 1961)

REFERENCES: Herbert Parmet, *Jack: The Struggles of John F. Kennedy* (1980); *JFK: The Presidency of John F. Kennedy* (1983); Thomas Reeves, *A Question of Character: A Life of John Kennedy* (1991).

Robert Francis Kennedy (1925–1968)

Kennedy was the younger brother of President John Kennedy who became a leader of the anti–Vietnam War movement before his assassination during the presidential campaign of 1968.

The third of the Kennedy brothers, Robert had great difficulty keeping up with his older, favored brothers Joseph, Jr., and John. For much of his political career he operated in the background as John Kennedy's political manager and adviser.

Kennedy was long distrusted by liberals because of his association with Senator Joseph McCarthy, and by labor because of his involvement with Senate committees investigating union racketeering. During his years as attorney general (1961–1964), he carried on a fierce prosecution of Teamster boss James Hoffa and eventually saw him convicted.

Kennedy became deeply depressed after his brother's assassination, but revived once he resigned as attorney general and won election as U.S. senator from New York in 1964. He disliked Johnson intensely, but at first hesitated to break with him because he thought Johnson would regard Kennedy's antiwar position as a purely personal vendetta.

Quote: "Few will have the greatness to bend history itself, but each of us can work to change a small portion of events, and in the total of all those acts will be written the history of this generation." (*To Seek a Newer World,* 1967)

REFERENCE: Arthur M. Schlesinger, Jr., *Robert F. Kennedy and His Times* (1978).

GREAT DEBATES IN AMERICAN HISTORY

GREAT DEBATE (1961–1973): Vietnam. Should the United States fight a major war in Vietnam in order to save the anticommunist government of South Vietnam from falling to the Communist Vietnamese?

Yes: Vietnam "hawks," led by President Johnson and his administration; the Cold War foreign-policy establishment; many political conservatives, led by Barry Goldwater and Richard Nixon; many labor groups, led by George Meany.

No: Vietnam "doves," led by Senators Morse, Fulbright, and McCarthy; some foreign-policy experts, led by George Kennan, Walter Lippmann, and Hans Morgenthau; many students and other young people.

ISSUE #1: Should the United States fight a war to preserve freedom and independence for the South Vietnamese anticommunists?

Yes: "Hawk" President Johnson: "The first reality is that North Vietnam has attacked the independent nation of South Vietnam. Its object is total conquest....Women and children are strangled in the night because their men are loyal to their government. And helpless villages are ravaged by sneak attack....Our objective is the independence of South Vietnam and its freedom from attack. We want nothing for ourselves—only that the people of South Vietnam be allowed to guide their country in their own way."

No: "Dove" journalist Neil Sheehan: "The regimes [of South Vietnam] were and are composed of men...who are allied with mandarin families....Most of the men who rule Saigon have, like the Bourbons, learned nothing and forgotten nothing. They seek to retain what privileges they have and to regain those they have lost....The Communist party is the one truly national organization that permeates both North and South Vietnam. The men who lead the party today...directed the struggle for independence from France and in the process captured much of the deeply felt nationalism of the Vietnamese people."

ISSUE #2: Should the United States fight a war in Vietnam to prevent the spread of communism to the rest of Asia and beyond?

Yes: "Hawk" President Johnson: "Let no one suppose that a retreat from Vietnam would bring an end to conflict. The battle would be renewed in one country and then another. The central lesson of our time is that the appetite of aggression is never satisfied....There are those who say that all our effort there will be futile—that China's power is such that it is bound to dominate all Southeast Asia. But there is no end to that argument until all of the nations of Asia are swallowed up."

No: "Dove" Senator J. William Fulbright: "The war is described as an exemplary war, a war, that is, that will prove to the communists once and for all that so-called 'wars of national liberation' cannot succeed. In fact, we are not proving that. It is said that if we were not fighting in Vietnam we would have to be fighting much closer to home, in Hawaii or even California. I regard this contention as a slander on the U.S. Navy and Air Force....I do not accept your [Secretary Rusk's] version as to why there may be an intrusion of communist forces into Thailand....As long as the war is going on, isn't this fact an incitement to intrusion by the other side?"

ISSUE #3: Should the United States fight a war in Vietnam to fulfill the commitments it has made and preserve its national credibility as a great power?

Yes: "Hawk" President Johnson: "Our power, therefore, is a very vital shield. If we are driven from the field in Vietnam, then no nation can ever again have the same confidence in American promise or American protection....Three Presidents—President Eisenhower, President Kennedy, and your present President—over 11 years have committed themselves and have promised to defend this small and valiant nation....We just cannot now dishonor our word, or abandon our commitment, or leave those who believed us and trusted us to the terror and repression and murder that would follow."

No: "Dove" Senator Stuart Symington: "I believe what is going on now in Vietnam has hurt the concept of our capability in the minds of our friends and allies as well as our enemies. It has hurt the national will in this country because of increasing dissension and I am afraid it has made the people who are opposed to us reduce their belief in our capacity."

ISSUE #4: Are the goals in Vietnam worth the cost to the United States of fighting the war?

Yes: "Hawk" President Johnson: "Peace will come also because America sent her sons to help secure it. It has not been easy—far from it....I have lived daily and nightly with the cost of this war. I know the pain it has inflicted....Throughout this entire long period, I have been sustained by a single principle: that what we are doing now, in Vietnam, is vital not only to the security of Southeast Asia, but it is vital to the security of every American....I believe the men who endure the dangers of battle...are helping the entire world avoid far greater conflicts, far wider wars, far more destructive than this one."

No: "Dove" Senator Joseph Clark: "Vietnam is a cancer which is devouring our youth, our morals, our national wealth, and the energies of our leadership. The casualty list from this war only begins on the battlefield. As victims we must count the programs of the Great Society, the balance of payments, a sound budget, a stable dollar, the world's good will, détente with the Soviet Union, and hopes for a durable world peace. The toll of this war can never be measured in terms of lives lost and dollars spent—they are only the tip of a vast iceberg whose bulk can never be accurately measured."

REFERENCES: Marilyn B. Young, *The Vietnam Wars, 1945–1990* (1991); Jeffrey P. Kimball, ed., *To Reason Why: The Debate About the Causes of U.S. Involvement in the Vietnam War* (1990).

QUESTIONS FOR CLASS DISCUSSION

1. Did Kennedy fulfill his promise to "get America moving again"? Why or why not?

2. Was the nonviolent civil rights movement of the 1960s a success? Why or why not?

3. What were the causes of the Vietnam War?

4. Were the cultural upheavals of the 1960s a result of the political crisis, or were developments like the sexual revolution and the student revolts inevitable results of affluence and the "baby boom"?

EXPANDING THE "VARYING VIEWPOINTS"

- Todd Gitlin, *The Sixties: Years of Hope, Days of Rage* (1987).

    A view of "the sixties" as fundamentally constructive:

    "Say what we will about the Sixties' failures, limits, disasters, America's political and cultural space would probably not have opened up as much as it did without the movement's divine delirium....This side of an ever-receding millennium, the changes wrought by the Sixties, however beleaguered, averted some of the worst abuses of power, and made life more decent for millions. The movement in its best moments and broadest definition made philosophical breakthroughs which are still working themselves out."

- William O'Neill, *Coming Apart* (1971).

    A view of "the sixties" as fundamentally destructive:

    "Though much in the counter-culture was attractive and valuable, it was dangerous in three ways. First, self-indulgence frequently led to self-destruction. Second, the counter-culture increased social hostility. The generation gap was one example, but the class gap another. Working-class youngsters resented the counter-culture. The counter-culture flourished in cities and on campuses. Elsewhere, in Middle America, it was hated and feared. The result was a national division between the counter-culture and those adults who admired or tolerated it, and the silent majority of workers and Middle Americans who didn't. The tensions between these groups made solving social and political problems all the more difficult and were, indeed, part of the problem. Finally, the counter-culture was hell on standards."

40

The Stalemated Seventies, 1968–1980

CHAPTER THEMES

Theme: As the war in Vietnam finally came to a disastrous conclusion, the United States struggled to create a more stable international climate. Détente with the two communist powers temporarily reduced Cold War tensions, but trouble in the Middle East threatened America's energy supplies and economic stability.

Theme: Weakened by political difficulties of their own and others' making, the administrations of the 1970s had trouble coping with America's growing economic problems. The public also had trouble facing up to a sharp sense of limits and a general disillusionment with society. With the notable exception of the highly successful feminist movement, the social reform efforts of the 1960s fractured and stalled, as the country settled into a frustrating and politically divisive stalemate.

CHAPTER SUMMARY

Nixon's "Vietnamization" policy reduced American ground participation in the war, but his Cambodia invasion sparked massive protest. Nixon's journeys to Communist Moscow and Beijing (Peking) established a new rapprochement with these powers. In domestic policy, Nixon and the Supreme Court promoted affirmative action and environmental protection.

The 1972 election victory and the cease-fire in Vietnam were negated when Nixon became bogged down in the Watergate scandal and congressional protest over the secret bombing of Cambodia, which led to the War Powers Act. The Middle East War of 1973 and the Arab oil embargo created energy and economic difficulties that lasted through the decade. Americans gradually awoke to their costly and dangerous dependence on Middle Eastern oil, and began to take tentative steps toward conservation and alternative energy sources.

Nonelected Gerald Ford took over after Watergate forced Nixon to resign. The Communist Vietnamese finally overran the South Vietnamese government in 1975. The defeat in Vietnam added to a general sense of disillusionment with society and a new sense of limits on American power. The civil rights movement fractured, and divisive issues of busing and affirmative action enhanced racial tensions. The most successful social movement was feminism, which achieved widespread social breakthroughs though failing to pass the Equal Rights Amendment.

Campaigning against Washington and Watergate, outsider Jimmy Carter proved unable to master Congress or the economy once he took office. The Camp David agreement brought peace between Egypt and Israel, but the Iranian revolution led to new energy troubles. The invasion of Afghanistan and the holding of American hostages in Iran added to Carter's woes.

DEVELOPING THE CHAPTER: SUGGESTED LECTURE OR DISCUSSION TOPICS

- Examine Nixon's domestic policies, including his corruption and resignation after Watergate. Explain the connection between the immediate Watergate scandal and the wider attacks on "the imperial presidency" as reflected in, for example, the War Powers Act.

    REFERENCES: Stephen Ambrose, *Nixon* (1989); Stanley Kutler, *The Wars of Watergate* (1990).

- Analyze the ebb and flow of American foreign policy in the seventies, from Nixon's Moscow-Beijing (Peking) visits to Afghanistan. Particular attention might be paid to the difficulties in implementing Kissinger's plans for a stabilizing agreement among the three great powers in a still-volatile world, and to Jimmy Carter's attempt to bring a stronger moral dimension to American foreign relations.

    REFERENCE: Robert D. Schulzinger, *Henry Kissinger: Doctor of Diplomacy* (1989); Gaddis Smith, *Morality, Reason, and Power* (1986).

- Explain the closely interrelated problems of the Middle East, energy, and economics in the seventies, perhaps focusing on the way America's growing economic difficulties made it more vulnerable to Middle East events, which in turn added to economic trouble. Consider the U.S. crisis with Iran in relation to the general political tensions of the region.

    REFERENCE: Michael B. Stoff, *Oil, War and American Security* (1980); James Bill, *The Eagle and the Lion: The Tragedy of American-Iranian Relations* (1987).

- Examine the reasons for the successes of American feminism at a time when most social movements spawned in the 1960s had fragmented and lost broader public appeal. Consider the relationship between more liberal or radical feminist activists who actively promoted social and culture changes and the large numbers of American women who entered the workforce and altered family roles even if they were not politically engaged.

    REFERENCE: Susan M. Hartmann, *The Other Feminists: Activists in the Liberal Establishment* (1998).

FOR FURTHER INTEREST: ADDITIONAL CLASS TOPICS

- Focus on Nixon and Watergate. Consider whether Watergate was in the end a victory for democracy or whether it created national cynicism about leaders and weakened Americans' faith in democracy and the presidency.

- Examine the rise of the environmental movement. Consider the relations of environmental concerns to economic issues in the 1970s, including oil and other energy sources.

- Consider the origins of the conflicts over busing and affirmative action. Explain how the broad American consensus in favor of civil rights, voting rights, integration, and economic opportunity fell apart on the questions of positive government action to advance African-Americans' economic and political standing.

- Discuss the Iranian revolution in relation to the rise of militant Islam in the Middle East. Consider why Americans (including government officials) had such difficulty comprehending Islamic fundamentalism.

CHARACTER SKETCHES

Richard Nixon (1913–1994)

Nixon was the most controversial politician of his generation and has remained a source of intrigue and puzzlement for scholars and the public.

The second of five sons of a devout Quaker family, Nixon was third in his class of twenty-five at Duke Law School. He wanted to be an FBI agent but instead became a local California attorney and later joined the Office of Price Administration and the navy.

He defeated Jerry Voorhis, a prominent New Deal Democratic congressman, in 1946 and won national fame for his work on the Hiss case. His 1950 campaign against Helen Gahagan Douglas was dominated by his red-baiting charges against her.

Thomas Dewey promoted Nixon for the vice presidency in 1952. His 1962 defeat for the California governorship was generally considered to have marked the end of his political career, so his recovery to win the 1968 GOP nomination was nearly miraculous.

Quote: "You won't have Nixon to kick around anymore, because gentlemen, this is my last press conference." (Press conference after election loss, 1962)

REFERENCE: Joan Hoff Wilson, *Nixon Reconsidered* (1994); Rachel Barron, *Richard Nixon* (1999).

Henry Kissinger (1923–   )

At the height of his power in the 1970s, Kissinger exercised more influence over American foreign policy than any secretary of state since George Marshall, and perhaps since William Seward.

Born in southern Germany, the son of a high school teacher, Heinz Kissinger (his original name) was frequently beaten up by anti-Semitic gangs. His father lost his job, and the family was forced to flee to the United States in 1938. Many writers have seen a connection between the instability of Kissinger's youth and his strong pursuit of order and stability in international relations.

His family never fully assimilated to America, and Kissinger retained his thick German accent throughout his life. In the U.S. Army he became a translator and eventually administered a small district in occupied Germany.

His book *Nuclear Weapons and Foreign Policy* (1957), which advocated the use of limited nuclear weapons, brought him to the attention of Nelson Rockefeller and began his career as an influential foreign-policy and defense theorist.

Quote: "The deepest international conflict in the world today is not between us and the Soviet Union, but between the Soviet Union and Communist China....Therefore, one of the positive prospects in the current situation is that, whatever the basic intentions of Soviet leaders, confronted with the prospect of a China growing in strength...they may want a period of détente in the West."

REFERENCE: Walter Isaacson, *Kissinger: A Biography* (1993).

Sam Ervin (1896–1985)

Ervin was the North Carolina senator who gained fame for heading the Senate Watergate investigations.

After growing up in rural North Carolina, Ervin was wounded and decorated for valor in World War I and earned a Harvard law degree in 1922. He helped defeat a North Carolina law banning the teaching of evolution. He was also a longtime judge and U.S. congressman.

Ervin was considered the Senate's most noted authority on the U.S. Constitution and was a strong advocate of civil liberties and legal rights for the indigent.

His bobbing eyebrows, thick jowls, and down-home sense of humor made him a popular hero during the Watergate hearings. He had a vast fund of quotations from the Bible, Shakespeare, English history, and American constitutional history at his command and often used them to enliven the proceedings. Although he always called himself a "simple country lawyer," he was in fact a highly learned and skilled jurist.

Quote: "As long as I have a mind to think, a tongue to speak, and a heart to love my country, I shall deny that the Constitution confers any autocratic power on the President, or authorizes him to convert George Washington's America into Caesar's Rome....When all is said, the only sure antidote for future Watergates is understanding of fundamental principles and intellectual and moral integrity in the men and women who achieve or are entrusted with governmental or political power." (*Report of Senate Watergate Committee*, 1974)

REFERENCE: Dick Dabney, *A Good Man: The Life of Sam Ervin* (1976).

QUESTIONS FOR CLASS DISCUSSION

1. Could any of Nixon's achievements in office compensate for his Watergate crimes?

2. What were the short- and long-term consequences of the communists' victory in Vietnam? How do these affect an assessment of the war?

3. How was the civil rights movement affected by federal policies in the 1970s, especially affirmative action?

4. What were the consequences of America's new economic vulnerability? How did it affect politics at home and abroad during the 1970s?

MAKERS OF AMERICA: THE VIETNAMESE

Questions for Class Discussion

1. How do the Vietnamese immigrants fit into the long tradition of immigration to America? How did the particular conditions of their initial migration—the loss of an unpopular war—affect their entry into American society?

2. In what ways do the Vietnamese-Americans appear to be preserving their traditions? In what ways might they likely adapt their traditions to American conditions, as previous immigrant groups have done?

Suggested Student Exercises

- Compare the experience of the Vietnamese with other immigrants from Asia (e.g., the Chinese (Chapter 24), the Filipinos (Chapter 30), and the Japanese (Chapter 38). Consider whether the term "Asian-American" is too broad to describe all these groups.

- Given the history of earlier immigrant groups, consider what issues will likely face the Vietnamese-American communities in the near future. Examine whether there is a "natural" generational transition that can be expected to affect the children and grandchildren of those who have immigrated.

MAKERS OF AMERICA: THE FEMINISTS

Questions for Class Discussion:

1. In what ways is the feminists movement similar to other movements for equality and social justice in American history (e.g., the abolitionist movement, the labor movement, and the civil rights movement), and in what ways is it different? How is feminism affected by the fact that most women have intense personal relationships with men?

2. What are the roots of the disagreements between "equal rights" feminism and those feminists who advocate attention to "gender difference"? What are the implications of each position for government policy (e.g., regarding workplace protections, regulation of pornography, or separate-sex education)?

Suggested Student Exercises

- Select one nineteenth century or early twentieth century women's leader (e.g., Lucretia Mott, Frances Willard, Jane Addams, or Charlotte Perkins Gilman), and compare and contrast their ideas about women's issues and roles in society with that of a prominent "second wave" feminist leader (e.g., Betty Friedan, Gloria Steinem, Bella Abzug, Catherine Mackinnon). Consider which differences are due to the different times in which they lived, and which reflect underlying philosophical disagreeements about gender and society.

- Trace the changing numbers and roles of women in the U.S. Congress from the 1950s to the present. Examine a few female representatives' and senators' careers and voting records to uncover their relationship to the visible feminist movement. (Perhaps compare two female officials from different party affiliations or different regions of the country.)

41

The Resurgence of Conservatism, 1980–2000

CHAPTER THEMES

Theme: Leading a conservative movement to power in Washington, Ronald Reagan vigorously pursued "new right" economic and social policies. Under Reagan and his successor George Bush, these policies brought both economic growth and massive budget deficits that put severe constraints on the federal government.

Theme: The 1980s saw a revival of Cold War confrontation, but the decade ended with the collapse of Communism, first in Eastern Europe and then in the Soviet Union itself. With the end of the Cold War and the U.S.-led victory over Iraq in the Persian Gulf War, America remained the world's only superpower. A series of relatively small military interventions in the Caribbean, Africa, and the Balkans raised questions about the proper use of American force in the underdeveloped world.

Theme: Elected as the first baby-boom president, Bill Clinton tried to turn the Democratic party in a more centrist direction. Ideological conflicts and sharp partisan battles in the 1990s were partly overshadowed by a booming economy and America's search to define its role in the increasingly global economy and system of international relations.

CHAPTER SUMMARY

Reagan led Republicans to sweeping victories in 1980 and 1984 over divided and demoralized Democrats. Riding a conservative national tide, Reagan pushed both his "supply-side" economic program of lower taxes and the "new-right" social policies, especially opposition to affirmative action, abortion, and drugs. These policies brought economic recovery and lower inflation, as well as record budget deficits that severely restricted "big government." The Supreme Court under Reagan and his successor, George Bush, became increasingly conservative, while the confirmation hearings of Justice Clarence Thomas highlighted issues of sexual harassment.

Reagan revived the Cold War confrontation with the Soviet Union, and engaged the United States in assertive military support for anti-leftist forces in Latin America and elsewhere. The ratcheting up of military spending, along with the attempted reforms led by Mikhail Gorbachev, contributed to the unraveling of Communism in Eastern Europe and the Soviet Union in 1989–1991. With America as the only remaining superpower, George Bush led an international coalition to victory in the Persian Gulf War, but the Middle East remained a dangerous tinderbox despite new efforts to resolve the Israel-Arab conflict.

The dynamic young "baby-boomer" Bill Clinton defeated Bush in 1992, and promoted an ambitious reform agenda within the context of his centrist "new Democrat" ideology. Clinton's stumbles over health care reform and foreign policy opened the door to aggressive conservative Republicans, who gained control of Congress in 1994 for the first time in fifty years advocating a "contract with America." But the Newt Gingrich-led Republicans' over-reaching enabled Clinton to revive and win a second term in 1996.

In his second term, Clinton downplayed reform and successfully claimed the political middle ground on issues like welfare reform, affirmative action, smoking, and gun control. A booming economy created budget surpluses, and encouraged Clinton's efforts toward ending international trade barriers. Conflicts in the Middle East and the Balkans led to American diplomatic and military involvements, with mixed results. A series of scandals, culminating in the Monica Lewinsky affair, led to Clinton's impeachment and acquittal in 1999. Texas Governor George Walker Bush defeated Clinton's vice president, Al Gore, in a contested cliffhanging election that was finally decided by a Supreme Court decision.

DEVELOPING THE CHAPTER: SUGGESTED LECTURE OR DISCUSSION TOPICS

- Describe the rise of conservatism in the 1980s. Explain Reagan's unique ability to link economic, social-policy, and foreign policy conservative principles into a potent political coalition. Discuss the successes and failures of Reagan's "supply-side" economics, as well as the ideological polarization of America's "culture wars."

    REFERENCE: William C. Berman, *America's Right Turn: From Nixon to Bush* (1994).

- Explain the revival of the Cold War in the 1980s. Examine the relation between American policies and the internal changes within the Soviet bloc, culminating in the collapse of Communism, the reunification of Germany, and the dissolution of the Soviet Union. Include consideration of the new problems for the United States created by the breakup of Communism in places like the former Soviet Union and the former Yugoslavia.

    REFERENCE: Theodore Draper, *The Devil We Knew: Americans and the Cold War* (1993).

- Examine the increasing importance of religion in American politics and culture in the 1980s and 1990s. Include consideration of both the "religious right" and evangelical movements, as well as other religious voices like those of the Catholic Church, the black churches, and rapidly growing religious groups like American Muslims and Buddhists affiliated with the immigration boom of the period.

    REFERENCES: Garry Wills, *Under God: Religion and American Politics* (1990); James Davidson Hunger, *Culture Wars: The Struggle to Define America* (1991).

- Examine the ideas and politics of Bill Clinton in relation to the changed ideological climate of the 1990s. Consider how Clinton attempted to steer a middle course between the more aggressively conservative Republicans and his own party's traditional liberal base on issues like welfare, social security, civil rights, and the environment.

    REFERENCE: James MacGregor Burns and Georgia Sorenson, *Dead Center: Clinton-Gore Leadership and the Politics of Moderation* (1999).

FOR FURTHER INTEREST: ADDITIONAL CLASS TOPICS

- Focus on Reagan as personality and political leader. Discuss why his personal popularity seemed to transcend his politically controversial policies, and what legacy he left to the Republican party and American politics generally.

- Examine the growing role of women and women's issues in the politics of the 1980s and 1990s. Consider the increasing impact of women in public and political life, perhaps by examining the careers of prominent figures such as Sandra Day O'Connor, Dianne Feinstein, Hillary Rodham Clinton, and Ruth Bader Ginsburg.

- Discuss the new importance of the "Third World" in American foreign policy of the 1980s and 1990s. The involvement of the United States in the underdeveloped world can be considered in relation to both military issues (e.g., the Latin American civil wars of the 1980s and the Persian Gulf War), as well as economic issues involving NAFTA and trade with countries like Mexico and China.

- Compare Clinton's impeachment and trial to that of Andrew Johnson in the 1860s. Focus on the parallel claims that the impeachment was fundamentally motivated by partisan spite and personal disdain for the president, as well as on the substantial differences in the political circumstances and in the charges themselves.

CHARACTER SKETCHES

Edward Kennedy (1932–)

Kennedy is a Massachusetts senator and heir to the Kennedy legacy in American politics.

The ninth child and fourth son of the family, Kennedy was indulged by his father and not pushed into competitive activities as the older children had been.

In his freshman year at Harvard, Kennedy was expelled for having someone else take a Spanish exam for him. He later returned to graduate from Harvard and the University of Virginia Law School.

His first run for the Senate came in 1962, only a few days after his thirtieth birthday, and provoked much criticism. But he conducted a successful campaign with the slogan "He can do more for Massachusetts."

The 1969 accident at Chappaquiddick Island, in which a young woman drowned, has remained Kennedy's greatest political liability. He was most sharply criticized not for the accident, but for his failure to report it until the next morning and for his unconvincing explanations of the events surrounding it.

Quote: "I understand that people feel strongly about me, as they felt about my brothers before me….[Some] people have been enthusiastic supporters, and others have been harsh critics. I would expect that to be the case as long as I'm in public life." (1974)

REFERENCE: James MacGregor Burns, *Edward Kennedy and the Camelot Legacy* (1976).

Ronald Reagan (1911–)

The oldest president before Reagan was Eisenhower, who was about seventy when he left office; Reagan was that age when he first took office.

Reagan's unemployed father worked for a time for Roosevelt's WPA program. As a youthful lifeguard, Reagan saved over seventy people from drowning, and he was amazed that many of them later criticized him and claimed that they had not been in danger.

His break into movies came in 1937, when Warner Brothers signed him to a seven-year contract for $200 a week. In the movie *King's Row* (1941), he played an amputee who said, "Where's the rest of me?" Reagan used this line as the title of his 1965 autobiography.

His involvement with many liberal causes continued until the late 1940s, when he took the lead in driving communists from the Screen Actors Guild. His second marriage, to the daughter of a politically conservative doctor, also helped turn him into a staunch conservative.

Reagan first won national political attention for a speech on behalf of Barry Goldwater in 1964. His first try for the presidency came in 1968, when he lost the nomination to Nixon.

Quote: "Either we accept the responsibility for our own destiny, or we abandon the American Revolution and confess that an intellectual belief in a far-distant capital can plan our lives for us better than we can plan them for ourselves. You and I have a rendezvous with destiny. We can preserve for our children this last best hope of man on earth or we can sentence them to take the first step into a thousand years of darkness." (1964)

REFERENCE: Lou Cannon, *President Reagan: The Role of a Lifetime* (1992).

Sandra Day O'Connor (1930–)

O'Connor is the Arizona judge who became the first woman U.S. Supreme Court justice.

Her childhood was spent on a ranch in Arizona. At Stanford Law School, Chief Justice William Rehnquist was first in her law class, and she was third.

She served as an assistant attorney general and was elected to two terms in the Arizona state senate, where she became majority leader. A Democratic governor appointed her to the state appeals court in 1979.

In her early days on the Supreme Court, O'Connor was considered a conservative who almost always followed the lead of Justices Rehnquist and Powell. She showed an independent streak, however, in breaking with them on some civil rights and civil liberties issues. She also began as a strong critic of the *Roe* v. *Wade* abortion decision and was widely expected to join other Reagan-Bush appointees in a new majority to overturn it. But in *Casey* v. *Planned Parenthood* and recent decisions, O'Connor sided with two other justices (David Souter and Anthony Kennedy) in upholding *Roe,* while accepting various state restrictions on abortion. In the 1990s, O'Connor was usually the key "swing vote" on the Court, especially on issues of affirmative action and abortion.

Quote: "Our decisions...establish that the party seeking to uphold a statute that classifies individuals on the basis of their gender must carry the burden of showing an 'exceedingly persuasive justification' for the classification....That this statute discriminates against males rather than females does not exempt it from scrutiny or reduce the standard of review." (Opinion in *Mississippi University for Women* v. *Hogan,* 1982)

REFERENCE: Vincent Blasi, ed., *The Burger Court* (1983).

George Herbert Walker Bush (1924–)

George Bush is the longtime Republican politician who won the presidency as Ronald Reagan's successor in 1988 but lost his bid for reelection in 1992.

Bush was the son of wealthy Connecticut senator Prescott Bush. His private-school and Ivy League education at Yale were long seen as political handicaps, but he counteracted them by emphasizing his World War II service in the navy and such down-home pursuits as eating pork rinds and pitching horseshoes.

During Bush's youthful oil-business career, and his two terms in Congress as a representative from the Houston area, he formed strong alliances with the Texas business community. An associate from those days, James Baker, became his closest political ally and later served as his secretary of state.

Bush held a long series of appointed positions—chairman of the Republican party, head of the CIA, ambassador to China—before becoming Reagan's vice president. Bush's extensive foreign-policy experience led him to focus his administration on international rather than domestic affairs, at considerable political cost. In the 1988 election and afterward, Bush denied any knowledge or involvement in the Iran-contra affair, although other Reagan officials, among them George Schulz and Caspar Weinberger, maintained that Bush was not "out of the loop."

After his defeat in 1992, Bush retired to Texas. His son, George Bush, Jr., was elected governor of Texas in 1994 and president in 2000.

Quote: "We are not the sum of our possessions. They are not the measure of our lives. In our hearts we know what matters. We must give [our children] a sense of what it means to be a loyal friend, a loving parent, a citizen who leaves his home, neighborhood, and town better than he found it." (Inaugural address, 1989)

REFERENCE: Peter Golman and Tom Matthew, *The Quest for the Presidency, 1988* (1989). Bill Minutaglio, *First Son: George W. Bush and the Bush Family Dynasty* (1999).

William ("Bill") Jefferson Clinton, (1946–   )

Bill Clinton served many terms as Arkansas governor before being elected the nation's forty-second president in 1992.

Clinton was born William Blythe in Arkansas. His father died in an automobile accident before Bill was born, and after his mother remarried, Bill took her new husband's last name. Perhaps the most decisive event in Clinton's early life was winning a scholarship to Georgetown University, a Catholic university in Washington, D.C. He so impressed some of his teachers that they suggested that he might consider becoming a priest, until he told them that he was a Southern Baptist.

After graduation from Georgetown in 1968, Clinton won a Rhodes Scholarship to study politics at Britain's Oxford University. After graduation from Yale University Law School, Clinton returned to Arkansas in 1973 to teach at the University of Arkansas Law School. In 1975 he married Hillary Rodham, a fellow Yale Law graduate and Arkansas law professor. Clinton ran for Congress in 1974 but lost to a popular Republican. In 1976 he won election as attorney general of Arkansas.

At the time of his election as chief executive of Arkansas in 1978, Clinton was the nation's youngest governor. He lost a race for reelection but regained the office in 1982 and every two years thereafter until his election as president.

Quote: "We are on the verge of a new way of doing things, grounded in our most enduring values, a philosophy that says America owes all of us an opportunity if we will assume responsibility for ourselves, our community, and our country. No more something for nothing. We're all in this together." (Speech, July 1993)

REFERENCE: David Maraniss, *First in His Class* (1994).

George Walker Bush (1946–)

The presidency of the United States is only the second public office to which George W. Bush was elected, after the governorship of Texas.

George W. Bush was born in New Haven, Connecticut, and moved with his family to Texas at the age of two. He is the oldest of five living children (four boys and one girl) of George H.W. Bush and Barbara Bush (another girl died of leukemia in 1953 at age 3). While his father was a rising star in Republican politics, George W. attended Philips Andover Academy in Massachusetts and Yale University, graduating in 1968. After several years of dissolution, drifting, unemployment, and occasional political work in Texas, Alabama, and Florida, he entered Harvard University, earning a Master of Business Administration degree in 1975.

He then moved to the west Texas town of Midland, and married a school librarian, Laura Welch. His younger brother Jeb, now governor of Florida, was considered the future politician of the family, while George W.'s talents were widely disregarded. This judgment seemed confirmed when he ran for Congress from Midland in 1978, but lost to the Democrat.

The several oil business ventures he attempted, the Arbusto and Spectrum Companies, were not very successful either, but earned enough, along with family support, for him to become the lead investor in buying the Texas Rangers baseball team for $600,000 in 1988 (he eventually sold his share a decade later for $15 million).

In 1986 he underwent a "born again" religious conversion, and moved from his family's traditional Episcopal faith into the Methodist Church. In 1994 Bush was nominated by the Republicans to run against the popular Democratic Texas governor Ann Richards, and his victory was considered a great upset. His re-election victory with 65% of the vote propelled him into the leading position for the Republican presidential nomination in 2000.

Quote: "Our country has been through a long and trying period, with the outcome of the presidential election not finalized for longer than any of us could imagine…I believe things happen for a reason, and I hope the wait of the last five weeks will heighten a desire to move beyond the bitterness and partisanship of the recent past." (Victory speech, December 13, 2000).

QUESTIONS FOR CLASS DISCUSSION

1. To what extent was the election of Reagan an endorsement of his conservative ideology, and to what extent was it a repudiation of the perceived failures of federal government policies in the stalemated 1970s?

2. In what ways might the 1980s and 1990s be compared with the 1920s in economic, social, and foreign policies? Did the economic boom of each period represent a genuine revival of American innovation, or was it fundamentally marred by the growing gap between rich and poor?

3. What were the successes and failures of American foreign policy in the post-Cold War era? Was the use of American military power in the Persian Gulf War and the Balkans a model for how American power could be effectively brought to bear, or did it demonstrate the limits of even the sole superpower's ability to resolve regional conflicts?

4. What is likely to be the enduring legacy of Bill Clinton in American politics? Did the focus on his personality and the scandals leading to impeachment drastically alter the way he is likely to be viewed by future historians, or will his economic policies and his political success in steering the Democratic party toward the political center be viewed as substantive achievements outweighing the weaknesses?

EXPANDING THE "VARYING VIEWPOINTS"

- Daniel Bell, ed., *The Radical Right* (1963).

    A view of modern conservatism as an extremist and paranoid fringe movement:

    "Anti-elitism oriented toward groups that cannot be regarded as oppressed minorities or victims of bigotry, or anti-Communism directed against the agents or dupes of an evil foreign power, can serve as palatable outlets for those who require a scapegoat....Intolerant movements, while often powerful, have never been able seriously to endanger the normal processes of American democracy....But if such movements can not come to power, they can damage the democratic process for short periods of time, and they can and have injured innocent people."

- Kevin Phillips, *Post-Conservative America* (1982).

    A view of modern conservatism as more deeply rooted in American history:

    "I submit that the New Right combines three powerful trend patterns that recur in American history and politics. First, to some measure it is an extension of the Wallace movement, and as such represents a current expression of the ongoing populism of the white lower middle classes, principally in the South and West....Second, the New Right is closely allied with the sometimes potent right-to-life or antiabortion movement, the current version, perhaps, of the great one-issue moral crusades of the American past....And this one-issue element, in turn, folds into the third phenomenon—the possible fourth occurrence of the religious revivals or 'Great Awakenings' that have swept across the land since the middle of the eighteenth century. If so, the religious wing of the New Right may be the political wing of a major national awakening."

42

The American People Face a New Century

CHAPTER THEMES

Theme: The United States underwent drastic economic and social change in the final decades of the twentieth century. The economic transformation from an "industrial age" to an "information age" produced new economic advances as well as a rapidly increasing income gap between the wealthy and the poor. Changes in women's roles, the family, and the arrival of new immigrant groups substantially altered the ways Americans live and work.

Theme: Despite the weaknesses of television and problems in U.S. education, American culture, literature, and art remained the most dynamic and influential in the world. The new diversity of gender, ethnic, and racial voices contributed to the vital energy that made American democracy not simply a political system but an ever-changing source of fresh ideas and popular images.

CHAPTER SUMMARY

In the 1980s and 1990s, the American culture and economy underwent dynamic changes from an age of heavy industry to an age of computerized information and mass culture. Science and education increasingly drove the new forms of wealth, and growth of new media and the Internet helped fuel a new economy linked with the rest of the world. The benefits of the new wealth did not reach everyone, however, as the gaps between those with education and those without contributed to an increasingly severe inequality in Americans' wealth and income.

The decades-long movement into the workforce of women, including mothers of young children, opened ever-wider doors of opportunity, and contributed to changes in men's roles as well as in family life. Women's concern for issues of health and child created a persistent political "gender gap" between Democrats and Republicans in national elections. With fewer families being formed, and fewer children being born to native-born Americans, the population began to age and the elderly became a potent lobbying force.

A vast new wave of immigration, especially from Asia and Latin America, brought newcomers seeking economic opportunity and liberties unavailable in their homelands. Hispanics, Asians, and Indians all asserted their own identity and pride, and made areas like the American Southwest a "bi-cultural zone."

The problems of poverty, increasingly concentrated in inner cities ringed by affluent suburbs, remained stubborn and frustrating to millions of Americans, including many minorities. The African-American community made great strides in education, politics, and other areas, but there was a growing gap between the upwardly mobile and those left behind. America's cities were plagued by problems of drugs and crime, but the soaring crime rates of the 1980s were reversed and turned downward in the 1990s. In the same decade many cities began to show signs of renewal.

American culture remained incredibly dynamic and inventive, both in "high culture" and "pop culture." The new voices of westerners, women, African-Americans, Asians, and others were increasingly influential and popular, contributing to the variety, energy, and humor of U.S. society. Beginning with the postwar "abstract expressionist" movement in New York City, American visual arts and architecture also led worldwide revolutions in taste and transformed the nature of urban life.

America was born a revolutionary force in the world. In the twentieth century it became more conservative in a world swept by global change. Yet the powerful values of American democracy presented persistent challenges to Americans to live up to their high ideals as "the last, best hope on earth."

DEVELOPING THE CHAPTER: SUGGESTED LECTURE OR DISCUSSION TOPICS

- Explain the broad changes in American economic and social development since 1975. The emphasis might be on the severe difficulties caused by the new vulnerability of the United States in the world economy, as well as innovations in technology and business management. Consider the way economic change has altered American society, including family transformations and population migrations.

    REFERENCE: Paul Boyer, *Promises to Keep: The United States Since World War II* (1995).

- Analyze the impact of the feminist movement on women, men, and U.S. culture and society as a whole. Examine not only the structural changes in women's economic and political roles, but the transformation in values, images, and perceptions in the last two decades. Consider the real gains women have made, as well as the issues and concerns that remain.

    REFERENCES: Rosalind Rosenberg, *Divided Lives* (1992); William Chafe, *The Paradox of Change: American Women in the Twentieth Century* (1991).

- Examine the "new immigration" to America in the 1980s and 1990s, including its impact on the American economy and society. Perhaps compare late twentieth century immigration to earlier waves of immigration—including some of the reactions of native-born Americans.

    REFERENCE: David Reimers, *Still the Golden Door: The Third World Comes to America* (1986).

- Look at the transformations of American culture and literature, especially the challenges to "traditional" views of proper culture and education. Consider whether the "culture wars" of the 1990s represented a real change from the American past, or whether the influence of new female and minority writers and artists was actually a revitalization of traditional American values of individualism, democracy, and equality.

    REFERENCE: Henry Louis Gates, Jr., *Loose Canons: Notes on the Culture Wars* (1993).

FOR FURTHER INTEREST: ADDITIONAL CLASS TOPICS

- Contrast the economic, social, and cultural life of a "typical" family of the 1970s with a similar family of the 1990s.

- Select one of the less-well-known "new immigrant" groups, e.g., Asian Indians or West Indians. Look at their reasons for immigration, their patterns of occupation and settlement, and the opportunities and obstacles they have experienced.

- Examine the new patterns of population movement, urbanization, and suburbanization as represented in the 2000 census. Consider particularly the population explosion in states like California, Texas, and Florida, and the corresponding growth in political strength of groups like Hispanics and the elderly.

- Select one novel and one painting as exemplary of the new forces in postwar American art. Perhaps consider why a once-neglected work like Hurston's *Their Eyes Were Watching God* has been rediscovered and celebrated in the 1990s.

CHARACTER SKETCHES

Betty Friedan (1921–)

Friedan is the author of *The Feminine Mystique* (1963) and the founder of the National Organization for Women (NOW), which became the principal arm of the postwar feminist movement.

Born Betty Naomi Goldstein in Peoria, Illinois, Friedan graduated from Smith College in 1942 and studied psychology at the University of California. While raising her family, she worked as a writer for women's magazines like *Redbook* and *Ladies' Home Journal*. A 1957 article for *Ladies' Home Journal* about her Smith classmates gave her the idea for *The Feminine Mystique,* which she wrote during five years of work at the New York Public Library. The book was an instant success and eventually sold millions of copies.

NOW was founded in her Washington hotel room after a 1964 federal government-sponsored conference in which women's concerns were ignored. Friedan created the name "National Organization *for* Women" in order to include men. She later came under sharp attack from more militant feminists for not supporting their more radical ideas.

Quote: "Who knows what women can be when they are finally free to become themselves?…The time is at hand when the voices of the feminine mystique can no longer drown out the inner voice that is driving women to become more complete." (*The Feminine Mystique,* 1963)

REFERENCES: Justine Blau, *Betty Friedan* (1990); Daniel Horowitz, *Betty Friedan and the Making of 'The Feminine Mystique'* (1998).

James Baldwin (1924–1987)

James Baldwin was the black writer whose powerful fiction and nonfiction works expressed his personal vision of the world and helped awaken white America to the depths of the racial crisis.

Baldwin was born in Harlem and spent most of his early life there. His father was an authoritarian, often cruel, Fundamentalist preacher. Many of Baldwin's more autobiographical works, including *Go Tell It on the Mountain* (1953), the work that first gained him literary fame, reveal the difficulties of his childhood and relations with his father.

Baldwin spent much time abroad, especially in Paris, where he felt he could escape the racial restrictions of the United States. However, he always returned to what he felt was his "home" in America. His book *The Fire Next Time* (1963) caused great controversy when it was published because of its predictions of racial violence but was later considered prophetic of the crises of the 1960s.

Quote: "The nation, the entire nation, has spent a hundred years avoiding the question of the place of the black man in it.…Any honest examination of the national life proves how far we are from the standard of human freedom with which we began. The recovery of this standard demands of everyone who loves this country a hard look at himself." (*Nobody Knows My Name,* 1961)

REFERENCE: David Leeming, *James Baldwin: A Biography* (1994).

Jackson Pollock (1912–1956)

Pollock was the most influential American artist of the immediate postwar era and is considered one of the great modern masters of painting.

The son of an unsuccessful Wyoming rancher, Pollock developed a deep love of nature while working summer jobs at the Grand Canyon.

In school Pollock was interested only in art and frequently got into academic and disciplinary difficulty. He studied with Thomas Hart Benton, the great American "regionalist" painter. Pollock's early nature paintings show Benton's influence but also reflect a tendency toward the abstraction that he later developed.

From 1935 to 1943 Pollock worked for the federal WPA Art Project. In the early 1940s he was influenced by Jungian therapy and the work of Picasso and André Breton. He made his breakthrough to abstract expressionism and later developed his techniques of dripping and splattering paint on the canvas to create complex special effects. Some of his works that originally sold for $600 were later bought for over $2 million.

Pollock seldom appeared in public and cultivated an image as a somewhat rough and mysterious character. He died in an auto accident in 1956.

Quote: "When I am *in* my painting I'm not aware of what I'm doing....I have no fears of making changes, destroying the image, etc., because the painting has a life of its own. I try to let it come through."

REFERENCE: Steven Naifeh and Gregory White Smith, *Jackson Pollock* (1990).

QUESTIONS FOR CLASS DISCUSSION

1. Was the growing inequality in American wealth and incomes the result of "natural" economic market forces, or was it encouraged by deliberate political policies, especially the tax cuts and trade policies of the 1980s?

2. Has the American family been in "decline," or has it simply changed forms while developing different kinds of strengths? What causes the fears of a "generational war" between the expanding numbers of elderly and younger Americans?

3. Has the nature of American race relations been substantially altered since the 1960s civil rights movement, or are relations between whites and African-Americans fundamentally the same? Has African-American society itself undergone substantial changes?

4. Why has "culture" become the focus of a series of "wars" between different intellectuals and social groups in the past ten years? Why are many of these "wars" over issues fought in American colleges and universities?

MAKERS OF AMERICA: THE LATINOS

Questions for Class Discussion

1. What distinctive conditions have shaped the experience of Latin American immigrants, especially Mexican-Americans, in the United States?

2. How has the proximity of Mexico to the United States affected the relations of Mexican-Americans with both their old and their new countries?

Suggested Student Exercises

- Examine those areas of the United States that have been most affected by Hispanic or Mexican immigration. Consider the likely impact of a large Hispanic presence on the politics, economics, religion, and culture of those areas.

- Examine the changing image of Hispanic-Americans in films, television, music, and other forms of popular culture. Perhaps use some samples of earlier stereotypes from the 1940s or 1950s to demonstrate the changes.